EDUCATIONAL
DEVELOPMENT
through INFORMATION *and*
COMMUNICATIONS TECHNOLOGY

The Staff and Educational Development Series
Series Editor: James Wisdom

SEDA is the Staff and Education Developmental Association. It supports and encourages developments in teaching and learning in higher education through a variety of methods: publications, conferences, networking, journals, regional meetings and research – and through various SEDA Accreditation Schemes.

SEDA
Selly Wick House
59–61 Selly Wick Road
Selly Park
Birmingham B29 7JE
Tel: 0121–415 6801
Fax: 0121–415 6802
E-mail: office@seda.demon.co.uk

SEDA
STAFF AND EDUCATIONAL
DEVELOPMENT ASSOCIATION

**Staff and Educational
Development Series**

EDUCATIONAL DEVELOPMENT
through INFORMATION *and*
COMMUNICATIONS TECHNOLOGY

Stephen Fallows and Rakesh Bhanot

**KOGAN
PAGE**

First published in 2002

Kogan Page Limited
120 Pentonville Road
London N1 9JN
UK

Stylus Publishing Inc.
22883 Quicksilver Drive
Sterling VA 20166–2012
USA

British Library Cataloguing in Publication Data

A CIP record for this book is available from the British Library.

ISBN 0 7494 3565 8

Typeset by Saxon Graphics Ltd, Derby
Printed and bound in Great Britain by Clays Ltd, St Ives plc

Contents

vi *Contents*

Notes on contributors

Kyriaki Anagnostopoulou is the Learning Technologies Adviser in the Centre for Learning Development at Middlesex University. Her role encompasses collaborative initiatives aimed at promoting and supporting the pedagogically effective uptake of learning technologies. She has a background in design and media arts. She is also a visiting lecturer in graphic information design for the University of Westminster. Her previous research includes improved methods of representing research data and the role of design in the learning and teaching process.

Rakesh Bhanot is the Programme Manager for the Postgraduate Courses in Learning and Teaching in Higher Education in the Centre for Higher Education Development at Coventry University. He has worked in several European countries and delivered seminars and workshops on a variety of educational topics in many parts of the world. Prior to his current post, Rakesh was the European Co-ordinator and Programme Manager for Public Broadcasting for Multicultural Europe (PBME), a pan-European organization of which he was a co-founder. He has also worked in the adult and further education sector and was a National Project Officer with the Further Education Unit. He considers himself to be a reformed 'technophobe'.

Paul Blackmore is Director of the Centre for Academic Practice at the University of Warwick and is responsible for leading the university's policy and strategy in academic staff development. He has 15 years' experience in professional development for staff in both higher and further education, and has developed and managed a number of accredited programmes. He has research interests in conceptualizations of professional expertise and in research-based teaching and learning.

Susan Chandler has worked as an instructional designer developing educational materials for both primary to secondary education and adult audiences. She currently coordinates the Distributed Learning Unit at Royal Roads University in Victoria BC, Canada. She designs online courses for midlife learners. Susan has studied at the University of Victoria (undergraduate) and at Saint Mary's University in Halifax (postgraduate).

Anne Davidson is a lecturer in the School of Health and Social Sciences at Coventry University. Although her original academic background was in biomedical research, her most recent activities have involved promoting ICT skills in a variety of professional contexts. She currently holds a part-time teaching fellowship, and was previously a member of the university's Teaching, Learning and Assessment Taskforce with a special interest in the potential of electronic learning environments to support subject-based teaching and the associated staff development issues.

Jacqueline Dempster is Head of Educational Technology in the Centre for Academic Practice at the University of Warwick. She has an academic background in biological sciences, and worked at the University of York and the University of Nijmegen in the Netherlands before taking up a post as manager of one of the former national CTI support centres. She has spent the last eight years in promoting and supporting educational development in the use of communications and information technologies (ICT) in higher education both at Warwick and at national levels. She currently manages three national projects to develop the use of ICT in learning and teaching and is actively involved in developing national professional development schemes for learning technologists.

Sue Drew is a Senior Lecturer in the Learning and Teaching Institute at Sheffield Hallam University. She is the joint author of two books and a CD ROM that provide Key Skills support materials, and of a number of articles about Key Skills. From 1998 to 2000 she was the manager of the 'Key to Key Skills' project funded by the Teaching and Learning Technology Programme (TLTP3), for which Sheffield Hallam University was the lead institution. This project provided invaluable experience of adapting and implementing Web-based learning support both within and across institutions.

Stephen Fallows has recently taken up employment as Research Co-ordinator for the Centre for Exercise and Nutrition Science at the Chester College of Higher Education. He was previously Reader in Educational Development at the University of Luton. Dr Fallows made a move to educational development from his original discipline of food and health policy via the use of computer-based teaching as manager of the pioneering ELF Project at the University of Bradford in the late 1980s. ELF (Electronic Learning-package Factory) was an early attempt to support the transfer of teaching materials from traditional modes into computer-based formats. He has now moved to a role that is focused on the management of the postgraduate learning experience.

Susan Foster is Vice President for Information Technologies at the University of Delaware, USA. She is a former chairman of the board of directors of CAUSE, served on the combined board to oversee the merger of Educom and CAUSE, and served on the inaugural board of the newly merged Educause. She is presently a member of the Educause professional development committee. Susan has served on the steering committee of the Coalition for Networked Information and is the University of Delaware's representative to the Educause National Learning Infrastructure Initiative. In 1995 Susan was a recipient of the American Management Systems and Carnegie Mellon University Graduate School of Industrial Administration Award for Achievement in Managing Information Technology. Susan serves on the board of directors of the State of Delaware Center for Educational Technology.

Mike Fuller is Senior Lecturer in Econometrics and Social Statistics in the Canterbury Business School at the University of Kent. He has been involved with supervising projects and dissertations over many years, and is currently enhancing the role of project work within Kent's undergraduate business administration degrees. He has co-authored an introductory statistics text, published papers applying statistics to a wide range of social and economic contexts, and writes regularly on the use of ICT in statistical education. He also manages electronic discussion groups concerned with statistical topics, management research and staff and educational development.

David Grantham is a Senior Lecturer in the School of International Studies and Law at Coventry University. He also has a staff development role in the Centre for Higher Education Development. Between September 1997 and August 2000 he was assigned to the university's Learning and Teaching Task Force, his main project being to design Web pages for undergraduate and postgraduate programmes. These have been presented at conferences and to colleagues in other law schools throughout the UK. In June 2001 he was awarded a National Teaching Fellowship. He will be using the opportunity provided through this award to continue to develop his work in Web design and to support other innovators in the field, nationally and internationally. He has a background in teaching law, management and industrial relations. His current professional interests are curriculum research and development, effective use of electronic learning environments, and staff and student development.

Michelle Haynes is the Open and Distance Learning Adviser in the Centre for Learning Development at Middlesex University. She works across the university with staff on the development of open and distance learning materials and on other issues connected to the enhancement of learning and teaching. She is also a tutor in educational management and educational research for the Open University. She is writing her PhD thesis on ethnicity, identity and race as experienced by Jewish women teachers in non-denominational schools.

Raja Maznah Raja Hussain is an Associate Professor at the Faculty of Education, University of Malaya. She was formerly the Director of the University of Malaya Learning Improvement Centre and was responsible for developing programmes to help improve teaching and learning skills of academic staff. She is currently on sabbatical at the Multimedia University in Cyberjaya as a visiting professor and Chair of the Instructional Design Committee for the Multimedia Learning System Project. She has a PhD from Indiana University in instructional systems technology. Her research areas are instructional design for Web-based learning, teaching and learning in higher education, and knowledge management in learning organizations.

Maggie Hutchings is a Senior Lecturer in Academic Services at Bournemouth University, contributing to staff development in Web-based learning, computer-mediated communication, and supporting student learning through her teaching on the university's staff development programme and the MA in Professional Development (Post-Compulsory Education). She has been involved in a number of learning and teaching projects using computer conferencing, computer-assisted assessment and Web based learning. She has an Honours degree in Social Sciences from the University of East Anglia, a

Master's in Information Studies from Sheffield University and a Cert Ed. She has published in the areas of study support, computer-mediated communication, staff development and computer-assisted learning. She is currently researching the contribution of online learning environments to learning in higher education.

Gillian Jordan is a Principal Lecturer in Open Learning in the School of Health at the University of Greenwich. Her background is in physiotherapy and she has extensive experience of both undergraduate and postgraduate education. She is responsible for developing open and distance learning opportunities for health professionals and is the leader of the MSc CPD (Health) programme. Her academic interests are in the areas of continuing professional development and the use of computers as communication tools. She is a member of the Chartered Society of Physiotherapy's Council, where she sits on the Education Committee, the Scientific Panel and the CPD and Lifelong Learning Panel.

Donna Wood McCarty holds a BA in English and a PhD in educational psychology. She is an Associate Professor of Psychology at Clayton College and State University in a suburb of Atlanta, Georgia, USA. Dr McCarty has extensive teaching experience at the undergraduate level and has had the opportunity to serve the university and the academic community in a variety of ways in addition to her teaching. She currently coordinates the academic assessment and faculty development programmes on her campus.

Marina Möller is an Education Media Technologist in the Department of Professional Education at Vista University, Sebokeng Campus, South Africa. She holds a Masters degree in computer-assisted education from the University of Pretoria. She is also directly involved in teacher education. She is particularly interested in using the computer in the classroom and has presented papers on this topic at national and international conferences.

Ivan Moore became Director of Learning at the University of Portsmouth in February 2002. Prior to this, he was Director of Learning and Teaching at the University of Wolverhampton for three years. During this time, he was responsible, among other things, for leading a university-wide project designed to make use of information and communications technology to support student learning. This major university initiative made use of the University of Wolverhampton's own online learning framework, the WOLF. The university now has a substantial proportion of its undergraduate portfolio supported by various forms of technology, including e-learning.

Marina Orsini-Jones is Subject Leader for Italian within the School of International Studies and Law at Coventry University and is seconded half-time as Teaching and Learning Fellow to promote staff development within the school. She developed a constructivist model of ICT integration within her teaching of Italian which was disseminated to other disciplines both within Coventry University and outside it. She has published a CD ROM to teach Italian language and society and various articles focusing on the pedagogical issues underlying effective ICT integration and related staff development issues.

Paul Orsmond is a senior lecturer in the School of Sciences at Staffordshire University where he is a Learning and Teaching Fellow. His interest is in educational development with particular reference to assessment and student learning. He has published and presented workshops on a range of educational matters including peer and self-assessment.

Estelle Paget is an educator and an entrepreneur. She has taught extensively in universities in France and Canada and is President of Paget Communications. She was formally educated at York University, Toronto, Canada (undergraduate) and at the Faculté des Lettres, Besançon, France (postgraduate). From 1993 to 1999 she designed and implemented a campus-wide mentoring programme for University of British Columbia faculty members. Presently, she is Director of Learning Facilitation Programs at Royal Roads University in Victoria, BC, Canada. She is developing and implementing an innovative certificate programme for faculty and deans in learning facilitation.

Mick Roach is an Educational Developer with the TELRI Project, a national project funded under Phase 3 of the Teaching and Learning Technology Programme. With an academic background in engineering, he has held teaching and research posts in both old and new universities as well as in industry. He has been responsible for developing educational frameworks to support problem-based learning in engineering and research-led teaching across a range of disciplines, with a particular expertise in the application of ICT to support high order thinking skills in student learning and assessment.

Christine Steven has experience teaching in secondary and further education as well as higher education. Her subject specialism is computer science but she maintains an interest in pedagogic issues and much of her research is in this area. Christine was for some years a teaching fellow at the University of Luton, where much of her work centred on issues of assessment, particular emphasis being on the use of computer aided assessment packages and their effectiveness. She is now a teacher in a secondary school in Kent where she has responsibility for key skills development and the use of computer aided teaching and assessment.

Mark Stiles is Professor of Technology Supported Learning and Co-Director of the Learning Development Centre at Staffordshire University. The centre has the proactive role of leading the transformation of the way learning takes place at the university. He is a regular national and international conference speaker on the educational aspects of the electronic support of learning and has published papers in the field. He is also Director of the Joint Information Systems Committee supported COSE Project which developed the COSE Virtual Learning Environment (VLE), now published as a commercial product. The COSE Project is still further developing the COSE VLE, and, using more recent JISC funding, is working on interoperability of VLEs/Managed Learning Environments (MLEs).

Stan Zakrzewski has recently been appointed as a Principal Lecturer in the Department of Computing, Information Systems and Mathematics at London Guildhall University. He was previously Head of Research (Learning Resources) at the University of Luton where he managed the implementation of computer based assessment at the university and researched implementation models for computer-based course delivery and assessment.

Preface

This volume owes its origins to the Annual Conference of the Staff and Educational Development Association (SEDA) held at the TechnoCentre, Coventry University in April 2000. This conference took the theme 'Reaching Out' and included presentations on widening participation, supporting networks and partnerships, and the challenges associated with the management of change within higher education.

Conference delegates interpreted 'Reaching Out' in a wide variety of ways. However, there was a strong cohort of presentations that focused upon the ways in which information and communications technologies (ICT) can be used to permit universities and other higher education institutions to reach out beyond the confines of the traditional lecture hall, seminar room or laboratory. Conference delegates discussed the ways in which ICT can be utilized to provide opportunities for the enhancement of learning for students both on campus and located at a distance. Delegates also considered the issues and difficulties associated with the adoption of such technologies, and steps that can be taken to deal with these.

The 2000 SEDA conference provided the 'seed ideas' from which this book has been developed; however, it should be noted from the outset that this is not a volume of conference proceedings. A minority of the chapters derive directly from conference presentations and associated discussions. Others have been included to provide examples and illustrations of the various issues that need to be addressed.

As editors, we have deliberately attempted to provide examples from around the world and from a variety of different styles of institution and circumstance. We have drawn together a collection of chapters that we hope will be informative and useful to colleagues. In developing the structure of the book we have been mindful of three key observations which remain central to our thinking:

- While the adoption of information and communications technologies is the theme of this book, it is merely the latest educational development. Thus, there are always lessons to be learnt from earlier innovations (whether these were short-lived or became a feature of the established fabric of education).

- Whatever medium is utilized (from the most simple through to the most complex), education requires 'good' teachers. By this we mean that a new approach or a new technology is not a panacea that will instantly maximize the learning experience. We have observed many instances in which those teachers who are most able to develop strong ICT-based teaching are those who were previously highly regarded in 'lesser' media. (Or to put it another way, just being a technological wizard is never enough.)

● The introduction of new approaches to learning brings with it a need for personal learning on the part of each teacher. This personal learning can take place in a variety of settings: attendance at a formal staff development occasion; the hit and miss, personal trial and error approach; and the sharing of ideas and professional practice. We hope that this book contributes to the third of these methods, as our contributors have reflected on their practice and have shared their ideas for wider benefit.

Also, as editors we took the view that this volume should not be a book through which ICT specialists speak solely to other ICT specialists. Rather, we have taken the view that in this book educators with strong interests in ICT based education should speak to other educators world-wide who wish to learn about this current educational development.

The book itself covers a range of themes. These have been grouped broadly as follows:

● Strategic management of ICT-related initiatives in higher education institutions.

● The use of online learning environments and associated communications technologies.

● The uses of ICT in a variety of learning and educational support situations.

● Matters associated with the introduction of ICT into the classroom.

Although we have (somewhat arbitrarily) grouped the chapters broadly as above, in practice most (if not all) contributions are really not confined to a single category and touch on a number of cross-related issues.

As editors, we cannot but note the increasing use of Internet-based sources within the references section of chapters in books such as this one. This is testament to the increasing prevalence and hence academic influence of ICT based modes of information dissemination and publication. Readers are (hopefully unnecessarily) reminded of the need to judge each document on its provenance and currency: while a uniform resource locator (URL) may remain constant, this is not necessarily also the case for the documents attached to it.

Finally, we must point out that while contributors make necessary reference to specific software and other commercial products in their descriptions, these mentions do not constitute product endorsements by either the editors or the publisher. Mention of specific commercial products is given solely as a matter of record.

Acknowledgements

The editors wish to record the receipt of a grant provided to the Staff and Educational Development Association (SEDA) by Peugeot Motor Co plc which was used to support the development of this volume.

Thanks must also go to those many colleagues who provided comments and advice on the chapters included in this book.

1

Educational development and ICT: an introduction

Stephen Fallows and Rakesh Bhanot

SUMMARY

The uses of information and communications technologies (ICT) provide us with some of the latest examples of the way in which technological developments have been taken up and used by educators. In the past hundred years alone, educators have adopted, to some extent or other, developments such as film, radio, television, video (recording and/or playback); each has been utilized as an adjunct to the established practices of face to face lectures, seminars and tutorials. Now it is the turn of ICT. This chapter provides a short introduction to the use of ICT in higher education and is intended to give a lead into the series of detailed chapters that follow.

THE MEANING OF EDUCATIONAL DEVELOPMENT

An 'educational development' can, for the purposes of this book at least, be considered as any novel action taken with the intention of either enhancing the teaching of a particular subject or enhancing of the students' learning of the subject. Many educational developments seek to achieve both of these objectives. In addition, it is increasingly the case that educational developments take place with a view to increasing the efficiency or productivity of teaching and learning. Often the institution, department or individual teacher is seeking to increase the educational outcomes while maintaining the direct face to face teaching at a constant level. A push for efficient and 'more productive' education has often been a feature of ICT based initiatives.

The concept of a 'novel action' needs a degree of clarification, since for most educators it is novelty within a particular context or set of circumstances that is important, rather than the absolute introduction of that which has never been tried before. Indeed, within the context of education, there is little that is absolutely new; most educational developments rest upon the adaptation of existing approaches and skills to changed circumstances.

Within the context of this book, the 'changed circumstances' centre upon a series of technological developments that have been taken up by educators around the world. The examples cited in the book are by no means unique; rather they offer illustrations of practice in a range of higher education institutions. We can note that technologically driven/supported educational developments may take place within the teaching of a single class by a lone pioneer educator or, as is increasingly the case, they can form the basis of strategic institution-wide teaching and learning initiatives that can have profound impact.

THE MEANING OF ICT

The term 'information technology' (IT) was adopted some years ago as a global term designed to include all matters relating to computers and the software that was utilized by these computers. The term was sufficient when each computer was essentially a stand-alone entity. More recently, increasing numbers of computers are interconnected in order that communication can take place between them. Initially, this interconnection was limited to local networks within organizations, but nowadays it has become the norm for communications to reach out worldwide using the international network referred to variously as the Internet, the World Wide Web or simply the Web or Net. In recognition of the addition of communications technologies, the term IT has evolved into ICT (information and communications technologies). (C&IT is used as an alternative configuration of these initial letters.)

It is the use of computers as communications tools (as well as aids to learning, teaching and assessment) that presents the key educational development upon which this volume is centred.

A BRIEF HISTORY

It is worthwhile for us to reflect briefly on the speed with which developments in the use of ICT in education have taken place. This reflection is by no means a definitive history text; it is not intended to be so. Rather, it serves to remind us of the multiplicity of changes that have taken place over recent years. The story illustrates the progression that has taken place within IT- and ICT based education with movement from the domain of the enthusiastic technologically driven pioneer to (almost) universal acceptance within some institutions. We are moving to a domain in which the basic usage of the technology is established, and what still requires further development is the broad raising of awareness of the educational benefits that can be achieved through effective use of ICT. Raising awareness of the potential is the first step; subsequent steps will realize this potential. The key trick will be to steer these steps in the direction that is most appropriate for the institution, teacher(s) and student(s).

It should be remembered that computers have been used in universities and other higher education establishments since the dawn of electronic computing in the late 1940s/early 1950s, but for the first 30 or more years they were essentially research facilities used for calculations and analysis rather than educational tools.

The introduction of personal desktop computers during the 1980s stimulated major changes within education, as elsewhere in the economy. The introduction of IBM's first PC on 12 August 1981 at a price of $1,565 (without monitor) was a major step: the desktop PC had gained respectability.

Computers were no longer simply remote and mysterious devices that required special locations and skilled operators and programmers; they rapidly came to be everyday productivity tools to be used universally for a range of tasks. While the first generation personal computers still required the use of programming skills, by the mid-1980s the early 'off the shelf' commercial software such as word processing packages and spreadsheets had begun to make their way from the business world into education.

By the 1980s pioneer enthusiasts were beginning to develop items of software that had specific educational functions. These were usually programs that provided specific instruction in a small element of the curriculum. Most of these pioneers were science based, and many of the early learning packages provided mathematical simulations of (for example) chemical reactions, physical situations or ecological interactions between different species. Such pioneers were distributed widely through education, from early years specialists through to university teachers.

Also in the 1980s, the business world was beginning to explore the use of computers in staff training, and a number of courseware development tools became available for the production of computer based training (CBT) materials. The early courseware development tools were often highly restrictive, very expensive to license and limited in their educational utility. Similarly expensive at the time was the delivery technology. Most commonly, CBT was adopted within large commercial organizations that needed to train large numbers of staff quickly (for instance a national bank introducing a new style of account could use CBT to train counter staff nationwide using the local office technology).

At the time, the economies of scale did not carry forward into higher education, in which each institution (and generally each teacher) maintained autonomy and flexibility in curriculum development. The fixed nature of early CBT material was sufficient for dedicated training in relatively mundane matters but lacked the sophistication needed for large scale adoption within higher education.

The serious development of computer-assisted learning (CAL) from the mid-1980s onwards began with enthusiasts preparing materials for their own students. Materials were often very specific and not cost-effective (in view of the development time that was required and low levels of usage). On reflection, the hours spent developing course materials (at that time) never had a direct payback.

There was a strong suspicion of material 'not invented here', and the majority of courseware remained confined to single institutions or even in many instances to a single educator. In the UK, the establishment of the discipline-related Computers in Teaching Initiative (CTI) Centres was a direct publicly funded attempt to encourage the sharing of expertise and course materials between institutions. More recently the CTI Centres have been replaced by the Learning Technology Support Network (LTSN), with a similar but updated mandate to stimulate the efficient and effective use of learning technologies.

Further support for the more efficient development of CAL materials came (in the UK) with the Teaching and Learning Technology Programme (TLTP) which has largely supported the operation of consortia to produce teaching and learning materials that are specifically intended to be used in several institutions. This initiative has undergone three funding phases. Although the educational return on the financial investment of public moneys into TLTP remains open to question, there can be no doubt that the initiative made significant steps in the development of usable and useful teaching packages that were appropriate for the university curriculum. Moreover, the collaborative nature of the programme has improved the degree of take-up away from the home institution, but in practice each university teacher has retained control of delivery as students have largely been directed towards 'fixed' subject specific learning packages. A study undertaken in 1998 provides a useful review of the take-up of TLTP materials (University of Edinburgh, 1999).

All the early CAL initiatives were essentially local in nature, with the 'educational products' being delivered via disk (later CD ROM) to a particular location for organized and controlled delivery. Over time, single machine courseware has been replaced by networked equivalents, with the courseware held on a central server, but the general controlled delivery concept remains. As CAL developed through the 1980s and 1990s it did so in a context of rapidly moving developments in personal computing. The personal experience of one of the editors of CAL development at the end of the 1980s was characterized by delivery ambitions which largely outstripped the capabilities of computers available for general student use. During the following decade computers became much more powerful and perhaps more importantly, more affordable. 'More powerful' meant that the aspirations of the CAL pioneers could begin to be achieved technically on everyday computers, rather than requiring specialist equipment. The 'affordable' issue was similarly important since it allowed institutions to offer greater availability on campus. At the same time, the supply of personal computers moved from specialist suppliers to high street retailers. With their ability to supply 'bundles' of computer systems and associated software at discounted prices, this meant that significant numbers of students (or their parents) were able to purchase their own systems.

In parallel with the developments in CAL summarized above, the 1990s were characterized by the development of the Internet. The Internet *per se*, the now global interconnection of millions of computers via a mix of direct hardwire connections and telephone modem connections, grew from a US initiative, the ARPANET. The ARPANET originated from military concern in the late 1960s about potential security of the computer linked communications of an America under nuclear attack. The ARPANET provided a solution: the system connected every station to every other through whichever route was most effective and quickest. The key idea was that if one message route became out of action then one or other of the other connections would be used to derive an alternative route for that crucial message. Michael Hauben of Columbia University provides a useful history of the ARPANET (Hauben, 2002). The principle of multiple routes from source to solution was carried forward into the development of the Internet which nowadays links both organizations and individuals worldwide.

The Internet is 'simply' the communications system that connects millions of computers through a worldwide web of connections. What are important are the benefits that can be achieved through use of such a communications system, and the associated issues.

In its first iteration, the Internet (like ARPANET before it) was concerned with the transmission of messages (whether simple text messages or more complex data streams) either from a single source to a single recipient or from a single source to multiple recipients. This is, of course, the basis of electronic mail (e-mail). The e-mail model continues and is today available to all and not confined to the 'techie' pioneers and their acolytes.

Later iterations of the Internet have shifted the balance of innovation from the active sending out of information to the provision of systems through which information is made available (generally freely) to others who wish to access it. Using earlier communications tools to provide an analogy, this is the shift from sending a private letter to posting a note on a notice board or placing a book or other document in a library. In principle, the Internet generally makes the notice board (or library) available world-wide to anyone with the necessary technology.

In practice, just as with a physical notice board or library, access to certain sites may be restricted to a particular group of users. Restriction can be based on membership of a particular organization or group. In educational terms this could be students of a particular institution or even of a specific programme of study. In the commercial sector access to many information sources (Web sites) is restricted to those willing to pay the required fee. The material available ranges from the contents of academic journals (generally purchased by universities and the like) to hard core pornography.

Finally, the range and quantity of materials available via the Internet is increasing exponentially. This has profound implications for education as students now have the possibility of selecting from and utilizing an incredible wealth of information.

THE IMPORTANCE FOR HIGHER EDUCATION

We begin by looking quickly at the nature of education from its earliest origins to the Internet age.

In the ancient and distant past the student learnt from a 'master', and the extent of the master's knowledge set the limits of available material. The skills of the master set the degree to which transfer of knowledge could take place. The good master not only 'knew his stuff'; he could also communicate it in a manner that not only held the attention of his students, but also communicated the message and motivated the students to learn. This basic principle remains fundamental to teaching today, but now there is also much more. (The use of the masculine in this paragraph is intentional to denote the male predominance in early education.)

With the introduction of writing, and in due course books, information and other aspects of knowledge could be transferred from place to place. The direct link to, and dependence upon, the local knowledge base (of the master) began to decline and has continued to do so ever since.

The range of knowledge available to the learner initially increased to also include all that was available in the local library: with sufficient time and patience, the learner could read all the books and (at least in theory) accrue all the knowledge.

This model of education remained the essential norm until the late 1990s. True, the local library (even in the more modest institutions) now contained thousands of volumes, but the students' access to materials was generally physically limited to that available on the premises (either personally from the teacher or in the library). Some institutions held vast collections, and systems of inter-library loans (in theory at least) extended the range of material to everything published, but for most students the practical level of access was limited to the local collection.

'Local' collections remain important for almost all students; after all, we all know that students are not renowned for the forward planning necessary physically to locate and access materials held at remote sites in time for the completion of the required learning and/or assessment activities.

The Internet moves matters to a new level. The college library is now just the local hands-on starting point. The true resource base is now world-wide, with the Internet providing an easy route to a previously untold range of sources. The concept seems perfect on first look, but re-examination reveals a number of potential issues.

- What is the provenance of the materials that students are actually accessing?

- Are the students sound in their analysis and evaluation of these materials?

- What was the motivation of the information provider (governmental, scientific, commercial, campaigning, or even pure mischief)?

Previous 'library' systems provided a degree of screening that is not found with Internet resources.

The quick review above illustrates a major educational development issue that surpasses the need for educators merely to engage with the current technologies. The technology represented by the Internet is all-persuasive for those who wish to utilize it.

But the Internet with its international ramifications is not the sole concern; returning to the local level there is the matter of how local teachers utilize the technological options to provide for the supposed needs of their students. There is as yet no consensus of best practice: how much information, and how it should be presented, remain open for debate.

THIS VOLUME

The contributors to this book do not provide the answers. Answers can apply only to individual circumstances: this means to specific programmes of study delivered by specific individuals, in specific locations to specific groups of students and at specific times. The experienced educator has always made day by day adjustments to both curriculum and delivery method to take account of circumstances; this will not change as ICT becomes embedded. The pace of change may be increasing but the primary functions of educators remain the same: that is to inspire students to wonder in their subject and to maintain this interest to promote active learning.

The book gives a selection of case examples of how educators around the world are adopting the new technological options to their personal, local and institutional needs. It is clear from these examples that we remain far from the universal solution. Perhaps that is a good thing: a universal solution suggests a single style of education. We are not advocating such an approach: rather we continue to favour the individualistic mix based on the teacher's personal knowledge and abilities. But we have to note that ICT in its various forms gives an increasingly important additional dimension to the educational mix.

REFERENCES

Hauben, M [accessed 28 January 2002] *History of ARPANET: Behind the Net: The untold history of the ARPANET* [online] http//www.dei.isep.ipp.pt/docs/arpa.html

University of Edinburgh (1999) *Use of TLTP Materials in UK Higher Education: A HEFCE Commissioned Study,* University of Edinburgh [online] http://www.flp.ed.ac.uk/LTRG/TLTP.html [accessed 28 January 2002]

2

Implementing an institution-wide ICT strategy for university education

Susan Foster

SUMMARY

To introduce, maintain and make good use of information technologies in university education, several essential ingredients are required. Establish a flexible, upgradable, ubiquitous, easy to use technology infrastructure. Streamline administrative services and relieve the burdens of students, faculties and staff in conducting university business. Make sure that students, faculty and staff are skilled in the use of the technology. Adopt and apply the appropriate learning model to instruction and apply technology accordingly. Participate with other higher education institutions, government, and industry to further the good use of technology. Don't drift!

THE CHALLENGE

By the time traditional US students receive their baccalaureate degrees they have spent eight or nine months, eight hours or more a day at the job of learning the necessities for successful, productive citizenship. Every generation of those students has used the tools of their era in that learning process. Now we are in the information age where computing and communications technologies are an integral part of all that we do in government, commerce, social service and life generally. Think of how disadvantaged students can be if a substantial portion of their waking hours are devoid of opportunities to gain experience with these technologies in every way possible. So, why not in education as well?

One reason is that our faculties largely have been unprepared for teaching generally and teaching with new technologies specifically. The reward system for higher education faculties in the US primarily still focuses on discipline expertise and research. As graduate students, members of US faculties largely are untrained in teaching and once they begin teaching, their professional development often has been weak. The result is that they can be under-motivated and under-developed; a very sad waste of superb resources. This is not to say that there are not outstanding teachers everywhere in US higher education. However, they have tended to be born, not made.

THE PROCESS

Ten years ago, in 1990, the University of Delaware embarked on weaving an information technology infrastructure into the fabric of the institution. We began with a high-speed network that goes everywhere: to every campus desktop, dormitory pillow, classroom, gathering place, laboratory, general use computing site, to and within the library. A modem pool provides access to the network from off campus. The university's goal was to use the network and information technologies to positive effect in four areas: administrative change, reassignment of tasks, academic support and an intranet to enhance student living and learning.

By 1994, the university had been singled out from among peers with the CAUSE Award for Excellence in Campus Networking. Progress was made not because computer enthusiasts persuaded the university administration to acquire 'new toys', but because people at the heart of the institution shared a vision of what they wanted to achieve and how information technologies could help to achieve it. It was this focus that made colleagues enthusiastic, that motivated them to join in to make the vision real.

With the network in place, it was time to decide how to approach enhancing the living and learning environment. We defined steps to meet this goal and recognized that they would impact every part of the university. We knew that some of these steps, perhaps many, would be hard to achieve while everyone was working heads down at their jobs as they were. As a result, we decided on a tactical approach to make the most of our ability to seize opportunities as they came along. We began first by using the intranet as a means of streamlining how the business of being a student was conducted.

The network has enabled reassignment of many tasks in many ways. Registration and routine administrative tasks can be done online using the Web, and interactive voice response systems greatly reduce the demand for person to person assistance. Staff are now free to provide other valuable services to students who do require personal attention. Voice synthesis of stored information to respond to telephone inquiries eliminates a layer of routine administration. Automation of these services means that students can easily maintain some of their own records. This can ensure, for example, that the university can more correctly know their current local addresses. There is no more runaround to many places to solve problems or complete transactions. Students find answers and complete transactions online and with interactive voice technologies. When problems are too complex for online solution, students go to one place on campus to resolve them. All faculty and staff members have their own office computers, and many academic tasks have been reassigned to the network. E-mail and class e-mail lists speed communication with instructors. Online advising makes it possible for students and their advisers readily to review students' progress and programmes, and to assess options.

The university's booklet about responsible computing for employees opens with these words:

> On virtually every office desktop at the University of Delaware, you will find a computer. It is probably used for communication as often as is the telephone. It is surely used to produce memos, letters and reports. In fact, you probably couldn't find a typewriter in many offices.
>
> Your desktop computer is a vital university connection. It puts you just keystrokes away from the information you need to do your work, and to do it efficiently. That information used to be delivered to you on paper – maybe coming once a month or after you wrote or telephoned a request for it, or maybe, you were never able to get it at all. That was in the past.
>
> Today, the business of the University of Delaware is done by computer.

Routine administration is just one aspect of student life that is now performed much more efficiently and effectively using information technologies. Library resources are online along with 'books I have checked out' information and electronic book loan renewal. Electronic reserves and full text journal and periodical databases are available. The library Web site also guides students to Internet sources appropriate to their research or areas of study. A list of this and other Web sites of interest is provided as Appendix 1 at the end of this chapter.

Textbooks can be ordered from the bookstore online, purchased with a credit card or with a university debit card. They are bundled and ready before classes begin. Students can buy computers and peripheral equipment through the university at attractive discounts and have them configured and Internet-ready when they arrive on campus. Ninety per cent of University of Delaware students own their own computers.

Several considerations were taken into account as a result of the need for students to use information technology resources to live and learn at the university. One is the appropriate use of these facilities. Students entering the university take an online 'Electronic Community Citizenship Exam'. The exam is an education tool that points out the appropriate use of the information technologies and provides students with the opportunity to demonstrate that they understand university policies. Students demonstrate their understanding by passing the exam with all correct answers. They may take the exam as many times as are necessary to achieve 100 per cent accuracy. The questions are randomly selected from categories in a database to assure different questions each time the test is taken. The database is updated from time to time to reflect the current state of Internet and resource use and misuse. A current problem among students in the United States is violation of copyright of music and video available on the Web.

THE MEANS

Having prepared an environment for easy use of information technologies for conducting student, faculty and administration business, the university turned to the teaching and learning environment of the classrooms. It was clear that faculty wishing to adopt information technologies into their teaching would be hindered, and probably discouraged, by the need to schedule specific rooms and have equipment such as VCRs, monitors and projectors carried to their location. A plan to equip classrooms with the right equipment based on size and use has allowed instructors to have ready access to the technologies they require without logistical concerns. Regular and frequent demonstration sessions are held in the classrooms for faculty members who plan to use the information technologies available.

With the network and equipment in place and administrative services available to streamline business activities of students, faculties and staff, a lifecycle replacement schedule ensures that the technology on desktops, in general use computer sites and in classrooms remains current. This is accomplished through an annual capital funding programme that assures technology refreshment as required, about every three or four years. Through this annual refreshment process faculty members who are adopting information technologies into their teaching can switch to laptops for easy transport to classrooms.

Is the University of Delaware's use of information technologies representative of US higher education generally? Let us stop here for a moment and consult Kenneth C Green's 1999 *Campus Computing* survey. Annually, Green surveys US higher education institutions in five categories: public universities, private universities, public four-year colleges, private four-year colleges and community colleges. His findings show that overall, US higher education institutions are well on their way to having high quality ubiquitous data networks (averaging a score of 5.7 of a possible 7) and have made great strides in using technologies to deliver administrative and library services. Universities rate highest among the survey groups in these areas (Green, 1999).

PEDAGOGICAL REFORMATION

The University of Delaware is a land-grant, space-grant, sea-grant and urban-grant privately chartered university with public (state) support. Its seven colleges and 38 research centres teach more than 21,000 matriculated undergraduate students and 3,250 graduate students. During the 1980s, the university was a pioneer in instructional technology using PLATO, the Control Data Corporation mainframe based instructional courseware. By the early 1990s, however, it was clear that the technologies available for teaching were inadequate to the task. It was not until the mid-1990s that technology in teaching, at least for materials presentation, became a reasonable option. Even so, technology was difficult to use and still offered little assistance with pedagogical reformation.

During this time there were early adopters of presentation technology in the classroom. These were individual faculty members who saw that technology could deliver information in new and perhaps more effective ways. However, these individuals were not focused on pedagogical transformation, curriculum enhancement, or learning outcomes. It was not until a group of faculty members at the university began to pursue their common interest in student learning styles and style effect on course outcomes that the potential for real instructional transformation was glimpsed. Based on this interest they began to investigate ways to improve undergraduate education. This group sought and received a small grant to form the Institute for Transforming Undergraduate Education. Institute members train and mentor their colleagues to adopt active and problem based learning into their courses. The effect of this concerted effort to affect pedagogical change has become widespread at the university in the last few years (Watson and Groh, 2001). Approaching 40 per cent of the faculties have participated in Institute training and workshops to incorporate active learning strategies into their teaching, shifting the emphasis from instruction to learning. More than 160 courses have been revised or identified for revision.

By adopting and applying this new learning model to courses the university has garnered and matched more than \$3 million from grants to sustain course restructuring and faculty development. In 1997, the National Science Foundation selected the University of Delaware and nine other institutions to receive its Recognition Award for the Integration of Research and Education. More than 65 per cent of University of Delaware faculties and 90 per cent of the science faculties integrate research into the undergraduate curriculum. Student participants in the undergraduate research programme conduct research with their faculty advisers, often working alongside their advisers' graduate students on projects that result in journal publication (Lyons and Foster, 2000).

With the network infrastructure in place, the time-consuming burdens of administration alleviated, and widespread pedagogical transformation underway, it has been relatively easy to introduce use of technology into the mix. A university collaborative formed of the Institute, the library, the Center for Teaching Effectiveness, and the Office of Information Technologies, and named the Teaching, Learning and Technology Institute, offers multi-week workshops to faculty members during the winter and summer holidays. Nearly 80 percent of faculty members have attended these sessions.

Faculties also have a teaching and learning technology centre where educational technology experts help them choose appropriate technologies for their courses and where they can pilot their ideas. The centre is helped immeasurably by faculty volunteers, exemplars, who have gone through the programmes, are using technology in teaching, and who want to help their colleagues. The centre uses Arthur Chickering and Zelda Gamson's seven principles for good practice in undergraduate education to help faculty members select technologies and use them well (Chickering and Gamson, 1987).

1. Good practice encourages student/faculty contact. Faculty members are encouraged to consider electronic mail, electronic bulletin boards, threaded discussions, and chat rooms.

2. Good practice encourages cooperation among students. Faculty members are encouraged to consider structured collaborative assignments facilitated

by Web based resources, electronic mail and mail lists, threaded discussion, and chat rooms. Informal spontaneous collaboration can take place when the means are simple and at hand.

3. Good practice encourages active learning. Faculty members are encouraged to consider the Web as a repository of information for student active learning. Guided searches and discussion through chat rooms can make students proactive and full participants in the learning process.

4. Good practice gives prompt feedback. Faculty members are encouraged to consider the University's instructional management system or other already available Web based means for students to do self-assessment of their progress with course materials and toward learning goals.

5. Good practice emphasizes time on task. Faculty members are encouraged to consider structuring their courses so that a wide array of materials need to be dealt with in order to achieve learning goals. This can increase the time that students spend working toward those goals and can reinforce the learning process.

6. Good practice communicates high expectations. Faculty members are encouraged to consider online syllabi and course Web pages to set expectations for student participation and performance. These standards are then readily available to students as they use other online materials for courses, helping to remind students and reinforce expectations.

7. Good practice respects diverse talents and ways of learning. Faculty members are encouraged to consider the potential of providing rich resources on the Web and of using many methods of faculty to student and student to student interaction. Students can then discover those resources and means that best fit their learning styles and permit them to achieve the learning goals.

The university has recently adopted a Web based course management system as the standard environment for faculty moving to Web enhanced courses. Faculty can use all or parts of the system appropriate to the teaching and learning goals of the course. The university has also pioneered streaming video, which has lowered the barrier for some faculty to get started with the technology without having to redesign the course. The experience of faculty members using streaming video is that they move quickly to integrating it with the course management system to provide interactivity.

Is the University of Delaware a bellwether for what is going on in the rest of the nation? Let us pause again to consult Kenneth Green. Taking all higher education institutions together, technology in instruction, in particular Web technology, lags behind the infrastructure and online library resources, with these averaging 4.6, 5.7 and 5.3 respectively out of a possible 7 (Green, 1999). This rating, by the way, is not external but is how the institutions rate themselves. What it says is that higher education institutions in the US generally are technologically ready for curriculum transformation and that this transformation has begun. It appears that the University of Delaware is typical of US higher education institutions in the order in which technology adoption has been undertaken on campuses.

CONSORTIA, PARTNERSHIPS AND LIAISONS

Institutions' individual efforts are assisted and informed by the higher education community as a whole. Although they are competitive, they find great value in working together. Unlike countries where the higher education instruction agenda is set by national government, the majority of the US national effort related to educational technology and infrastructure is the result of institutional consortia and collaborations that form from time to time and continue as needed. The largest and most broadly based of these is EDUCAUSE. Most of its members are US institutions. However, it also has member institutions in Canada, South America, Australia, Europe, Asia, and partnerships with higher education information technology associations in Europe, Great Britain and Australia. The US consortia and collaborations frequently garner funding from both public and private sources and receive substantial contributions from the higher education members through fees and participation commitments. The National Learning Infrastructure Initiative (NLII) of EDUCAUSE is a consortium of colleges, universities and commercial partners which focuses on the need for standards, clearinghouses and assessment of information technology based teaching materials and outcomes. The NLII spawned the IMS Global Learning Consortium; a standards and specifications body working on sharable instructional modules that can interoperate in a networked environment. The NLII has also encouraged collaboration among its members resulting in the MERLOT project and the Learning Technology Consortium. Each of these groups offers a courseware clearing house and evaluation service.

Another EDUCAUSE initiative, Net@EDU, is a thought-leadership coalition of college and university chief information officers and state network directors. Net@EDU works to advance national networking for research and education through joint projects with higher education institutions and government, and by informing federal policy. Yet another is the University Consortium for Advanced Internet Development (UCAID). UCAID members, which include the software, hardware and telecommunications industries and government agencies, are researching, building, and testing the next generation Internet (I2). EDUCAUSE also spawned I2 and UCAID.

Some states in the US have begun to take a more active role in fostering common instructional standards and media and infrastructure. This is particularly true of those states that are looking to asynchronous or distance education to provide higher education to a burgeoning population, a geographically disbursed population, and those in need of professional development to promote regional economic development.

GOOD NAVIGATION

In discussing the course redesign challenge, Janet DeVry and David Brown summarized:

> In this rapidly changing technological world, we need proven guideposts to help us know where we are going. Just as forming learning objectives is critical in determining what students will learn in class, forming objectives about the purpose and function of technology is critical to whether or not the promise of technology to transform education will ever be realized. Without guidelines, we are adrift. We do not have time to drift. We have students to educate for a world far more technologically complex than we can imagine. They need to be well equipped. (Brown and DeVry, 2000)

REFERENCES

Brown, D G and DeVry, J R (2000) A framework for redesigning a course, in *Teaching with Technology*, ed D G Brown, Anker, Bolton, Mass., p 15

Chickering, A W and Gamson, Z F (1987) Seven principles for good practice in under-graduate education, *AAHE Bulletin*, **38** (7) (March), pp 3–7

Green, K C (1999) *Campus Computing 1999: The tenth national survey of computing and information technology in higher education*, Campus Computing Project, Encino, Calif.

Lyons, L C and Foster, S J (2000) Computing environment at the University of Delaware, in *Teaching with Technology*, ed D G Brown, Anker, Bolton, Mass., pp 20–21

Watson, G and Groh, S E (2001) Faculty mentoring faculty: the institute for transforming undergraduate education, in *The Power of Problem-based Learning: A practical 'how to' for teaching undergraduate courses in any discipline*, Stylus, Sterling, Va.

CONSULTED SOURCES

Foster, S J and Hollowell, D E (1999) Integrating information technology planning and funding at the institutional level, in *Information Technology in Higher Education: Assessing its impact and planning for the future*, ed R N Katz and J A Rudy, no 102, (Summer), Jossey-Bass, San Francisco, Calif.

Green, K C (1999) First to the ballroom, last to the dance, in *The 'E' is for Everything: E-commerce, e-business, and e-learning in the future of higher education*, ed R N Katz and D G Oblinger, Jossey-Bass, San Francisco, Calif., pp 13, 15

Luker, M A (ed) (2000) *Preparing Your Campus for the Networked Future*, Jossey-Bass, San Francisco, Calif.

Mackenzie, E O (1999) *Report on Technology Use in the Classroom at the University of Delaware*, White Paper

Oblinger, D (1999) *Putting Students at the Center: A planning guide of distributed learning*, EDUCAUSE Monograph Series, no 1

Twigg, C A (1999) *Improving Learning and Reducing Costs: Redesigning large-enrollment courses*, Pew learning and technology program, Center for Academic Transformation, Rensselaer Polytechnic Institute, Troy, NY

APPENDIX 1: WEB SITES OF INTEREST

Bibliography and Bookmarks for Teaching, Learning and Technology
http://www.clunet.edu/iss/lib/culpep/online.html

California Virtual Campus
http://www.cvc.edu

Center for Teaching Effectiveness, University of Delaware
http://www.udel.edu/cte

EDUCAUSE
http://www.educause.edu

IMS Global Learning Consortium, Inc.
http://www.imsproject.org

Institute for Transforming Undergraduate Education, University of Delaware
http://www.udel.edu/inst

MERLOT: Multimedia Educational Repository for Learning and On-line Teaching
http://merlot.cdl.edu

Minnesota Virtual University
http://www.mnvu.org

National Learning Infrastructure Initiative
http://www.educause.edu/nlii

Net@Edu
http://www.educause.edu/netatedu

Problem-based Learning, University of Delaware
http://www.udel.edu/pbl

Streaming Video Courseware, University of Delaware
http://www.udel.edu/UMS/itv/demo

Teaching Learning and Technology Center, University of Delaware
http://www.udel.edu/present

Teaching, Learning and Technology Institute, University of Delaware
http://www.udel.edu/cte/tlt600.html

University Consortium for Advanced Internet Development
http://www.ucaid.org

University-based Teaching and Learning Centers
http://www.wfu.edu/organizations/TLC/resources.htm

University of Delaware Library
http://www.lib.udel.edu

Virtual College of Texas
http://www.vct.org

Western Governors University
http://www.wgu.edu

World Lecture Hall, University of Texas at Austin
http://www.utexas.edu/world/lecture

3

Institution-wide implementation of ICT in student learning

Ivan Moore

SUMMARY

The University of Wolverhampton is a 'modern university' with a strong regional role in the centre of England. It has a strong widening participation mission, and engages students from a range of cultural, educational and socio-economic backgrounds. It is constantly striving to find ways of improving the learning environment for its students, and several years ago it set up a department to support the Development and Evaluation of Learning Technology Applications (DELTA). More recently, it established a Centre for Learning and Teaching (CeLT) and, together, these two departments have been key in encouraging the widespread involvement of teaching staff in using information and communications technology (ICT) to provide support for students. This chapter describes how this has been achieved and discusses some of the critical success factors.

BACKGROUND

The beginning of a project to implement ICT in student learning at the University of Wolverhampton arose from a coming together of four separate activities:

1. In 1996, DELTA won a European Union grant to develop online learning materials for small and medium-sized enterprises (SMEs) in the centre of England (the Midlands) and to deliver them through a Midlands Metropolitan Network (MIDMAN). The project became known as 'Broadnet'. The director of DELTA evaluated the various commercially available learning environment software packages and decided to produce an in-house learning environment – the Wolverhampton Online Learning Framework (WOLF) – which he felt would be better suited to the needs of the project.

2. In 1998, the Pro Vice-Chancellor for Academic Development was preparing a planning framework, which outlined a six-year development plan for the university. In this, she highlighted the need to 'exploit the potential of ICT' in student learning. The following are specific actions that are outlined in the planning framework:

   – Within the learning and teaching policy (LTP), adopt WOLF as the standard for the delivery of technology supported learning.

   – Create a provider/client service relationship between DELTA and the university.

   – Make sufficient end user technology available to make use of technology supported learning (TSL).

   – Provide appropriate support, including training, for teachers and learners.

   – Run a university-wide programme to have at least all level 0 and level 1 modules available for engagement through TSL (by 2004/5).

   – Create appropriate quality standards for TSL.

3. Also in 1998, the senior management team of the university organized a seminar at which several key projects were investigated. Staff were identified to coordinate investigations into different areas of the university's development portfolio, and one of these areas was the potential for ICT in student learning. And so was born the 'ICT task group'. This group met over the following year and investigated both the pedagogic implications of ICT and the infrastructure needs of implementing ICT. The report gave cautious but positive support for the implementation of ICT in student learning.

4. Finally, the university developed a learning and teaching policy in 1998. A key outcome of this policy was the recommendation to invest in a Learning and Teaching Institute with responsibilities for 'quality evaluation and production of learning resources, staff development and support'. This recommendation was implemented by the establishment of the Centre for Learning and Teaching (CeLT). With the appointment of a director, the role of CeLT was expanded to include strategic leadership and advice in learning and teaching and support for policy formulation.

Extracts from the report of the task group in July 1999

The group and its wider representation
This task group met several times throughout the year to discuss the implementation of a technology supported learning (TSL) programme within undergraduate and sub-degree programmes of study. Initially, the group comprised of representatives from schools and some support departments and views were communicated between the group and the schools and departments via these

representatives. As time progressed, the constituencies of representation were widened to include a representative from each school and representatives from each of the university's committees. This allowed wider consultation and feedback to be achieved. The final outcomes of the group were communicated to senior management staff of the university during the senior staff conference in June 1999.

The findings of the task group

The group noted that considerable progress had already been made in TSL in some schools. These developments were often the result of individual, unsupported effort, and were not achieved in any way as a result of any school or university-wide strategy. Staff involved in these developments are to be congratulated. There was considerable expertise in pockets across the university. Centrally, the Broadnet programme had allowed the university to develop a market lead in the area of TSL and it seemed appropriate to make use of the expertise and products gained through this project. The DELTA Institute had developed the Wolverhampton On-line Learning Framework (WOLF) and this was seen as a useful TSL learning environment to promote through the TSL project.

The following recommendations are made:

- All level zero and level 1 modules should develop some form of engagement with TSL within the next three calendar years.
- The university should provide a strategic goal for the engagements along with a harmonizing framework, and schools should determine their own local strategies for achieving the outcomes set by the university.
- The outcomes will be established on behalf of the university by a TSL project management team. This team will also be responsible for harmonizing and monitoring the progress of the school strategies.
- Progress will be reported annually through executive and Academic Board.
- WOLF should be promoted as the university's first choice of TSL environment.
- Other courseware may be used at the discretion of the relevant school.
- The management team will advise the DELTA Institute of the functional requirements and enhancements necessary for WOLF.
- They will determine the forms of support necessary for schools, departments and staff in pursuing the project outcomes.
- Funding must be provided, at least for the first phase of the project. This should be managed through the project management team.

THE PROBLEMS

In attempting to implement the actions in the planning framework, several issues became apparent:

- WOLF had been developed for a specific purpose: to provide a platform for the delivery of learning content to adult learners at their workplace in SMEs. WOLF was not perceived as an appropriate framework for full-time undergraduate students.

- Although the planning framework was set over six years, the university expected these engagements to be achieved within one academic year.

- The university expected a single strategy to deliver the intended outcomes within this short timescale.

- Although the university wished to 'exploit the potential of ICT', there was no understanding of what that potential might be. It was not clear if it might be in improving the quality of the learning environment, in making efficiency gains, in facilitating international market penetration, or simply in providing an exciting variation in the learning experience which would satisfy the expectations of our ICT-literate students.

- The ICT task group report referred to learner 'engagements' with ICT. There was no information about what was meant by these 'engagements'. However, it was intended that they would be the same for all modules across all schools.

THE PROBLEMS SOLVED

Once the issues that were creating a barrier to progress had been identified, a management executive team was established to identify the means of overcoming these barriers. A number of principles were established:

1. WOLF would be the university's preferred framework. The DELTA Institute, the CeLT and IT services would provide support for developments using WOLF, and IT services would provide and ensure an appropriate server and infrastructure for WOLF. Staff or schools could use any other framework, or indeed, technology, which they thought would better suit their purposes. If this were to be the case, then the school would be responsible for providing the necessary support. An agreement was made between CeLT, who were now managing the project, and DELTA whereby requirements for functional enhancements to WOLF would be routed through the management team to DELTA, who would implement these enhancements. In this way, concerns over the effectiveness of WOLF would be addressed and the capacity to develop WOLF in a manner appropriate to student learning would be exploited. Additionally, academic staff would have a feeling of some influence over the shape of the framework.

2. Rather than producing a single strategy, the project team determined the outcomes of the project, and schools were required to devise their own 'local' strategies. The project team provided a framework for school strategies in order to ensure conformity with the principles of the project and to harmonize school strategies.

3. The timescale for achieving the outcomes was established as four academic years, beginning in September 1999.

4. Initial engagements were not defined centrally, but rather, schools defined their own starting points and were required to show how these would develop. This was to allow staff to start from different places and to develop an understanding of different aspects of an online learning environment. For example, some could begin by simply providing their module guides or notes on the framework, some might begin by exploiting the online communications, and others still might begin by using the online self assessment facility.

A prototype phase was introduced, during which time the functionality of WOLF was tested and a small number of pioneering academics tested some of the potential of the system.

THE TSL PROJECT

The following boxes provide summaries of the project outcomes, the makeup and role of the management team and the framework for school strategies. The Gantt chart in Figure 3.1 provides details of the project timescales.

The TSL project strategy

Defined outcomes of the project

- All level 0 and level 1 modules will engage with TSL in some form.
- There will be a phased roll-in of modules over the three calendar years from 2000 to 2002.
- The university will promote the use of the Wolverhampton On-line Learning Framework (WOLF) as a standard environment for TSL.
- WOLF will not be the only means by which staff may choose to develop an engagement. Where some other means is chosen (commercial courseware, TLTP products, courseware application packages such as Question mark, CD ROM, intranet, Web pages, etc), this should be iden-tified and managed.
- Schools will be responsible for determining their own strategy, with priorities, for achieving these outcomes.
- The nature of the initial engagement for each module will be defined within the strategy, as will the criteria and means of evaluating the engagement. These engagements will be extended systematically to higher levels of modules.
- A framework will be provided to schools in order to facilitate their articulation of their strategy.

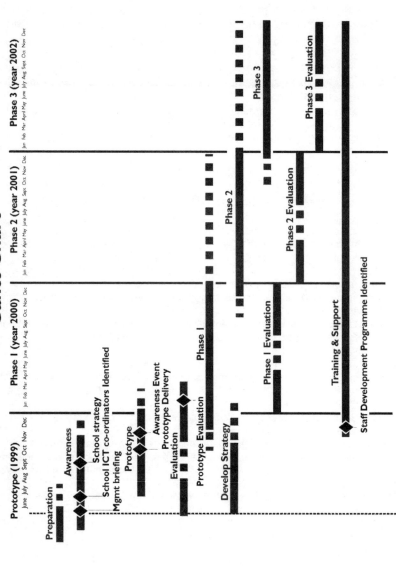

Figure 3.1 *Phases in the TSL project*
Source: Centre for Learning and Teaching

The role of the institution and the management team

The role of the institution
This project will be managed through the TSL project management team. This team will include representatives from Executive, the Centre for Learning and Teaching, the DELTA Institute, IT services, the Learning Centres, Registry, Finance, the University Quality Committee, Staff Development and the Schools.

The role of the TSL management team
The team will:

- Raise awareness across the institution of the potential for TSL and of the TSL project itself.
- Disseminate developments, initiatives and approaches to the use of TSL.
- Establish the functional specification of WOLF.
- Determine an initial functional specification for WOLF.
- Prototype initial engagements in order to determine a working functional specification.
- Provide functionality requirements to the DELTA Institute and ensure that these requirements are met.
- Determine and revise periodically the TSL strategy and timescales.
- Receive the initial school strategies and monitor and advise the school coordinators in regard to these strategies.
- Provide a conduit for the exchange of good practices across schools.
- Identify staff development and other support needs for the project.
- Coordinate, with other groups, the development of quality guidelines and procedures for the implementation of TSL materials.
- Manage and approve the development of relevant user guides etc.
- Develop appropriate project and materials evaluation tools.
- Make recommendations on infrastructure implications to the relevant departments and university committees.

The team will meet at least once per semester.

Framework for school strategies

Strategic framework for the TSL project
Schools are asked to prepare a strategic plan, which will identify how they intend to meet the objectives of the project. Schools have different approaches to learning within their disciplines, and have varying levels of expertise and experience in the implementation of TSL, so each school will identify its own strategy. However, this is an institutional project and there is benefit to be gained from a harmonized and coordinated approach to its pursuit, so school strategies will be developed according to a common framework. The framework is set out below.

School coordinator for the project
The strategy will need to identify a school TSL coordinator. This person will have certain responsibilities, which include:

- assisting the dean to develop the school strategy;

- raising awareness of the project amongst school staff;
- disseminating information on existing and developing materials;
- liaising with the academic staff in identifying priorities and modules for inclusion at each stage;
- coordinating the activities of those involved in the development work;
- representing the school on the TSL management team;
- assisting the dean in managing the school strategy to ensure successful completion of its objectives.

Phases and timescales
The strategy should identify the modules to be involved in each phase of the project. Schools will want to determine their own priorities and these should be clearly articulated. For each module, the nature of the initial engagement and the person with first responsibility for the development work will be identified.

Engagement with TSL
The nature of the initial engagement in a module is not defined centrally and should be articulated by the module coordinators. The strategy should encourage a rich variety of means of engagement and it should be remembered that engagement means more than simply populating an environment with course notes or other forms of delivery.

Development model
The strategy will need to identify the process for deciding whether to use WOLF or some other courseware, or server, for initial engagements. The means by which materials will be developed will need to be described. Schools may wish to choose from a number of options including:

- developing a mechanism for identifying appropriate, existing, externally available materials;
- establishing a school courseware development unit (CDU);
- releasing academic staff from teaching hours to facilitate their development work;
- attaching staff to the Centre for Learning and Teaching (CeLT);
- buying in technical or other expertise;
- establishing a TSL project self-help team.

Continuation
A description of horizontal and vertical continuation strategies should be provided:

Horizontal: A module might identify engagement by way of, say, self-assessment materials. On completion of this programme, the module coordinator should be encouraged to identify the ways in which further engagement might be developed.

Vertical: Once students have been introduced to TSL in their first year, they will expect to encounter TSL in their level 2 and eventually level 3 modules. The mechanism for achieving this and for building on the first-year experience should be outlined in the strategy.

Evaluation and quality
All materials, learning processes, engagements and outcomes of the intro-duction of TSL into any module should be evaluated. Criteria for evaluation

should be established at the beginning of each phase of the project. Key staff involved in the evaluation (module leader, project coordinator and school staff) should be identified. The strategy should identify the *mechanisms* for achieving this (eg special evaluation group, school learning and teaching committee) and the *means* of evaluation (student questionnaires, module surveys, staff evaluations, outcomes analysis etc).

Schools will need to assure themselves of the quality of the TSL environment. Their quality development and assurance procedures and guidelines should be in harmony with those established by the institution and adopted by the TSL management group.

Support
Based on a clear and realistic appraisal of the various forms of support currently available centrally, the school strategy should identify the support, which the school will provide, and the support, which the school may require from the institution. Suitable headings might include staff development, technical, pedagogic, infrastructure, financial and other.

School strategy papers should be presented to the TSL management group for its consideration at its next meeting in September 1999.

A key development in the project was establishing a TSL coordinator in each school and department. The school coordinators developed school strategies and represented the interests of the school on the project management team.

An early process in the prototype phase was to produce an independent evaluation of just exactly what WOLF could really do. This 'functional specification' was carried out by a member of staff from CeLT along with one from IT services. Figure 3.2 shows the functional specification model used. The first row identifies the main functions provided by WOLF at that time. As you move down through the rows, more detail is provided about the particular function under investigation. A full report was produced and this report led to the development of several 'WOLF guides' and training booklets. The two independent evaluators became the TSL advisers and provided the university's central support and staff training resource for WOLF. For further details, see O'Donoghue *et al* (2000).

The strategies required schools to identify training and staff development needs. These focused initially on technical training and support. The view taken here was that academic staff had at least some understanding of learning and teaching, whereas they had little understanding of WOLF. They would be expected to utilize their pedagogic skills when developing engagements with WOLF. Clearly there was a huge training need, but there was little training resource. A cascade model of training and support was provided (Dalziel, Childs and Moore, 2000). This is represented in Figures 3.3 and 3.4. This cascade system was used to provide training (top-down), support (bottom-up) and feedback (bottom-up). The feedback path was to be the mechanism for academic staff to suggest functional enhancements to WOLF. A 'bug report'

WOLF features	Teaching materials	Tutoring and mentoring	Learning Ssupport	User tools	Tutor admin	System requirements:
Overview	**Course** Structured course materials	**Tools** Communication & collaboration	**Search** Learning support facilities	**My folder** Module related tools	**Tutor** Module administration	• for developers • for users • infrastructure implications **Enhancements**
Summary of features	• course notes • presentations • case studies • activities	• calculator • chat & forum • e-mail tutor • events/notices • references	• content • library • e-mail • phone	• bookmarks • check progress • notepad • personal diary • e-mail	Tools for: • scheduling events • tracking progress • structuring module	**Developments**
Feature functionality						
Technical functionality						

Trainer ← WOLF Guide → Developer

Support staff → User

Figure 3.2 *WOLF functional specification*

form within WOLF was used for staff to report functions that did not work as intended. Bugs reported directly to DELTA in this way were investigated within 24 hours and fixed within a further 24 hours.

Cascade training model

Figure 3.3   *Cascade training model*

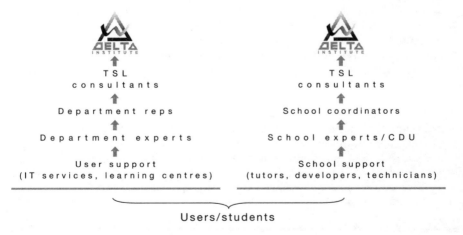

Users/students

Cascade support model

Figure 3.4   *Cascade support model*

OTHER SUPPORT MECHANISMS

Clearly, the regular project management meetings provided a forum for sharing practice among the school coordinators, but academic staff developing their engagements were often working in isolation. As the project developed, the management team introduced regular 'showcase' events. Staff would come together to demonstrate their engagements and discuss any issues, concerns or successes they were having. In this way a rich resource of practical implementations of different approaches was shared around the teaching staff.

A recent development, introduced by DELTA, is the Wolfpack. This is an informal user group, which consists of staff from within the university and beyond who are using WOLF in one of its various internal or commercially available external forms to support their students in their learning. The group communicates through a mailbase and occasional meetings within the university.

RECENT DEVELOPMENTS

In order to track and support developments in schools, each coordinator provided a module action plan (MAP). This was necessary to ensure that initial engagements developed by the staff were developed. The map took each level 1 module and identified the nature of the initial engagement, the intended first development and suggested further expansion into the learner space in the framework.

WOLF has itself developed in many ways since the beginning of the project. The 'my folder' option has been supplemented with a 'group folder'. This allows groups of students to work in a number of ways. It can be used to support study cells or it can be used to support group projects. Materials held within a group folder are available only to the students identified as being within the group. A portal has been introduced, through which all students enter WOLF; student tracking systems have been developed; the online assessment facility has been enhanced and a student feedback form has been developed.

CONCLUSIONS

Although the project is only at the stage of the end of the first phase, over 200 modules are now registered on the database. Many level 2 and higher modules are using WOLF and some modules are now available fully online to students who wish to study remotely from the university. Some schools are now in a position to offer programmes of study or modules to a worldwide marketplace.

Factors that made it work

The following success factors have been identified (Moore and Childs, 2000):

- University-wide project objectives and management informing local strategies.

- This provides a combination of institution-wide cohesion for the project and empowerment of staff at a school level.

- Realistic timescales (three years).

- Appropriate training and support systems.

- In-house pedagogic and technological expertise.

- Staff and students having direct input into the development of the learning framework that they are using.

- School TSL coordinators having sufficient experience and resources to facilitate the development of ICT within their school.

Clearly, institutional support was necessary. The university identified TSL as a key development in its learning and teaching support infrastructure. A pro vice-chancellor and director of learning and teaching were given responsibility for developing the project and the DELTA institute was given ongoing support for its work in this area.

It was important to recognize the work that had been going on in the university in an uncoordinated way and to recognize the staff who had been involved in this work. Several of these staff became school coordinators for the project.

Although there was little financial resource, that which was available was put into people. The project coordinators were given time to carry out their work in the schools, and key central staff were appointed/seconded to support the project.

A clear strategy was crucial. The strategy was sufficiently focused to be meaningful, but flexible enough to allow staff to feel they could engage in it. One important realization of this was to establish a university framework for the project, with clear objectives, but to allow schools to develop their own local strategies.

Above all else, the strategy needed to have staff at all levels who were accountable for the success of the project at their respective levels.

The barriers

Despite the fact that the project is important to the university and that it has the support of senior management, it is not known to all staff in the university. After two years, many academic staff still had not heard of the project, even though great efforts were made to tell everyone about it. The difficulty in disseminating this kind of information cannot be over-emphasized.

It has taken a long time for the school coordinators to come to recognize their role as project managers. Staff are used to sitting on committees and to representing the needs of their school on central committees. However, the role of the school coordinators is different. They are project managers who are accountable to the university, not for their own involvement with TSL, but for that of their colleagues and of their school. One way to overcome this was to require each school to develop a project plan. The school coordinators then became responsible, not only for the plan, but also for its implementation.

Naturally, the project has always been under-resourced. It has always, therefore, been important to use resources effectively. Much of the emphasis here has been on supporting the school coordinators. The project team meets monthly for two hours, and these monthly meetings include staff development workshops for the coordinators.

This leads on to the key issue of staff development. It should always be understood that, while communication is essential for a project of this kind to be successful, it is equally important to recognize that many staff will not have the necessary expertise to carry out their roles. In many cases, once awareness has been raised with staff, they become enthusiastic, and support has to be available immediately. Staff development is therefore crucial. It must be relevant to their needs, pitched at their level of expertise, and timely. Staff development needs to include not only initial training, but also other forms of support for staff. Within the project, we have created a model for both training and support for staff. School strategies also include school-specific staff development and support needs.

REFERENCES

Dalziel, C, Childs, M and Moore, I (2000) *Supporting Staff in the Delivery of Technology Supported Learning at the University of Wolverhampton*, 7th International ALT Conference on Integrating Learning Technology, Manchester, September

Moore, I and Childs, M (2000) *The TSL Project at the University of Wolverhampton*, European Association of Distance Teaching Universities Annual Conference, Paris, September

O'Donoghue, J, Fleetham, L, Dalziel, C and Molyneux, S (2000) *The Wolverhampton Online Learning Framework*, 7th International ALT Conference on Integrating Learning Technology, Manchester, September

4

The impact of ubiquitous laptop computing

Donna Wood McCarty

SUMMARY

This chapter focuses on the impact of a ubiquitous laptop computing project on teaching and learning at a medium sized, public commuter university in the United States. The implementation of this information technology project is described as a three-phase process, with each phase having its own unique characteristics. Data from a qualitative research project, *The Chronicles of Change*, as well as faculty and student survey results are discussed throughout. The benefits and challenges of technology use in an educational context as well as the key lessons learned at each implementation phase are highlighted.

INTRODUCTION

As anyone who is cognizant of trends in higher education is well aware, institutions around the globe are utilizing technology for educational purposes with increasing frequency. This is certainly the case in the United States, where more and more colleges and universities are adding technological components to their curricula. The extent to which this is happening and the rapidity with which these changes are occurring vary widely from institution to institution; to date, relatively few have made information technology a ubiquitous part of campus life. The University of Minnesota at Crookston, Wake Forest University in North Carolina and Seton Hall University in New Jersey are among those institutions that have undertaken the maximal infusion of information technology into the curriculum. One such institution is Clayton College and State University (CCSU), and this chapter will elucidate some of the outcomes of this total immersion into information technology for educational purposes.

As context for the analysis that follows, it is important to understand that CCSU is not a privileged private institution comprised of affluent students with high entrance test scores. In fact, it is a part of the public University System of Georgia, and its student body is composed of many first-generation college students, with many from blue-collar or rural backgrounds and approximately half from a minority group. Many of the entering students are less than fully prepared for college and have relatively low scores on entrance tests. While CCSU enrols many students of traditional college age, the average student age is 27, and a large portion of the student population are working adults who are returning to school to further their educational goals. CCSU is a commuter campus in a suburb of metropolitan Atlanta, and currently serves just under 5,000 students each semester.

INFORMATION TECHNOLOGY PROJECT (ITP) DESCRIPTION

During the Fall of 1997, Clayton College and State University implemented a rather bold educational experiment known as the Information Technology Project (ITP). This project was intended to achieve a total infusion of information technology into instruction. In preparation for the implementation of the programme, faculty had been equipped with laptop computers and unlimited Internet access both from campus and from home, and had received an array of training in the applications that were to be common to all students and faculty. From late Fall 1997 into early 1998, students were issued laptop computers with the Microsoft Office suite of applications (like those of the faculty) as part of a technology package which included unlimited Internet access (from home and campus). They were also provided a help desk for support and repair, and training in the use of the technology. The experiment in ubiquitous computing began in earnest.

There was certainly a desire on the part of all involved to promote a facility with computer technology to prepare students for careers in the next century; but it is important to understand that the major concern was that the project have a positive impact on the faculty's pedagogy and the quality of student learning. Educational outcomes like the ability to communicate in writing and to think critically are of primary importance to the faculty and administration at the institution, and everyone involved wanted to be certain that ITP was serving as an enhancement (and at least not a detriment) to these overriding educational goals. While grades, standardized test scores and other indexes are of use in ensuring that a programme such as ITP is of benefit to students, these measures would not capture the richness of the experience that the faculty and students were to undergo. Furthermore, the standardized measures would not provide detailed information useful for improvement and to share with those at other institutions considering an infusion of technology into their programmes.

ITP EVALUATION STRATEGY

A strategy for examining the impact of ITP on teaching and learning was established, and the major question for the investigation was as follows: will learning productivity be enhanced by the systematic use of information technology as an instructional strategy?

In turn, learning productivity was defined with respect to three parameters:

- the *effectiveness* of instructional approaches;
- the *efficiency* of resource use;
- the *satisfaction levels* of faculty, students, and employers with the preparation of CCSU students.

Information technology for instruction was defined as student and faculty use of notebook computers, the Internet and other technology for educational purposes. Surveys, standardized tests and other measures were to be given to the students, but the need existed for a method of data collection that would 'tell the story' and provide a more detailed and contextual source of information about the impact of the project. Two faculty members at CCSU determined that a qualitative study would help provide such a record and developed the concept for *The Chronicles of Change* (McCarty and Robinson, 1999).

The basic premise of *The Chronicles of Change* was that an infusion of technology at a university would be successful only if the faculty support the effort and believe that technological tools can enhance student learning. Therefore, the project consisted of journal entries provided by a group of faculty volunteers from a variety of disciplines. Over the course of two years, the faculty responded at various intervals to prompts such as, 'In what ways has ITP enhanced/detracted from the teaching/learning process?' and 'How has ITP changed the campus culture at CCSU?' Initially, there were 23 faculty across all four schools at the university in a range of disciplines from English to nursing to paralegal studies. These faculty also varied in how positively they regarded technology. After the first three months, there were still 18 of the volunteers who remained committed to the project; fortunately, the proportionality by school and range of attitude toward ITP remained constant despite the loss of 5 of the original participants.

The analysis of the data was facilitated through use of a widely used software program for the analysis of qualitative data: Non-Numerical Unstructured Data Indexing Searching Theorizing (QSR NUD*IST). A conceptually ordered display (Miles and Huberman, 1994) was utilized in the analysis, as data were separated into individual conceptual text units by idea or by concept. Data were then imported into the software and coded by topic. Each conceptual text unit could be reported to as many categories as appropriate. The software provided the means to examine all comments within an individual category, overlapping categories, or the union of two or more categories. The journal data were then examined for patterns and the exceptions to those patterns.

An examination of the data revealed that time was an extremely important factor in the events following ITP implementation. The patterns within the data suggested that implementation occurred in a three-phase process with each phase exhibiting markedly unique characteristics. The periodic examination of the data during implementation provided diagnostic information enabling the administration to make important modifications to implementation strategies. The data suggest that these alterations have been critical to the success of ITP.

PHASE I OF THE PROJECT

In Phase I of the project, optimism and enthusiasm ran high. Satisfaction levels for both faculty and students indicated that each group anticipated that ITP was going to have a very positive impact on teaching and learning at CCSU. In a pre-ITP survey, 89 per cent of faculty and 71 per cent of students were moderately to entirely positive when asked how they felt about students having their own notebook computers to use. Similarly, 97 per cent of the faculty and 91 per cent of the students believed that technology would enhance the student learning experience (Clayton College and State University, 1999).

Clearly, most faculty and students had faith in 'technology as change-agent' and believed that ITP would enhance learning. In the words of one of the faculty chroniclers:

> I believe that students' critical thinking skills will be strongly enhanced as a result of ITP, beginning at the moment that they first use the laptop. Getting an e-mail account, learning to connect from remote locations, using the Internet, and generally learning to use the computer are just the beginning of the critical thinking and problem solving skills that will be required of students. As they become more experienced users, critical thinking will be a natural part of using the Internet more efficiently. Students will be encouraged to work independently and to discover the vast array of information that is at their fingertips. Also, as they learn to use Microsoft Office, their problem solving skills will develop. I think this will be one of the major accomplishments of ITP.

The optimism expressed in the survey results and some of *The Chronicles of Change* comments was tempered with a healthy sense of realism about the impact of ubiquitous technology. Another faculty member stated that:

> Critical thinking skills will be greatly improved if classes engage in activities based on interactive tasks. Learning how to type with a word processor or to complete exercises on the computer will not move students to think more critically. If activities are designed to stimulate thinking on several levels, however, the students will think more critically. In other words, if they combine reading, discussion, and writing with the power of the computer to generate group discussion, research, and peer evaluation, they will improve their critical thinking skills.

Yet another expressed cautious optimism about the impact of the project:

> I do not believe that ITP by itself will enhance the teaching/learning process. The teaching/learning process will be enhanced if teachers and students regard the program with enthusiasm and put it to good use. The process will be degraded if teachers or students get so bogged down, or caught up in the technology that the process gets away from

them. It is completely up to the humans involved to use these tools as such in creative ways.

A very small subset of the chroniclers were not at all optimistic about the benefits of ITP and predicted that the technology would not have any major impact on teaching and learning. One faculty member expressed this view as follows:

> To date there is no recognized diet pill that really works and allows people to lose weight, yet millions of people try these pills every year. We constantly look for the 'quick' fix to problems. I think the computer is the new diet pill in education. We hope (expect, think, etc) that this will cause students to be better critical thinkers, more educated, use more resources, study longer, harder, more thoroughly. I do not think this will be the case (especially since I have not lost any significant weight in the last years).

In addition to critical thinking, the faculty were quite concerned about how the project would impact communication skills. Virtually everyone associated with the project noted a rapid escalation in the amount of communication going on between faculty and students and between students. Most of the comments submitted to *The Chronicles of Change* in Phase I of implementation focused on the joys and frustrations of burgeoning e-mail use. The extent to which an actual improvement in writing skills was occurring as a result of all of this communication was unclear; while some faculty members seemed to be using the technology to enhance writing, others seemed to focus almost entirely on technology for sharing information. The potential to enhance writing skills was apparent, however, as faculty commented on uses such as students sending in successive drafts of assignments, and on students being more likely to try different kinds of sentences, patterns of development, word choices and so on because of the ease of word processing.

Very early in project implementation, the faculty expressed a great deal of optimism regarding the ways in which ITP would enhance the efficiency of their instructional efforts. An analysis of *The Chronicles of Change* data support the notion that ITP had a dramatic effect on efficiency. It is clear that innovations such as the ability to send messages to entire classes at once via a class 'listserv' and to place class materials onto a faculty member's Web site for student access added greatly to the efficiency of both teaching and learning. However, the ability to communicate with students 24 hours a day made teaching a round-the-clock job, and the volume of communication was rapidly becoming burdensome. The rapidity with which the project caught on led to huge demand on the infrastructure supporting the project, and this led to persistent problems of usage reliability for faculty and students. Students turned out to be less technologically savvy than expected, and much time and energy was expended in assisting students with basic skills like saving files and file management. Therefore, while the project produced many positive effects early on, the negatives created frustration and somewhat diluted the benefits accrued.

Overall, Phase I of ITP implementation was characterized by both widespread optimism and frustration. It was a time to adjust to the many challenges of technology use. While the overriding goal was to approach instruction in new ways, the very real practical constraints of the infrastructure, student and faculty preparedness, and rapidly increasing e-mail communication made this a time of obsession with technology rather than the hoped for innovation.

PHASE II OF THE PROJECT

Phase II could be summed up as a time of reality-checks and mid-course corrections. By early Phase II, the novelty of the project had diminished somewhat and the faculty chroniclers' entries were characterized by less optimism and a heightened sense of realism and, in some cases, frustration. The fact that making ITP a success required a very steep learning curve was becoming increasingly apparent to the faculty; their skill levels at the use of technology for instruction were building rapidly, and so were their concerns over the difficulties of implementation. It is interesting to note, however, that when asked whether or not they would continue with ITP implementation if it were up to them, the faculty journalists unanimously expressed their desire to continue the project.

As the faculty's comfort level with technology use increased, their frustration levels at the difficulty of using technology effectively for instruction increased. It became apparent that the attempt to build faculty skills in the software applications and basic skills had been quite effective; the translation of these skills into innovative and effective instructional practice was quite another matter. Those faculty who were already of a highly creative and adventurous inclination seemed to find solutions to problems and ways around the frustrating obstacles. Others seemed to become 'blocked' during Phase II and to become mired in a focus on difficulties with the reliability of access to the campus network and other frustrations. Many workshops on building technology skills were provided on campus and technical support was available as well; however, support targeted at the faculty desire to use technology effectively for instruction was not provided in any formal sense. The huge time commitment required to produce instructional technology was another obstacle that seemed to discourage the faculty chroniclers.

It is interesting to note that frustration levels were increasing within the context of so much development of skill and comfort level with the use of technology. Phase II was an interesting part of the implementation process because it encompassed both extremely positive experiences by faculty and students who were getting more and more proficient at the use of technology, and extremely negative experiences as they had expectations of reliability of access that were not being met. Underlying the growing frustration was the sense that substantive improvements in the quality of teaching and learning could be made if faculty support and system reliability could be improved.

An interim examination of the data revealed an alarming trend toward greater frustration, and it became increasingly clear that some mid-course corrections were needed. While faculty development surveys given to the faculty were also of great use in determining strategies for program improvement, *The*

Chronicles of Change data proved particularly useful in this regard. The faculty chroniclers expressed many ideas and suggestions that were useful in formulating a plan to enhance the effectiveness of ITP support. One extremely valuable insight was the observation that instructional technology support belongs in Academic Affairs as opposed to the Office of Information Technology Services. One chronicler clearly stated the key concern: 'I wonder why instructional technology doesn't fall under the oversight of the VPAA [Vice President for Academic Affairs] like everything else connected with curriculum.'

Based upon the faculty comments in *The Chronicles of Change* as well as responses on a faculty development survey, a faculty committee (the Faculty Development Coordinating Committee) devised a set of recommendations for the improvement of faculty support (Clayton College and State University, 1998). These recommendations centred around the establishment of an 'instructional technology center' which would have attributes such as these:

- hardware and software needed to produce instructional materials;

- careful staffing with academically oriented professionals with strong instructional design expertise (not 'techies');

- a faculty mentor/colleague tutor programme where faculty with expertise in instructional technology uses can assist their peers in a collegial atmosphere;

- workshops, online information and other instructional materials for beginning, intermediate, and advanced level faculty would be designed, taught, or distributed through the center;

- student assistants to work with faculty on projects;

- a pleasant, collegial, stimulating environment for faculty to come together to discuss instructional issues and work on projects of mutual or individual interest.

The data provided persuaded the administration to find the resources necessary to implement the recommendations of the faculty committee. A Center for Instructional Development (CID) and a Faculty Instructional Development Lab (FIDL) were created under the aegis of Academic Affairs. Once these targeted improvements in the support systems were implemented, it remained to be seen whether or not satisfaction levels with ITP would improve during Phase III of project implementation.

PHASE III OF THE PROJECT

Faculty comments during Phase III were strikingly different from those of the previous phases. The faculty journalists indicated in their comments that ITP had become a fully integrated part of CCSU, even for those initially resistant to the project. One chronicler stated this culture shift: 'ITP is part of our culture, for better or for worse. Personally and professionally, I think we are the better and our students in the long run will benefit greatly.'

The faculty also express satisfaction at what they describe as an increased student acceptance of ITP and the confidence students demonstrate in their use of technology: 'Student acceptance is way up... as they become more familiar with the tool they are using it more and in more ways. It would be hard to go back to the old way of doing things.'

These observations are supported by a follow-up survey of satisfaction with ITP of both faculty and students, which asked the same questions as were asked prior to implementation. When asked how they felt about students having their own notebook computers to use, 84 per cent of the faculty were moderately to entirely positive after almost two years of project implementation; this figure is only slightly down from the 89 per cent of faculty who expressed such positive responses prior to implementation. On the same item, 75 per cent of the students reported (post-implementation) that they were moderately to entirely positive about having their own notebook computers to use. Again, this figure is quite similar to those in the optimistic days prior to implementation; in fact, students are slightly more positive than they were pre-ITP, when 73 per cent reported positive feelings. When asked to what extent technology had enhanced the CCSU student learning experience, 91 per cent of the faculty and 84 per cent of the students still had faith in the technology's benefits in this regard after two years. These figures are down slightly from the 97 per cent and 91 per cent respectively who responded positively prior to implementation.

One aspect of the project that was controversial from the beginning was the use of laptops in the classroom during class time. Both faculty and students were much less positive about this prospect before implementation, with only 52 per cent of faculty and 65 per cent of students expressing moderately to entirely positive feelings. Following almost two years of implementation, these figures were down to 47 per cent of faculty and 53 per cent of students. For many faculty and students, computers are best used between and after classes as an enhancement to preparation. Ninety-nine per cent of faculty and 88 per cent of students believed that students would use their computers outside of class for coursework in general; these figures were 96 per cent for faculty and 76 per cent for students after two years of implementation (Clayton College and State University, 1999).

These results, taken as a whole, suggest that both faculty and students remain very positive about ITP, but that a 'reality check' occurred as the participants became increasingly experienced and sophisticated in the benefits and challenges of technology for instructional purposes.

The survey results are quite consistent with those found in *The Chronicles of Change* data, in that the faculty journalists express continued satisfaction with ITP and notably increased satisfaction with support services and infrastructure reliability. A second and extremely significant change in the comments is a steady decrease in the expressions of frustration that characterized Phase II. Satisfaction with the reliability of the infrastructure and support services increases throughout Phase III, as faculty consistently note the increased reliability of e-mail, the Web server, and other infrastructure-related aspects of the project. The area of faculty support garnered perhaps the greatest increase in satisfaction of any, as the faculty expressed unanimously positive reactions to the newly established Center for Instructional Development (CID) and Faculty Instructional Development Lab (FIDL).

These faculty comments typify those submitted throughout Phase III:

The FIDL is providing excellent support for a myriad of functions.

The Learning Center for the faculty (FIDL) has been a lifesaver... always available if I need help.

The CID is the best thing that we could have done for the faculty.

The faculty training center [FIDL] continues to provide wonderful classes, which improves our comfort level and our expertise.

The presence of 'faculty mentors' as a part of the programme provided additional stability and collegiality to the faculty support effort.

In Phase III of project implementation, frustration that was once focused on reliability issues and the lack of effective faculty support is channelled into a new area: an awareness of the challenges inherent in harnessing technology's power for true pedagogical improvement. In a positive trend, the faculty journalists noted that ITP was beginning to enhance instructional effectiveness in significant ways. For example, one faculty member noted that:

I think that ITP has caused me to reassess the way I teach and the materials I have created as a result of technology have, for the most part, been improvements over my previously used class materials.

Others noted a trend toward the faculty becoming more and more selective about their uses of technology:

Classroom sessions have had to be rethought with the new system. All of this work has made a good number of them [faculty] prioritize what is important to education and to dump things that are stylish, but provide no substance. Hence, many of them have dropped the grandiose [attempt] to use the computers for all aspects of their teaching. They are beginning, instead, to go with those few things that are proving to be useful like e-mail for communication after class and the Web for delivering documents they used to hand out.

Increasingly, the faculty journal entries reflected a significant shift in focus from mastering the technology itself toward striving to find the proper pedagogical uses of the technology. This shift in focus seems part of a natural, evolutionary process as the faculty became increasingly comfortable with the technology. As with any complex activity, the basic processes become more automatic with time, allowing greater attention to increasingly sophisticated aspects of the activity. More energy can also go into achieving balance between effort expended and benefits obtained. Throughout Phase III, the need to achieve a balance between time expenditure and instructional efficacy was expressed by many of the journalists.

It is, however, interesting to observe that time and experience were not eliminating all questions and concerns regarding the use of technology for instruction. Instead, time and experience were simply creating newer, more sophisticated challenges. What began as relatively simple problems of learning to use technology and adapt existing instructional materials to new formats was evolving into difficult pedagogical issues. For example, one faculty chronicler noted that she had found an unintended consequence when she developed her Web site:

> Making so much of the course material available on the Web causes students who are prepared for class [to be] bored when I review the material. I'm having to think of ways to create discussion points and classroom activities to augment the material. It is difficult, as it has always been, to design instruction that meets the needs of all types of students.

The faculty also expressed concern about a tendency on the part of some students to become too dependent on technology. One chronicler feared she might be creating more dependent students, although that was clearly not her intention:

> At the same time that I am assuming increased understanding of the software, I find students accepting the availability of the technology as if it has always been here. They commonly ask, 'Will this be on your Web site?' or 'Will you e-mail us these class discussion notes?' In one way, this is good because it shows familiarity with the computer technology, but in another way I see these questions as foreshadowing of my becoming an enabler for a lack of note-taking or listening in class. They might become too dependent upon my having everything posted on the Web or upon my willingness to save discussion notes and send as an attachment to a class e-mail.

Phase III, then, is an interesting time in which both the benefits and the limitations of technology become better understood and accepted by the faculty. This is a time of excitement, as substantive improvements in pedagogy become increasingly common. There are also clear indications that the faculty possess an increasingly sophisticated understanding of the need to apply technology to the principles of good instruction rather than the reverse. Future analysis will assist in the ongoing effort to understand the impact of technology on the teaching and learning process.

CONCLUSIONS

It can certainly be said that implementing the Information Technology Project has been a fascinating journey. While countless conclusions can be drawn, the following are among the most important:

- Despite the natural tendency for faculty and students to become 'obsessed' with the technology itself, it is important to keep the focus squarely on the teaching/learning process and on improving pedagogy.

- The expectation that technology will transform teaching and learning virtually overnight is unrealistic; adapting to the challenges of using instructional technology takes time and is a multi-phase process.

- Given sufficient time, the effort to infuse technology effectively into instruction can yield significant benefits for the student, faculty, institution and community.

- As faculty become more sophisticated users of technology, they become increasingly selective about when and where to apply each tool. They need instructionally oriented support services to assist them in the very challenging endeavour of learning to use technology effectively for instruction. Faculty colleagues can be a valuable key to providing such support.

Future analyses will be undertaken in an ongoing effort to understand the impact of the evolving Information Technology Project at Clayton College and State University. It is hoped that teaching and learning as well as the trend towards pedagogical improvement will continue to be the focus of this 'adventure in technology.'

REFERENCES

Clayton College and State University (1998) *Recommendations*, Spring 1998, Faculty Development Coordinating Committee, internal document

Clayton College and State University (1999) *Faculty and Student Satisfaction Survey Data: Academic effectiveness information*, Vice President for Academic Affairs [online] http://adminservices.clayton.edu/vpaa/academiceffectiveness.html [accessed 28 January 2002]

McCarty, D and Robinson, K (1999) *The Chronicles of Change Project, A Qualitative Study: Summary of results*, unpublished report, academic effectiveness information, Vice President for Academic Affairs [online] http://adminservices.clayton.edu/vpaa/academiceffectiveness.html [accessed 28 January 2002]

Miles, M and Huberman, A (1994) *Qualitative Data Analysis*, 2nd edn, Sage, Thousand Oaks, Calif.

5

Managing active student learning with a virtual learning environment

Mark Stiles and Paul Orsmond

SUMMARY

Staffordshire University is committed to providing the best learning experience it can for its students. This commitment is called 'building the learning community' (BLC). One goal of BLC is to shift the learning environment from an information transmission/teacher focus to one which is learner focused. Through BLC, greater flexibility in learning provision via a variety of technologies is offered. This chapter discusses the rationale behind BLC and addresses fundamental staff development concerns.

THE BACKGROUND: BUILDING THE LEARNING COMMUNITY (BLC)

Responding to challenges

There has, over recent years, been a shift in emphasis within higher education from teaching to learning. This shift is from a focus on teachers and information transmission, to a more student focused or centred perspective. The student centred perspective considers teaching in terms of the impact or potential impact on student learning. While for many in HE this has always been the case, there is now official recognition of the importance of how staff teach and students learn. There are various reasons for this shift.

- There is growing evidence of attempts to improve the quality of teaching and learning in HE using theory and research tools to understand and intervene in student learning (Gibbs, 1996).

- Internal pressures: for example, the shift from small homogeneous intakes to a diverse, mass system of HE has challenged teaching methods. The establishment of external monitoring bodies like the Graduate Standards Programme (HEQC, 1995) has formalized and strengthened existing activities to ensure academic standards. There is heightened awareness of employability and skills development (Fallows and Steven, 2000).

● Internal changes within universities have promoted a re-evaluation of learning and teaching activities in response to external pressures. For example, many universities now have or are developing a Learning and Teaching Strategy (Gibbs, 2000).

The tenets of BLC

In 1996 Staffordshire University developed a university-wide learning and teaching strategy, 'building the learning community' (BLC). The emphasis is on 'learning' and 'community'. In creating BLC, the university has drawn on best practice within the university and provided a focus for staff to develop and maintain a new commitment to students. Through BLC, the university hopes to meet the challenges discussed above: focus on student centred learning, widen participation, develop resource-based learning, enhance skills development and ultimately enhance student employability.

To achieve this, the university set up a BLC investment programme to cover development until 2004. The programme covers all aspects of BLC. A major aspect is 'Developments in resource-based learning, including information communication and technology', and this will be the focus of this chapter.

LEARNING AND TEACHING AT STAFFORDSHIRE UNIVERSITY

The BLC strategy necessities the continual re-evaluation of the learning and teaching methods employed. It is important that students, if they wish to be successful, become familiar both with subject specific knowledge and the learning ethos of Staffordshire University. Therefore, students need to adapt to the learning and teaching approaches promoted within the university, which have a strong emphasis on the autonomous learner. To facilitate adaptation, the university has been rigorous in defining effective student learning and tutor teaching.

Effective learning

To drive the implementation of these initiatives, the university required a learning and teaching strategy. *How* that strategy is implemented is discussed in the next section; *what* is implemented is considered here. The learning process is concerned with the acquisition of subject specific knowledge and skills, and the development of more general or strategic approaches and skills; one facet of expertise is being able to see the relationship between the 'specific' and 'strategic' (Alexander and Judy, 1998). This development must also take place in the context of the acquisition of discipline or professional culture if both sets of knowledge and skills are to be of utility to the individual in the face of new situations or changes of career (Stiles, 2000a).

This requires recognition that the sharing of learning activities within such a culture contributes to the social process in which development takes place

(Vygotsky, 1978) and that learning is situated in the contexts of this culture and the learning environment provided, within which learners and experts interact (Lave, 1988). Learning activities provided should be 'authentic' to this culture, requiring the development of expertise in the employment of the tools (including cognitive tools) and artefacts (resources etc) of the field or discipline (Brown, Collins and Duguid, 1989).

For the individual learner, this requires assistance in recognizing the relationship between individual and social learning activities (Salomon and Perkins, 1998). Also, they must be aided in acquiring the semiotic (meaning-making) tools of the field: a vital component of becoming part of ('adopting') the culture in question (Wells, 1996).

It is important that assessment rewards, and is seen to reward, understanding, and that it and learning activity are overtly related to syllabus and appropriate to the level of the learner (Entwistle, 1995).

This view has led to an approach to course design which is output driven and focuses on the learning process and the effect it has on the learner, rather than an input led view focusing on content and its absorption by the learner. This approach, described previously (Stiles, 2000b), can be summarized as:

- Identify and develop learning outcomes. What is the point of the course? How is the successful learner changed? Learning outcomes should make clear to learners 'where they will be' at the end of the course. They make the context for learning clear, as the learning activities and assessments making up the course should be clearly related to the learning outcomes.

- Design learning opportunities. What can a learner do to demonstrate that one or more learning outcomes have been met? Regardless of learner level, specifically and strategically, these opportunities should be 'authentic'.

- Ensure opportunities are appropriate to level. If necessary, higher level opportunities can be deconstructed into lower level opportunities to an appropriate extent. A model to assist in this was developed (Roach and Stiles, 1998) as part of the COSE (Creation of Study Environments) project.

- Collaborate. To what extent are the learning opportunities and/or assessments appropriate for collaborative or group working?

- Identify or create resources. A helpful approach has been the division of resources into subject specific information, advice on method or strategy, internal (prerequisite or inherent learning opportunities) and external resources (such as reading lists, the World Wide Web and other electronic resources, and lectures).

Effective teaching

Generally, the criteria for good teaching have the same outcomes as for good student learning. To respond to the challenges described earlier, and help students become effective learners, the following strategies have been employed:

- Staffordshire University wishes to see teaching in HE viewed as a professional responsibility. To build on the enthusiasm and knowledge of teachers, the university educational staff development programme attempts to provide staff with a good grounding in the learning and teaching process. This programme aims at giving staff the professional resources to enable them to respond appropriately in differing teaching contexts.

- Approaches are encouraged which develop empathy between students and tutors within the environment of a teaching session. It is important that teachers have an accurate perspective of students' learning and are able to effectively interpret, where possible, signals sent out by the students.

This emphasis on teaching, coupled to a more focused staff development programme, has led to tutors at Staffordshire University displaying greater belief in their teaching and developing a wider/deeper understanding about student learning.

DISTRIBUTED LEARNING: A MAJOR COMPONENT OF BLC

What distributed learning is

Distributed learning is about 'A4' learning: any time, any place, any pace or any subject. While not *requiring* the use of technology, it is unlikely to be effectively deliverable or supportable without its involvement.
    One definition of distributed learning is:

> Distributed Learning is an instructional model that allows instructor, students, and content to be located in different, non-centralized locations so that instruction and learning occur independent of time and place. The Distributed Learning Model can be used in combination with traditional classroom-based courses, with traditional distance learning courses, or can be used to create wholly virtual classrooms.
>
> (Saltzberg and Polyson, 1995)

We would characterize distributed learning as:

Using technology as a focus to provide a learning experience that is:

- learner centred;
- active;
- supportive;
- holistic;
- effective.

Such an approach challenges organization, infrastructure and staff development.

Tools for distributed learning

A plethora of names now describe the software and technologies being developed to provide distributed learning. It is important to recognize the main divisions between such systems:

- A 'virtual learning environment' (VLE) or 'learning management system' (LMS) is designed to act as a focus for students' learning activities and to provide tools for their management and facilitation. It should also enable the provision and management of content and resources required in helping make the activities successful.

- A 'managed learning environment' (MLE) includes the wider features of enrolment, course options management, student record and profile keeping. In addition, it should provide for the wider management, inter-change and publication of content beyond the MLE in question and have the features needed to allow learners to move or progress between courses and institutions.

A number of VLEs/LMSs are now available (examples include WebCT, Blackboard, Colloquia, Co-Mentor, Lotus LearningSpace, and COSE). However, despite vendors' claims to the contrary, no true single MLE exists, and given the varying needs of different institutions and national education systems, no single solution is likely. The future of the MLE depends on the provision of standards to allow a VLE to interoperate with student management and other back office systems, digital libraries, learning resource repositories and other VLEs. It is this interoperating whole that will constitute the 'true MLE'.

Relevant international initiatives include the US Instructional Management Systems (IMS) Project, the European PROMETEUS Project, and the IEEE Learning Technologies Standards Committee.

Staffordshire University is working with the JISC funded UK CETIS Centre at Bangor University in these areas of development.

Choice of VLE

One classification of VLEs is 'content centred' or 'learner centred' (Milligan, 1999).

In content centred systems, course material is aggregated into 'courses' to which learners are assigned, coupling the learner closely to the content. Such systems are intended to be pedagogically neutral, but without a strong approach to course design they tend to encourage the recreation of traditional delivery approaches. Examples of such systems include Lotus LearningSpace, WebCT and Merlin.

In learner centred systems, learners are organized into groups ('courses' or smaller collaborative groups). Content exists independently ('decoupled' from learners) and can be made available to learners in more flexible and dynamic ways in support of assigned activities or learning opportunities. Such systems lend themselves more readily to active, constructivist approaches. (COSE and Colloquia are examples of learner centred systems.)

A second dimension is in the emphasis and perspective placed on the use of communication. One categorization is as 'content oriented' or 'discussion oriented', but a more cogent distinction might be between 'activity oriented' and 'discourse oriented' systems, focusing on the *reason* for communication. VLEs are spread widely across this dimension, examples being COSE, which is heavily activity oriented, Co-Mentor which is effectively content free and focuses on synchronous communication in support of learning activities, and FirstClass, which evolved from being firmly discourse oriented into a wider system.

Pedagogic issues

Experience at Staffordshire (and elsewhere) indicates that successful use of VLEs (and distributed learning) is significantly dependent on the quality of course design (plus the subsequent management and support of learning).

Much of the current enthusiasm for distributed learning is grounded in the potential offered by the World Wide Web (WWW) and associated technologies. But within this enthusiasm lie the problems of over-concentration on the technology itself and institutional-level focus on wider 'strategic' goals. It is vital that an understanding of *how* the technologies will address these wider goals is reached, combined with a central focus on providing learners with effective learning experiences. If this is not done, common errors identified over the many years of use of ICT in learning could be replicated or compounded.

These errors have centred around pedagogic and course design issues and have resulted in poor learner engagement. The primary cause has been an 'information delivery' view of learning, compounded by a focus on the practice of method as the prime form of learning activity (Brown and Duguid, 1996). This is often evidenced by a preoccupation with 'interactivity', without recognizing that 'interactive' CBL (computer based learning) can often be mechanistic and un-engaging, whilst reading well chosen sources in pursuit of writing an essay can be very engaging! As a result, traditional CBL has often been the cause of 'technology refusal' by both staff and learners (Hodas, 1993).

In the context of technologically supported learning, duplication of traditional didactic approaches, focusing on content rather than how learning will take place, often leads to learner isolation and demonstrates a failure to recognize the social nature of learning (Brown and Duguid, 1996; Soloway *et al*, 2000).

Where this social aspect *is* recognized, there have still been problems caused by perceiving discourse as the prime collaborative form (Klemm and Snell, 1996). This may be partly due to misinterpretations of 'conversational models' of learning (Laurillard, 1993), dwelling on learners discussing a 'topic' rather than holding conversations in support of collaborative production of an artefact. Much 'positive' research involving computer mediated discourse appears to be based at the Masters or education course level, and overlooks the problems that learners at lower levels (where they may lack both specific and strategic knowledge and skills, and are at an early stage of 'culture adoption') have with practising discourse.

Organization of change

In late 1997 Staffordshire decided to adopt Lotus LearningSpace (LLS), a content centred VLE. This was a business decision based on the lack of evidence of mass use of VLEs internationally. Lotus/IBM were, at that time, able to demonstrate some large(ish) scale use elsewhere, and the product was based on a widely proven technology (Lotus Notes). The university's own learner centred VLE, COSE, was at that stage still in the development stage. Current policy supports course development using LLS, COSE and generic WWW-based approaches, but excludes any other VLEs.

The organizational issues are significant. The Staffordshire experience is that the introduction of distributed learning requires a strategic institutional approach, facilitating all the elements of change required. Unless this is done in the context of coherent learning and teaching strategy, developments are likely to remain with 'enthusiasts' and not impact on mainstream practice.

The IT elements are perhaps the easiest (if not the cheapest) to build once the choice of VLE has been made. A consistent and stable software platform, which nevertheless allows the incorporation of specialist software, is needed, as is a hardware provision and communications and technical support framework capable of supporting the intended scale of operation. Clear planning for support of off campus or distance learners is required if such modes of working are desired, particularly to ensure equity of treatment with on campus learners. All of this will involve development of technical and support staff and is likely to challenge traditional roles.

In the absence of a true MLE, the organizational issues of learner registration and enrolment are considerable, and must not be overlooked in both the decision-making and planning stages. Similarly, the needs of course validation and quality cannot be bypassed. For example: does a course previously validated require re-validation when elements of it are to be delivered via distributed learning? Is content to be quality assured? Not many teaching staff are used to their course notes being examined for quality prior to delivery. If content *is* to be quality assured, how will the fact that distributed learning is dynamic and new content will appear or be developed as the course progresses be addressed?

Staff development for distributed learning

Staffordshire University established a number of ways to bring about and monitor change. A Learning Development Centre (LDC) provides workshops and other staff development, and is the primary means of addressing staff educational development. The LDC was created in direct response to the planned introduction of distributed learning. It has a proactive role as well as a supporting one, coordinates the BLC plans of schools and manages the funding available for new developments as part of these plans. Its directors report directly to a deputy vice-chancellor.

It is considered essential that all staff development effort in distributed learning has a sound pedagogic underpinning. The overall staff development effort required to support distributed learning has involved staff from the LDC, the university's IT service and staff from other services as well as teaching staff, and has covered:

- IT Support staff training: systems support, support of staff and student computers, IT support of students.

  This required training of IT systems staff in Notes/Domino, Notes/Lotus LearningSpace (LLS) training for IT and LDC support staff, and LLS training for help desk staff. This training was bought in. The LDC itself has trained IT systems, support and help desk staff in support of COSE.

- Teaching staff training: involves educational/pedagogic training as well as training in the use of the VLE.

  BLC managers, IT managers and LDC managers received initial training in the use of LLS via consultants. Subsequently, the LDC has trained nearly 350 teaching staff in course design for distributed learning and the use of, and management of learning in, either LLS or COSE. Staff are not given access to VLE systems until they have undertaken this dual educational/IT training.

- Support of teaching staff: support in learning development and course design; support in use of VLEs; support in technical aspects of content creation.

  Teaching staff visit the LDC, or ask for LDC members to visit schools, to discuss specific issues. Staff can work through course designs with LDC staff and seek guidance once teaching has started.

With the advent of BLC there have been changes in practice, attitude, debate and discourse around learning and teaching across the university.

EVALUATION AND CONCLUSIONS

Creating a student learning environment

Distributed learning requires the generation of an effective learning environment. Distributed learning allows tutors to take a 'meaning orientation' as opposed to a 'reproducing orientation' in their teaching (Ramsden and Entwistle, 1981). One method used to achieve this is in applying 'deconstruction'. Breaking up learning opportunities into constituent or prerequisite opportunities appropriate to the learner's level allows the tutor and the student to gradually exchange both power and control in the learning process. The scaffolding that the tutor provides in the early stages of study is removed (faded) with increasing student experience by reducing the degree of deconstruction. This reflects the cognitive apprenticeship model of learning (Collins, Brown and Newman, 1989).

Engaging students fully in the learning process and encouraging them to take responsibility for their own learning requires academic staff to make an

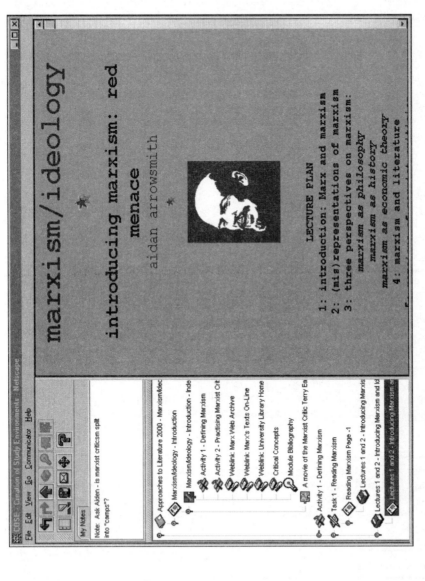

Figure 5.1 *A COSE learning opportunity showing scaffolding*

important shift from teaching to facilitating active learning. This in turn involves staff and students working in partnership and sharing conceptions of the teaching, learning and assessment process (Stefani *et al*, 1997). Prosser and Trigwell (1997) argue, 'teaching is less about what the teacher does (ie signs of teaching) and more about what the students do in relation to the teaching (ie what is signified by the teaching)'. At Staffordshire University, including distributed learning in the process of creating a positive student learning environment is leading tutors to realize that understanding the process by which students learn helps to improve the quality of student learning and influences course design. Moreover, this provides students with an opportunity to move from a surface approach to learning to a deeper approach. In surface-level processing the subject focuses on the 'sign', that is, on the discourse itself or on the recall of it. Deep-level processing indicates that students have concentrated on what is signified, that is, what the discourse is about (Saljo, 1979). The successful use of distributed learning has led tutors to use skills and techniques learnt through preparation and delivery of distributed learning in their non-distributed learning teaching.

This is strongly evidenced by a published detailed study (Holland and Arrowsmith, 2000) of the use of the COSE virtual learning environment with first-year English literature undergraduates at Staffordshire University. This work was done as part of a wider Fund for the Development of Teaching and Learning (FDTL) project consortium, 'Assessment and the Expanded Text', led by the University of Northumbria.

The COSE VLE is designed to facilitate active, constructivist approaches to learning (Stiles, 2000b). Feedback to interviewers from Northumbria by tutors and learners involved in the project above was extremely positive, and the report highlights the importance of putting the design of learning outcomes and learning opportunities first, and then providing guidance and resources to aid the learner in addressing them. One of the most telling quotes from the study is:

> We believe the primary advantage of COSE remains its ability to make explicit to students the strategies and stages they might make use of as they work through questions, concepts and resources in the process of preparing a piece of assessed work. However, we have also found that working with COSE has challenged us, as tutors, to reconsider our practice. Our work with a constructivist learning environment has encouraged us to provide our students with more structured and more helpful opportunities to practise the skills they use when they produce assessed work.
>
> This has had an impact on the ways we teach 'outside' COSE in other formats.

Active learning

The changes taking place in HE described earlier contain an implicit requirement for HE to fulfil the role of developing effective, independent, autonomous learners. Distributed learning is a powerful tool in achieving this aim.

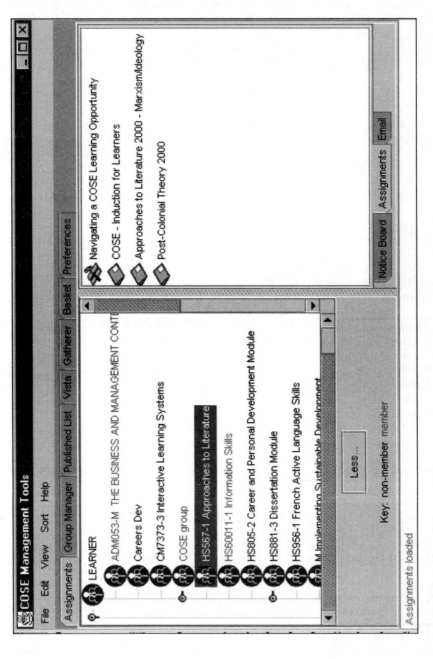

Figure 5.2 *The COSE learner tools*

An important concept within the overall learning programme is the promotion of 'active learning'. Active learning is not 'do it yourself' learning; the tutor must plan a learning programme for the student. Distributed learning enhances the opportunities for students to become active, autonomous learners because it facilitates those aspects of learning approaches required for active learning (Denicolo, Entwistle and Hounsell, 1992):

- Students are involved in searching for personal and academic meaning in their studies.

- Students need to take greater responsibility for their own learning, thinking things through, tackling problems, and discussing ideas with others.

- More mastery of a body of knowledge with the attitudes and tasks associated with it are required. Active learning places skills acquisition in a position of high priority.

CONCLUSION

If COSE or another VLE is to be used within an institution, the reasons for implementation must be clear. Institutions must ask '*Why* are we doing it'? For this to be answered successfully, senior management must perceive that implementation of distributed learning can be beneficial and managable. The commitment of the teaching staff is essential. Even if not in full agreement with every aspect of the initiative, they must be aware of the potential benefits to themselves and their students. Understanding its potentials will allow teaching staff to find ownership of the initiative and work with it rather than against it.

Implemented and managed properly, distributed learning allows students to be more than just 'interactive', they become 'engaged' in the learning process. Students are constructing an understanding of a subject.

The focus must be on learning outcomes rather than content. The constructive learning process the students are involved in must be designed to lead to desired outcomes and to develop appropriate learning skills. The skills/knowledge assessed must reflect the process the students have experienced or, preferably, assessment should be embedded in the learning opportunities provided.

REFERENCES

Alexander, P A and Judy, J E (1998) The interaction of domain-specific and strategic knowledge in academic performance, *Review of Educational Research*, **58** (4), pp 375–404
Brown, J S, Collins, A and Duguid, P (1989) Situated cognition and the culture of learning, *Educational Researcher*, **18** (1), pp 32–42
Brown, J S and Duguid, P (1996) Universities in the digital age, *Change: The Magazine of Higher Learning*, **28** (4), pp 10–19
Collins, A, Brown, J S and Newman, S E (1989) Cognitive apprenticeship: teaching the crafts of reading, writing and mathematics, in *Knowing, Learning and Instruction: Essays in honor of Robert Glaser*, ed L B Resnick, Erlbaum, Hillsdale, NJ, pp 453–94

Denicolo, P, Entwistle, N and Hounsell, D (1992) *What is Active Learning?*, CVCP Universities Staff Development and Training Unit, Sheffield

Entwistle, N (1995) The use of research on student learning in quality assessment, in *Improving Student Learning: Through assessment and evaluation*, ed G Gibbs, Oxford Centre for Staff Development, Oxford

Fallows, S and Steven, C (2000) *Integrating Key Skills in Higher Education*, Kogan Page, London

Gibbs, G (1996) *Improving Student Learning: Using research to improve student learning*, Oxford Centre for Staff Development, Oxford

Gibbs, G (2000) Learning and teaching strategies: the implications for education development, *Educational Developments*, **1** (1), pp 1–5

HEQC (Higher Education Quality Council) (1995) *The Graduate Standards Programme: Interim report*, HEQC, London

Hodas, S (1993) Technology refusal and the organizational culture of schools, *Education Policy Analysis Archives* **1** (10) [online] http://olam.ed.asu.edu/epaa/abs1.html [accessed 28 January 2002]

Holland, S and Arrowsmith, A (2000) *Towards a Productive Assessment Practice: Practising theory on-line*, University of Northumbria, Newcastle upon Tyne

Klemm, W R and Snell, J R (1996) Enriching computer-mediated group learning by coupling constructivism with collaborative learning, *Journal of Instructional Science and Technology* **1** (2) [online] http://www.usq.edu.au/electpub/e-jist/docs/old/vol1no2/article1.htm [accessed 28 January 2002]

Laurillard, D (1993) *Rethinking University Teaching: A framework for the effective use of educational technology*, Routledge, London

Lave, J (1988) *Cognition in Practice*, Cambridge University Press, Cambridge

Milligan, C (1999) *Delivering Staff and Professional Development Using Virtual Learning Environments*, Heriot-Watt University, Edinburgh [online] http://www.jtap.ac.uk/reports/htm/jtap-044.html [accessed 28 January 2002]

Prosser, M and Trigwell, K (1997) Relation between perceptions of the teaching environment and approaches to teaching, *British Journal of Educational Psychology*, **67**, pp 25–35

Ramsden, P and Entwistle, N J (1981) Effects of academic departments on students' approaches to studying, *British Journal of Educational Psychology*, **51**, pp 368–83

Roach, M P and Stiles, M J (1998) COSE: A virtual learning environment founded on a holistic pedagogic approach, *CTI: Software for Engineering Education*, **14**, pp 5–11

Salomon, G and Perkins, D N (1998) Individual and social aspects of learning, in *Review of Research in Education*, ed P Pearson and I Nejad, **23**, pp 1–24, American Educational Research Association, Washington DC

Saljo, R (1979), Learning about learning, *Higher Education*, 8, pp 443–51

Saltzberg, S and Polyson, S (1995) Distributed learning on the World Wide Web, *Syllabus*, **9** (1), pp 10–12

Soloway, E, Jackson, S L, Klein, J, Quintana, C, Reed, J, Spitulnik, J, Stratford, S J, Studer, S, Jul, S, Eng, J and Scala, N (2000) *Learning Theory in Practice: Case studies of learner centered design*, University of Michigan, Ann Arbour [online] www.acm.org/sigchi/chi96/proceedings/papers/Soloway/es_txt.htm [accessed 28 January 2002]

Stefani, L A, Tariq, V-N, Heylings, D J A and Butcher, A C (1997) A comparison of tutor and student conceptions of undergraduate research project work, *Assessment and Evaluation in Higher Education*, **22**, pp 271–88

Stiles, M J (2000a) Developing tacit and codified knowledge and subject culture within a virtual learning environment, *International Journal of Electrical Engineering Education*, **37** (1), pp 13–25

Stiles, M J (2000b) Effective learning and the virtual learning environment, in *EUNIS 2000: Towards Virtual Universities: Proceedings of the European University Information*

System 2000 conference held at INFOSYSTEM 2000, Poznan, Poland, Instytut Informatyki Politechniki Poznanskiej, Poznan, pp171–80

Vygotsky, L S (1978) *Mind in Society*, Cambridge University Press, Cambridge, Mass.

Wells, G (1996) *Working With a Teacher in the Zone of Proximal Development: Action research on the learning and teaching of science*, Ontario Institute for Studies in Education [online] http://www.oise.utoronto.ca/~gwells/teacherzpd.txt [accessed 28 January 2002]

WEB SITE REFERENCES

This chapter has made reference to a number of ICT projects and products; explanatory information is available at the following Web sites.

Blackboard
http://www.blackboard.com/

CETIS Centre
http://www.cetis.ac.uk/

Colloquia
http://www.colloquia.net

Co-Mentor
http://comentor.hud.ac.uk/

COSE
http://www.staffs.ac.uk/COSE/

FirstClass
http://www.softarc.com/products/

IEEE Learning Technologies Standards Committee
http://ltsc.ieee.org/wg12/

IMS Project
http://www.imsproject.org

Lotus LearningSpace
http://www.lotus.com/home.nsf/welcome/learnspace

Merlin
http://www.hull.ac.uk/merlin/

PROMETEUS Project
http://prometeus.org/

WebCT
http://www.webct.com/

6

Virtual learning environments as tools in learning and teaching

Michelle Haynes and Kyriaki Anagnostopoulou

SUMMARY

In this chapter we discuss the use of virtual learning environments as a means of providing quality learning and teaching. We begin by defining what we mean by a virtual learning environment and explaining how it mirrors the traditional or face to face university with which we are all familiar. Drawing on research, as well as our own workshops with lecturers and staff developers, we consider the effect that this method of working may have on learning and teaching. We also consider some of the concerns that people working in educational institutions might have about the impact of these changes on their own working practices. We do this by providing a discussion based on seven key questions:

1. What is a virtual learning environment?
2. Who is the teacher and who is the learner?
3. What then happens to the role of the lecturer?
4. When will they study and when will I teach?
5. Where will all this take place?
6. Why change the way we work now?
7. What will it cost and what is the damage?

INTRODUCTION

At the beginning of the third millennium, the seemingly overarching World Wide Web and the instant availability of information via the Internet are having profound changes on the environment in which education, particularly higher education, operates. As we write this, the year 2001 approaches and the spectre of computers which think and operate space-ships looms over us just as the world of

Big Brother and Newspeak loomed over the advent of 1984. Educational institutions want to take advantage of the World Wide Web to improve the quality of their learning and teaching and also to maximize their student numbers by using it as a tool for diversifying into distance education. Providers of post-18 education want to improve student learning – for both distance and face to face students – by creating structured opportunities for students to work together online. They also want to improve student skills in the use of information technology because these are what are needed in the 21st century. Meanwhile, for a variety of reasons, students are simultaneously demanding courses that do not tie them down to full time attendance on a campus. Many students in the UK are also in employment or have caring responsibilities. Others want to follow a course at the university of their choice but without having to change where they live.

Learning can take place in any structure; what is important is the process and the infrastructure. When parents visit schools or students visit universities they often say 'it is not the building that matters'. What do matter are the learning materials; the quality of the teaching, seminars and one to one discussions; assessment and support; opportunities for contact with other students and information resources: all the experiences and processes that turn an empty shell into a learning environment. Virtual learning environments can also offer these experiences to students and staff alike.

WHAT A VIRTUAL LEARNING ENVIRONMENT IS

A virtual learning environment can be compared to the empty shell of a building. It is a virtual structure created on the Web into which all aspects of a traditional learning environment can be placed. It can support both learning and teaching as well as administrative functions from enrolment through to assessment results and careers advice.

When trying to visualize the concept you may find that it helps to think about the building in which you work. What is it that has turned it into a learning environment? Our own offices are in a building that was once a bottling factory but is now a busy university: that is, a learning environment. This has been created by the use of the space and by the addition of certain facilities. For example, the library containing books, newspapers and journals; the lecture theatres; seminars; advice centres for students; examinations. All of these facilities can also be made available to students online through the use of a virtual learning environment. By using their password – as opposed to a swipe card – to go through the 'door' students can access learning materials as well as library facilities, newspapers, e-mail, the World Wide Web, the bookshop and their grades. They can also undertake assessments online, all accessed through one portal and one password. The shell itself includes the wherewithal for lecturers to make available course materials to their students. These can be inserted without the lecturers having involvement in the intricacies of Web design or specialist computer languages. If lecturers want to have a multiple choice assessment task all they have to do is insert the questions and indicate when access to the task is to be allowed and how often each student is to be allowed to access the task.

So the easiest way in which to visualize a virtual learning environment is to think of the plan of the campus of any educational establishment with which you are familiar. Where are the facilities mentioned above? Where would you find other areas such as a chat room? Where are the students' mail trays and how do they access their assessment records? Where are the notice boards? All of these can be included in a virtual learning environment along with seminar rooms where the discussion is moderated by the tutor, areas for the students to chat and areas for them to work in small groups. They may have a one-to-one with their tutor or enter into a discussion with their peer group. All the facilities required in a traditional university are needed in virtual learning environments too, and this is why many universities use a map of their physical campus as the home page for their virtual learning environment.

However, there is no need to think in terms of starting from scratch and designing the structure for yourself. Many different products are available and can be purchased ready for use just as you might purchase a building for use as an educational establishment. Also, these structures have already been adopted for use by other institutions which are usually willing to share their experiences and may be prepared to run a workshop for you. Some of the learning environments are available for preview or even trial over the Internet.

THE WORKSHOP

As an introduction to virtual learning environments we have devised a workshop in three stages:

1. On arrival the participants find on their seats an artefact representing some part of the contents of a learning environment, whether virtual or real. This could be an examination paper, a diary, a newspaper, an enrolment form, or study materials. They are then asked to share with the rest of the group, who discuss whether it would be part of the infrastructure and generic to the university or specific to a particular course.

2 In the second stage the participants are put into small groups, each with a moderator. Each group is given a topic to 'discuss' using written messages on sticky notes which are attached to a flip chart to show the thread of their discussion. Thus they are having a 'virtual' electronic conference.

3. Lastly, new groups are formed with members from each of the original groups and their feelings about the process they have just been through are discussed and then pulled together in a plenary.

It will be noted that Parts 2 and 3 mirror the experience of working in a virtual learning environment.

The discussion that follows is based on research and on our experiences of running this workshop in different locations and seeks to answer the ubiquitous five questions: who, what, when, where and why?

THE TEACHER AND THE LEARNER

An online learning environment can provide a mode of learning that empowers students to become autonomous learners controlling both the process of their learning and its speed. The use of chat rooms and both synchronous and asynchronous moderated discussion groups means that students have the opportunity to learn from each other and create knowledge and meaning between themselves. This is due to the nature of the conferencing software and in particular the provision of permanent records of learning conversations that can be accessed and shared flexibly. So the use of this medium can help an institution in its progress towards student centred pedagogy (Surry, 2000). Lecturers' roles become those of facilitators supporting effective learning. They no longer have to be the fount of all knowledge relevant to a module, and are able to share in the learning process with the students. Instead of 'knowledge transfer' students are able to construct their own knowledge with their peers (Inglis, Ling and Joosten, 1999). Communication is no longer on the basis of one to many but many to many, and students are encouraged as part of the learning process to communicate with each other.

This transfer of power and control is illustrated in Figures 6.1 and 6.2.

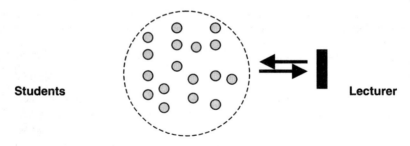

Figure 6.1 *One to many*

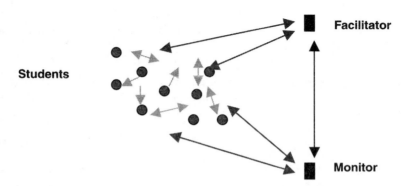

Figure 6.2 *Many to many*

Figure 6.1 shows the pattern of communication in a traditional lecture where the lecturer/teacher is communicating with the students and they may be responding to the lecturer but are not communicating with each other (at least not as part of the structured learning programme). In Figure 6.2, which depicts the change to working online, the students are communicating with the lecturer/teacher in the new roles of facilitator of their learning and monitor of their progress and also the process. Most importantly, they are also communicating with each other. It is also likely that the facilitator will have more interactions, and not fewer, with individual students. If one considers the scenario of a lecturer who has 200 students in a lecture every week, then an online learning environment may also provide for greater personalization within more traditional academic settings.

Rosie (2000) puts forward the view that 'deep and surface learning often intersect within a learning context and that the eventual outcome or chosen strategy owes much to a dialectical approach that tutors can encourage'. Tutors are often uncertain as to what they should be doing while students are working online. Researching via the Web can mean that 'a student works through a position, an argument or procedure and then confronts it with an alternative' and this is likely to lead to deep rather than surface learning. It is the tutor who is the person who is responsible for encouraging and guiding the students to develop 'both thesis and antithesis' necessary for deep learning to take place (Rosie, 2000).

Two areas of concern in this radically new method of studying are security and motivation. Regarding security, the system has to be programmed in such a way that the lecturer can be reasonably sure that the person online and participating in a seminar or taking an assessment is who they claim to be. It is also possible to track how many times an assessment is attempted or even to block students doing it more than once. Regarding motivation, the tone of the material, its structure and the way in which it engages the student in learning are vital since any student who is bored by the materials or the content of a seminar will simply log out or not log on at all. As we have already discussed, the involvement of the tutor in all the learning processes is vital. Adjusting the balance between the teacher directed structured learning and the student centred, self-paced learning for any given online context to ensure student motivation and promote personalized approaches to study is part of the art of teaching online (Mason, 1998).

To sum up, an online learning environment will not per se improve student learning. What matters is the pedagogical approach underlying its implementation (Barajas and Owen, 2000; Lian, 2000). Although the course may be differently structured and the delivery may be far from what we are used to, there will always be a need for educationalists, although they may be fulfilling different and maybe more rewarding roles; teachers may find that they have also become learners.

WHAT HAPPENS TO THE ROLE OF THE LECTURER

As well as having a role as teacher or facilitator of learning, the lecturer may have a role either as the author of learning materials or in gathering together pre-existing materials and writing wrap-around materials for them. (For example Athena University is able to carry out its mission by utilizing pre-existing Internet resources.) Writing distance learning materials is a complex task. It is not simply a question of putting lecture notes and handouts onto Web pages. Petre *et al* (1998) state that simply translating material from print into electronic form is rarely productive. The absence of additional support structures necessary for distance education hinders students from engaging in a 'community of learning'. Success lies in appropriate transformations that build upon the unique opportunities afforded by the new media: transformations for the Internet, not just translations. Inglis *et al* (1999) talk of three zones of expertise: information technology, instructional design and subject. It will not be necessary for a lecturer to be proficient in all three, but opportunities will arise for re- and up-skilling for those who are interested. However there is likely to be a division between those who are skilled in design and subject knowledge and those who are able to programme the information technology.

As mentioned above, materials for distance learning have to be carefully constructed to lead and engage the student in active learning with reflection, application and self-assessment built in to each chunk of learning materials. It should be remembered that the UK Open University employs hundreds of academics whose main task is to write course materials. They do not have a teaching commitment nor do they deal directly with students except at residential schools. Their main role is to write good quality distance learning materials.

Once the course is up and running in a virtual learning environment the lecturer's role changes to that of facilitator of the learning process through discussion groups, guiding them as appropriate and through one to one contact with students via e-mail. However the facilitator or moderator does not have to be the person who wrote the materials. The author may have moved on to write another module or may be lecturing in a face to face situation. Again, in the Open University all students receive the same materials and are allocated to their own associate lecturer who has expertise in their particular subject. But these associate lecturers are employed on a part-time basis and generally have no input into the materials.

The role and the involvement of the online moderator is vital for student learning in the medium of electronic conferencing and also contributes to the successful embedding of the technology in the learning situation.

Nevertheless, we can not often rely on electronic communications since these are initially the resources with which students experience difficulty. Some of the support traditionally provided in face to face situations is now inherent in the technology itself and provided at a completely different level. It may be thought that technology is objective and impartial but software design is in fact guided by the educational theories held by its developers; learning theories embedded in the technology reflect the pedagogical concepts held by the software developers at the time. Virtual learning environments need to support orientation, understanding the relationship between tasks and resources, the establishing and maintaining of new study habits, confidence building, integration, and allow personalization, tracking and provide feedback (Sumner and Taylor, 1998). Academics were often responsible and accountable for the provision of most of the above in a physical, face to face environment. In their new roles as online facilitators, they are called upon to provide support and guidance additional to that provided by the technology. Does this indicate loss of control and power, or does this mean that more tools are provided for more structure and detailed monitoring? Ultimately, it all depends on how the technology is used and what role and significance is assigned to it within the curriculum.

WHEN STUDENTS WILL STUDY AND WHEN TEACHERS WILL TEACH

Change is never easy and this issue, clearly related to time and timing, has been raised by the academics with whom we have worked. Because students are working online they are able to study whenever they wish. They are unimpeded by opening hours of buildings or times of lectures and seminars. The only limiting factor may be their access to suitable equipment. If they need access to online learning from within the institution, then issues of campus opening hours and support will have to be addressed, but in the UK many university computer rooms are already open late in the evening. When end of semester assignments are due our institution, like others, stays open all night. Research into students provided with computing facilities in their own rooms found that they tended to work late in the evening and into the night rather than in the morning (Crook, 2000). The difficulty with this is that they may well expect a lecturer to be online when they are, and guidelines have to be set and clearly laid out.

On the other hand, because it is possible to post an answer to a student query on a notice board, it may be that time is saved because the question only has to be answered once. Similarly, feedback mechanisms can be built into the assessment so they are installed before any assessment takes place and multiple choice assessments can be marked by the system and the results posted up automatically. Contractual time may become an issue and lecturers need very clear guidelines as to their responsibilities and duties. They cannot reasonably be expected to write course materials alongside all their other contractual commitments. Changes in teaching commitment, for example, may need to be negotiated.

There is probably more danger of students not spending enough time on their studies rather than overworking. Within a virtual learning environment it is possible to monitor the length of time that a student is logged on to the system and what pages were accessed. Of course there can be no way of establishing whether the student was reading the screen or was elsewhere in the room (at least, not yet) but neither can one tell how much time a student in a traditional university spends engaging with the course materials. If you wish to limit the distractions available, access to the Internet, references and resources through the virtual environment can be restricted to those that are thought necessary for the course of study, thus limiting distractions.

WHERE ALL THIS WILL TAKE PLACE

By its very nature a virtual learning environment means that students can study and learn in any location as long as they have suitable technology and their password. They do not have to be in the physical institution between prescribed hours on prescribed days, although some students may be enrolled to study online but may also attend the university or a local study centre for some face to face tuition. It also means that they may opt to study on a mix and match basis, selecting courses from different institutions to suit their learning goals.

There is an obvious loosening of control over the physical presence of the student. It may no longer be possible to monitor attendance at seminar groups but it will be possible to monitor the level of use of the technology and also individuals' contributions to discussions or small group work. In fact, it can be built in as a requirement for assessment.

Another aspect of location is that research has found that where students are attending a traditional campus but have online access in their own rooms, learning becomes a less social activity in terms of face to face interaction, and they spend less time in computer rooms and libraries (Crook, 2000).

WHY THE WAY WE WORK NOW SHOULD BE CHANGED

Britain and Liber (1999) believe that virtual learning environments may potentially support learning styles that are especially time-consuming for teachers using traditional methods such as collaborative learning, discussion-led learning, student centred learning and resource based learning. These styles of learning have been traditionally supported using tutorials and small group seminars and other such activities which are no longer possible due to increased time pressures on staff, increased student numbers and economic pressures. Many education providers make the transition to online learning for three main reasons: it can save on costs, provide greater access and improve the quality of the learning experience.

Costs

Whether it is cheaper to deliver online is not clear cut. However it is anticipated that cost will decrease with time. There is more discussion on the cost implications of online learning in the next section.

Access

Online learning is an innovation for both traditional and distance education and will change and enhance both methods of learning. Traditional face to face education is no longer working as well as it might for a lot of students. It is not meeting the demands of an increasingly client-led market, and online learning is part of the movement to widen access. Widening participation has already led to a demand for increased variation in the choice on offer. One side effect of introducing online learning is that it makes it possible to spread access to educational resources, specialist courses and renowned experts not only within the UK but beyond to those in remote areas (Mason, 1998). Within the growth of lifelong learning, this mode of study is ideally suited to mature students already in employment or with caring responsibilities. It offers all students the opportunity to study with the institution of their choice without having to relocate and without the isolation that can arise from studying written materials in isolation from others. It has also been shown that in some cases completion rates are higher for students studying online when compared to those following what has hitherto been thought of as a typical distance education course (Jung, 2000).

There are a lot of would-be students for whom the expense or inconvenience of attending from 9 am to 5 pm five days a week for three or even four years means that traditional forms of education are no longer an option to even be considered; but they want the interactivity that is offered by learning online. There will be others who choose to put together their own programmes from what is on offer via the Internet. Still more will want to stay with one institution but will want to complete their course in two years by doing extra modules online, while some will study for three years but take some of their credits online each year, thus being able to maintain their employment or caring responsibilities.

Quality

The use of virtual learning environments allows for collaborative learning so that students also learn from the process of learning and even for collaborative authoring (Nachmias, 2000; Olguin *et al*, 2000). Students can learn some of the skills of collaboration by working online with each other, and the socialization and communication encouraged by this method of working are part of the process of learning (Robson, 2000). Because of the new routes of communication that this opens up it is possible for learning to also take place through such activities as peer review, role playing and problem-based learning, enabling socio-cultural learning which is both contextualized and culturally based (Robson, 2000). This is what Marton and Booth termed 'social constructivism' (Richardson, 1999). The use of virtual learning environments will make it possible to give greater stimulation and variety to students and enable links to a wide range of resources such as video, multimedia and animation (Inglis *et al*, 1999). The use of virtual learning environments allows for the use of multimedia, simulations, role plays, video conferencing and the regular, if not immediate, updating of information and references.

A complete virtual learning environment has to be a mix of inquiry based teaching strategies and teaching conditions which support the goals of the strategies, allowing students to build on what they already know and reality outside of the (virtual) university (Lian, 2000). It can improve on current learning and teaching in many ways:

● It makes it possible to give group feedback on an assignment which can be less threatening than comments to individual students.

- It enables anonymous peer review of work (Macdonald, 2000).

- It forces students not only to be autonomous learners but to use deep learning.

- The careful design of the learning experience can lead to improved outcomes (Robson, 2000).

- Depending on what is being tested the use of online testing can give the lecturer greater access to the understanding and progress of each student.

- It enables individual contributions to collaborative projects to be tracked and monitored (Macdonald, 2000).

- There will be a rich mixture of students on each course, possibly drawn from around the world.

- For the new generations of students, 'raised on Nintendo, MTV and CompuServe, working with multimedia may be a more familiar, flexible and effective way to learn than sitting in huge classes' (Elfin and Wright, 1994).

- Delivery online as opposed to text based distance learning allows for the ongoing updating of materials and for immediate delivery of both study materials and assessment comments.

Online learning technologies can be used in a number of ways, some of which provide a richer learning experience than others, but whether the richness is exploited is subject to the approach taken by the teacher and the conceptions of teaching and learning that s/he holds.

WHAT IT WILL COST AND WHAT THE DAMAGE IS

This topic is wider than we are able to cover here. However, there will be issues of access to appropriate technology to be taken into account when establishing the learning environment.

- If students are studying at a distance then the cost of purchasing appropriate hardware will fall on them. Institutions may wish to consider hiring or loaning equipment or arranging for special discounts with particular suppliers.

- Similar schemes may need to be considered for academic staff not based within the institution.

- The costs of different virtual learning environment software can differ radically depending on their features. Packages may include learning materials, licences to online resources, complete student management systems, or may just offer an empty framework. Such software can be free of charge but can also range up to hundreds of thousands of pounds.

- For students who are working online but are also on campus, plug and play facilities for laptops may be necessary and adequate access to institutional hardware will have to be ensured.

- The institution will have to consider the provision of a suitable server and links to the Internet.

- Support will have to be provided for students both on campus and online. This will involve technical back-up, learning support and academic staff being available to deal with problems either in person, online or by telephone.

- However all these costs may be covered by the cost-benefits of a larger student body and reciprocal and cooperative arrangements entered into with other institutions (Elfin and Wright, 1994).

- Delivering courses online is not necessarily going to be cheaper (Inglis *et al*, 1999) although costs may decrease over time and also with economies of scale.

- Developmental costs may be higher than one might expect. For written materials it is recommended that the development time allowed per hour of learning time is 50 hours (Rowntree, 1990).

- Additional staff will be required either to design and write the courses or to replace the teaching time of pre-existing academics who divert their time and energies into this work.

There may also be personal costs to the academic staff – such as lack of promotion and limited research activity – if the use of technology for teaching is not embedded in the institution and given equal status with other forms of academic work (Ellis, 2000).

CONCLUDING COMMENTS

New media always hope to revolutionize education. When we decide to make a technological intervention we should aim to maintain and enhance peda-gogical principles. It is not the technology that matters but the approach to learning and teaching which is adopted by the stakeholders. The roles of these stakeholders are shifting and difficult to define, but we hope we have demonstrated that this will not be a matter of deskilling (or redundancy of skills) but of up-skilling and building on those already pre-existing. The knowledge and skills required for learning and teaching in the pre-techno-logical environment are needed to underpin future developments in online education in the 21st century.

As Surry points out, technology brings with it unique attributes which can be exploited as tools for learning, and it can be used to redefine the experiences available to learners (Surry, 2000). Within higher education there is a continuum, at one end of which is the traditional three year, residential degree studied by young people as a once and for all process. At the other is lifelong learning, courses on demand, the student as a customer (Inglis *et al*, 1999).

Brian Winston's theory is that technology is often available before the social circumstances enabling or forcing its use arise (Winston, 1998). For example, the telegraph was first demonstrated at the beginning of the 19th century when England had made peace with France, and so no use for it could be envisaged.

Just as it was once famously said that telephones were such a wonderful invention that one day every town might have one, so technology has swept the world. Those of us over a 'certain age' (that is, one of the authors) can remember when large companies installed mainframe computers housed in hangar-like buildings and they took three weeks to produce a print-out of all employees above a specified job level. It is hard for all of us to remember that well into the last decade in the United Kingdom, e-mail was a rarity found only in large businesses and only used for in-house communications. Now billions of people world-wide, whether in education or industry, expect to have a computer on their desk if not on their lap and in the palm of their hand.

People have become accustomed to finding out information at the touch of a few keys, instantaneously and at their convenience. In the new millennium it is the 'Martini approach' to life and education which is gaining ascendancy; the advertising slogan used to promote that beverage – 'any time, any place, any where' – is becoming the demand of an increasingly vociferous and well-informed 'clientele' as prospective students must now be called. The challenge for higher education is to meet that demand while maintaining the quality of the educational process, content and outcomes.

REFERENCES

Barajas, M and Owen, M (2000) Implementing virtual learning environments: looking for a holistic approach, *Education Technology and Society*, **3** (3) [online] http:// ifets.ieee.org/periodical/vol_3_2000/barajas.html [accessed 28 January 2002]

Britain, S, and Liber, O (1999) A framework for pedagogical evaluation of virtual learning environments, *JISC Technological Applications Programme* [online] http://www.jisc.ac.uk/jtap/word/jtap-041.doc [accessed 28 January 2002]

Crook, C (2000) *Re-mediating Study on the Networked Campus*, paper for Future Learning in the Virtual Society, Institute of Education, University of London, 4 February

Elfin, M and Wright, A R (1994) America's best colleges, *US News and World Report*, **117** (12), pp 86–88

Ellis, E M (2000) The Pennsylvania State University World Campus, *Open Learning*, **15** (3)

Inglis, A, Ling, P and Joosten, V (1999) *Delivering Digitally: Managing the transition to the knowledge media*, Kogan Page, London

Jung, I (2000) Distance education in Korea, *Open Learning*, **15** (3)

Lian, A (2000) Knowledge transfer and technology in education: toward a complete learning environment, *Education Technology and Society*, **3** (3) [online] http://ifets.ieee.org/periodical/vol_3_2000/lian.html [accessed 28 January 2002]

Macdonald, J (2000) *Innovative Assessment for Networked Communities*, paper at the 8th International Improving Student Learning Symposium, Improving Student Learning Strategically, Manchester UMIST

Mason, R (1998) *Globalising Education: Trends and applications*, Routledge, London

Nachmias, R (2000) Web-supported emergent-collaboration in higher education courses, *Education Technology and Society*, **3** (3) [online] http://ifets.ieee.org/periodical/ vol_3_2000/a05.html [accessed 28 January 2002]

Olguin, C J, Delgado, A L N and Ricarte, I L M (2000) An agent infrastructure to set collaborative environments higher education courses, *Education Technology and Society*, **3** (3) [online] http://ifets.ieee.org/periodical/vol_3_2000/a02.html [accessed 28 January 2002]

Petre, M, Carswell, P B and Thomas, P (1998) Innovations in large-scale supported distance learning: Transformation for the Internet, in Eisebstadt, M and Tome, V (eds) *The Knowledge Web: Learning and collaborating on the Net*, Kogan Page, London

Richardson, J T E (1999) The concepts and methods of phenomenographic research, *Review of Educational Research*, **69** (1) (Spring), pp 53–82

Robson, J (2000) Evaluating online teaching in open learning, *Journal of Open and Distance Learning*, **15** (2), pp 151–72

Rosie, A (2000) 'Deep learning': a dialectical approach drawing on tutor-led Web resources, *Active Learning in Higher Education*, **1** (1), pp 45–59

Rowntree, D (1990) *Teaching Through Self-instruction: How to develop open learning materials*, Kogan Page, London

Sumner, T and Taylor, J (1998) Media integration through meta-learning environments, in Eisebstadt, M and Tome, V (eds) *The Knowledge Web: Learning and collaborating on the Net*, Kogan Page, London

Surry, D W (2000) Strategies for motivating higher education faculty to use technology, *Innovations in Education and Training International*, **37** (2), pp 145–54

Winston, B (1998) *Media Technology and Society, A History: From the telegraph to the Internet*, Routledge, London

7

Motivational factors in students' online learning

Anne Davidson and Marina Orsini-Jones

SUMMARY

A campus-wide electronic learning environment (based on WebCT) has been integrated recently into teaching practice at Coventry University. This chapter reviews the student perspective of using the online resources, drawing on the experience of 270 students studying a variety of subject disciplines. We focus on whether the lecturer's perception of the pedagogic validity of specific learning resources is matched by student feedback. In particular we attempt to identify the positive and negative factors that affect students' engagement with the electronic learning environment. We use these, within a theoretical framework, to produce a set of guidelines that we hope will assist other teachers who are attempting to harness ICT to promote student learning.

INTRODUCTION

In September 1999, a campus-wide electronic learning environment, referred to as 'Learn Online', was introduced at Coventry University in the UK. Based on Internet technology, Learn Online consists of several thousand 'Study Webs' providing a password protected environment within which students and lecturers can interact with each other and with a variety of learning resources. The Study Webs were created using WebCT (Web Course Tools) software, which allows icons to be placed within a Web page, each icon summoning a subsidiary resource or application. A typical Study Web includes icons to call up e-mail, discussion (conferencing), calendar and assessment facilities. An additional 'resources' icon invokes a secondary Web page with a Contents area, as well as links to the University Library and Study Skills materials. The Contents area has been developed flexibly by different lecturers incorporating a spectrum of materials from lecture handouts and annotated hyperlinks through to online interactive tutorials, and instructional material collaboratively produced by the students themselves. The flexible interface allows the learner to switch easily between static and interactive resources.

Student user names were automatically associated with the relevant Study Webs, and a simple additional interface was created to allow students to view and log in to their Study Webs via a Learn Online link on the university home page. The approach offers students a uniformity of interface, while permitting lecturers to develop, customize and deploy the facilities according to their own needs and perspectives.

The development of the technical infrastructure was supported by parallel initiatives that encouraged academic staff to reflect on the pedagogical principles underlying their teaching, and how these might be expressed in the new medium. We have described previously how learning activities can be developed effectively within cycles of action and reflection in which both students and teachers participate (Orsini-Jones and Davidson, 1999).

However, simply making learning resources available did not necessarily imply that all students would be motivated to use them. Seymour Papert (1996) claims that 'the art of learning is an academic orphan'. This art, subsequently referred to as 'mathetics', may not come naturally, and according to de Corte (1995, 2000), the development of mathetics amongst undergraduate students in new universities can only take place if we create 'a powerful learning environment' which involves students in the negotiation of meaning. To determine the extent to which Learn Online was being used and perceived as a 'powerful learning environment', we undertook a survey of students' experience of using Study Webs six months after the campus-wide implementation. A questionnaire was administered to 270 students interacting with 12 different Study Webs across seven different subject areas including physiology, health informatics, languages, law, physiotherapy, psychology and women's studies.

The students were campus based as opposed to distance learners, but could access the facilities off campus if they had Internet access. Seventy-nine per cent of the sample were female and 96 per cent were studying full-time. The preponderance of female students closely reflected the gender distribution within the subject disciplines.

The questionnaire was designed collaboratively by the participating tutors and made available in paper or electronic versions. From the responses, we were able to determine students' general rating of resources and how these were affected by extrinsic factors such as access. Open-ended questions provided responses which illuminated the quantitative measurements, and enabled a content analysis to identify common themes.

The aims of this chapter are to:

- Highlight issues emerging from the survey, with particular attention to aspects which encouraged (or discouraged) students' active engagement with the online learning resources.

- Review student feedback, in the context of the online resources offered and associated educational research, in order to offer student centred guidelines for those teachers who are new to ICT (particularly in a campus-based environment).

STUDENTS' GENERAL EXPERIENCES OF ONLINE LEARNING

Overall, the students exhibited a positive attitude to the electronic learning environment. Thirty eight per cent of students claimed it had enhanced their study 'a lot or quite a lot', while 49 per cent said it enhanced their study 'a little'. Only 8 per cent said it had 'not enhanced their study' and 5 per cent said they had not used it (though the latter figures may be underestimated due to lower response rates in some modules where the questionnaire was administered online).

Interestingly, students frequently expressed a desire to see lecturers use Study Webs more extensively, and many students commented that they valued the flexible access it offered (Table 7.1). A number of students specifically commented on their learning experience: the spontaneous phrase 'different way of learning' recurred frequently.

Several distinct modes of WebCT use could be deduced from individual student comments. These could be roughly categorized as:

- 'Delvers': students who used it regularly for a variety of purposes and who felt their learning had benefited from the experience. Their comments portrayed enthusiasm and a desire to be able to use it for more of their study.

- 'Dippers': students who conveyed that they benefited from the online resources, but indicated that they used them intermittently for specific purposes.

- 'Uninterested': a small number of students who expressed a polite lack of interest or occasionally downright dislike. Some of these had experienced frustration in finding a working computer and/or preferred more traditional ways of learning.

THE FIRST STEP TOWARDS SUCCESSFUL ONLINE LEARNING IS GETTING ONLINE...

The Learn Online interface was designed to simplify student access. Students were able to use a single user name and password to access the Study Webs associated with any of the modules they had officially chosen to study, from any computer connected to the Internet, on or off campus. It appeared that this approach was largely successful, as the vast majority of students (82 per cent) reported that they were able to access their Study Webs when they wanted to. The inherent flexibility of access, together with a generous provision of open access computers on campus, apparently minimized any potential problem of reliance on communal resources.

However, while the actual number of students reporting access problems was relatively small, students in this group were three times less likely to report that the Study Webs had enhanced their study. Addressing the needs of those who experienced technical difficulties is an important step in maximizing the potential benefit of online learning.

Table 7.1   *Major themes identified from students' descriptions of their experience of using WebCT*

(Bullet points indicate sub-themes identified)	No. of students commenting
It was useful to be able to access lecture handouts prior to or after lectures/seminars: • to compensate for missed lectures or missed points • to maximize the learning opportunity of the lecture/seminar itself	39
It provided fast/convenient access to materials or links that supplemented face to face teaching	24
It was valuable when preparing for assignments, exams and presentations: • see model answers or previous students' work • have used or intend to use for exam revision • like revising by doing tests	35
Useful for communicating with and receiving timely feedback from the lecturer	16
Useful for communicating with fellow students: • discussion forum particularly useful • like to see views/get feedback from fellow students	31
Usefulness of discussion forum limited by poor participation or lack of time	10
Appreciated flexibility (time/place/mode of learning): • offers a new, different way of learning • particularly useful when accessed from home	28
Ability to benefit is related to computer skills/confidence: • avoided because of poor computer skills • benefited despite poor computer skills • IT/transferable skills improved as a result of using • need more training to use effectively	23
Should be used more extensively: • more lecturers should use it • more material should be made available via WebCT	29
Experienced difficulty accessing WebCT: • difficult to find a free/working computer • log in difficulties (not registered, password confusion)	31

Note: 222 (out of 270) students submitted free comments on the experience of using WebCT. A content analysis was performed to identify key themes contained within these comments. Multiple themes were identified in 76 of the responses while 24 responses gave too little detail for a theme to be identified.

Students' comments illustrated that some access problems arose from password/logging in difficulties, while others related to locating a computer (see Table 7.1). Confusion between different passwords required for logging into networks and Study Webs was not uncommon. Other students indicated that they had avoided the Study Webs because of poor computer skills. It is clearly difficult to distinguish the dimensions of cause and effect in a complex mixture of technical, motivational and confidence related factors. Significantly, research in the classroom and workplace has indicated that using computers seems to raise people's expectations that they can participate fully in and determine the shape of meaningful activity. Consequently they are even more frustrated when the opportunity is denied them (Sandholtz *et al*, 1997, Zuboff, 1988, both cited in Warshauer and Kern, 2000: 56). The findings of the Aster Project (1999) also identified adequate access and basic IT competence as critical factors in determining how students receive ICT materials.

In our study, it was particularly apparent that when lecturers supplemented the brief universal induction with additional, practical support, they were rewarded with higher levels of student engagement and perceived benefit. It seems sensible to propose that if the learning resources that lecturers work so hard to construct are to reach all those who could potentially benefit, lecturers must ensure appropriate technical and skills support, either directly or indirectly.

Off campus access to learning resources

Thirty-six per cent of the students reported they could access their Study Webs off campus, and many commented on the convenience of being able to access the resources from home. Once again this appeared to have a bearing on student-perceived benefit. Forty-eight per cent of students from the group who perceived the Study Webs had enhanced their study 'a lot' or 'quite a lot' claimed to have home access. Significantly lower levels of home access were recorded in the groups of students who reported that Study Webs had only enhanced their study a little, or not at all.

The higher levels of perceived benefit for students with home access have mixed implications for widened provision in higher education. The ability to access learning resources at a time and place that is convenient to the individual is an obvious benefit to mature students or part-time students who have many conflicting demands on their time. The advantages were specifically recognized in a number of comments, exemplified by, 'It has been a useful resource to enhance my learning, and it is convenient, as it is always there when I want to use it.'

On the other hand it is important to ensure that students from less privileged backgrounds are not disadvantaged. It was recently reported that in the UK the proportion of adults who have home access to the Internet varies according to gender and social class. Men are almost twice as likely to have home access as women, while people from social class AB are 15 times more likely to have home access than semi-skilled or unemployed people (Travis, 1999; National Statistics, 2000).

RESOURCES WHICH WERE PERCEIVED TO ASSIST STUDENT LEARNING

It was important to identify the aspects of the electronic learning environment that students found particularly useful. There are some obvious difficulties in seeking this type of information since the same facilities can be deployed in radically different ways depending on the learning objectives of individual modules and the perception of student needs. Nevertheless it was possible to identify some general areas of resource deployment. Figure 7.1 shows which resources were deployed in the modules surveyed. It also indicates which resources were perceived as being 'very useful' by more than 50 per cent of the students who used them.

It is clear that lecturers had used the Study Webs extensively to make lecture related material available and to support (coursework) assessment. Furthermore, in most modules, these learning aids were deemed to be very useful by a majority of students.

Making lecture handouts available in this way is a contentious issue within our institution, as elsewhere. Some lecturers feel it will have an adverse effect on attendance, or fail to develop students' note-taking skills. From the student perspective, many commented that it enabled them to catch up on lectures they had been unable to attend, or 'to identify points [they] had missed' (Table 7.1).

Biggs (1999) suggests that most lectures promote a surface learning approach: the emphasis on listening and copying detail are not conducive to the deeper learning approach encouraged by other learning activities. Exponents of the

Module	A	B	C	D	E	F	G	H	I	J	K	L
Discussion student/student			O	O	O				●	●	O	
Discussion tutor/student			●	O	O		●	●	●	●	●	
Module mail							O		O	●	O	
Lecture notes/ handouts		●		O	●	●	●	●	●	●	●	●
Interactive tasks				O	O		O		●		O	
Assessment related material	O	●		O	●	●	O	O	●	●	●	●

O- facility used in module; ● >50% of facility **users** found **very useful**

Figure 7.1   *Deployment of Study Web resources by module*

electronic delivery of lecture handouts argue that the lecturer is freed from a slavish emphasis on content delivery, and can substitute interactive activities for some (or even all) of the time allocated to the lecture. In turn, the student may be liberated from the unproductive elements of copying detail, and is free to engage mentally with the conceptual framework that the lecturer is attempting to portray. Several students identified this benefit in their comments:

> Printing the lecture notes beforehand gave me an opportunity to understand more of the lecture and have a more comprehensive set of notes.

> Personally I found [the topic] a difficult subject to understand, so being able to access this information in my own time and at my own pace was extremely useful.

Many of the lecturers in this survey had supplemented 'flat lecture notes' with added value activities (additional tutor notes, student led guidelines, links to Web resources, formative tests, access to external data and the like) to encourage students to engage in deeper learning (Orsini-Jones and Davidson, 1999; Grantham, elsewhere in this volume).

Frequently these resources were interwoven with discussion activities or interactive tests and problem solving tasks. A host of comments from individual students testified to the power of this approach and its ability to motivate students.

Biggs (1999) has pointed out that:

> teachers might worry less about motivating students, and more about teaching better. When they teach in such a way that students build up a good knowledge base, achieve success in problems that are significant and build up a feeling of ownership over their learning, motivation follows good learning as night follows day.

We have previously described how WebCT can be used to integrate these elements. Student input and feedback can be used to develop the learning resources, with a highly positive effect on motivation and ownership of learning (Orsini-Jones and Davidson, 1999). A number of the modules included in this survey were developed on this model.

At the same time there is a consensus that student motivation is directed by perceived outcome, or to put it more simply, 'Students learn what they think they will be tested on' (Biggs, 1999). When technology is involved, 'learning experiences are not directly linked to features of technology, but more crucially determined by students' perceptions of what the intended outcome is and how they can prioritize it within the many demands made on them' (Jones, 2000).

Taking all these considerations into account, we felt it was important to ascertain whether students singled out learning activities that were explicitly or implicitly assessment related.

Almost every WebCT module surveyed had resources dedicated to assisting students to prepare for assessment (Figure 7.1). These included: formative tasks, tests and activities; samples of good and bad work with marking schemes and commentary; links to key resources; individual or group project work mounted by the students on the module Web site. Figure 7.1 also shows that this was clearly a useful investment of lecturer effort since in 7 out of 11 modules, more than 50 per cent of students who utilized the resource found it very useful. Individual student comments identified other benefits such as being able to view other students' work including tutor feedback, formative tests and using WebCT resources as a general revision aid (Table 7.1).

Learning support offered by the communication resources

A substantial proportion of student comments centred around the helpfulness of timely communication with their tutor (Table 7.1). However the module mail resource was not widely used (except in one module with a high proportion of mature, part-time students). This may have been because the university's generic e-mail system offered a simpler and more familiar method of communication. The discussion forum, however, was widely used and highly rated for tutor–student communication.

The latter was used for a variety of purposes including seeded, academic discussion, online group work, and in many cases, simply to clarify points and answer queries. In some modules, the communication resources also played a role in peer support, as suggested from the comments of two part-time, mature students:

It... allowed me to contact other course members to discuss how we were coping or to pass on information.

It was like a security blanket – very useful to contact other students with similar problems.

The popularity of the resource gave rise to a different type of problem. In one of the larger modules the participating lecturer negotiated a 'last posting date for a guaranteed answer' policy in order to fulfil the raised expectations of her students.

Usefulness versus use

Obviously, students actually have to engage with learning resources in order to benefit from them. Table 7.2 makes the distinction between use and usefulness. For example, lecture support material was utilized by more than 80 per cent of students and also rated as very useful by more than 50 per cent of all students. Other resources, such as the assignment support, were rated as 'not useful' by only a tiny proportion of students but were not utilized by up to 30 per cent of the students to whom this resource was available. Surprisingly, relatively few students rated resources such as interactive activities and online discussion within student groups as 'very useful', despite the fact that these are the activities which might be expected to encourage deeper learning, and which were highly commended in individual comments from students.

Table 7.2 *Students' usage and rating of different Study Web resources*

Student rating	Study Web resource					
	Lecture notes/ handouts (n = 143)	Assignment related material (n = 212)	Discussion student– tutor (n = 141)	Module mail (n = 79)	Interactive activities (n = 106)	Discussion student– student (n = 95)
very useful	53%	37%	36%	34%	25%	21%
moderately useful	25%	31%	30%	28%	51%	37%
not useful	5%	4%	11%	14%	12%	16%
didn't use	17%	27%	23%	24%	11%	26%

Only responses from students whose modules actively deployed the listed resources have been included. The total number of students in each column (n) varies from resource to resource as different modules incorporated different combinations of resources.

It seems we cannot assume that all students will gratefully immerse themselves in such activities without encouragement and support.

Staff also need to develop strategies to encourage participation, as well as developing skills to facilitate online learning.

ORGANIZATION AND MANAGEMENT OF LEARNING ACTIVITIES

Many student comments testified to the value of 'being able to access the resources in [their] own time and at [their] own pace'. However some activities required students to participate within a given time frame (for example, online tutorials in which groups of students interactively engaged in problem solving activities).

While many students were highly positive about this type of learning experience, it was clear that the benefit could be negated if students experienced difficulty in coordinating their group activity, or were required to attempt the task at a time when there was heavy demand on communal computer facilities. It also illustrated how the most carefully designed learning materials can be undermined, if students have insufficient preparation for using the material. The preparation may involve a considerable amount of development activity and planning on the part of both students and tutors.

CONCLUSIONS

The students who participated in our survey broadly welcomed the electronic learning environment. Individual comments expressed a general goodwill towards the innovation, and often a realistic recognition that there was a learning curve for staff as well as students.

There was also evidence of pragmatism amongst students who fully appreciate the computer in its role of 'knowledge broker': 'What is important is to know where to find it (= *knowledge*), be able to find it, and be able to use it' (Murray, 1995: 125).

While all the participating lecturers have an active interest in pedagogy, none had been using WebCT for more than 18 months (some considerably less). Not surprisingly, there was wide variation in both the sophistication and extent of resource deployment. While no single facility or resource within the Study Webs was identified as a 'sure winner', there were also no marked 'losers'. Thus even the least demanding of resource deployments (such as making lecture notes available or using the discussion forum as a 'query answering' service) were appreciated by a substantial proportion of students, often for sound pedagogical reasons, as illustrated by their comments. This should be seen as encouraging to the novice ICT users in the teaching community. We have previously described a model where Study Webs have been allowed to evolve, driven by lecturer and student reflection, and the incremental skills of both (Orsini-Jones and Davidson, 1999). We are inclined to believe that this survey validates the model, irrespective of the starting point of the lecturer and student in the ICT skills curve. It has to be borne in mind that electronic learning environments offer a fluid, cumulative learning resource that can be built, honed and tailored over many years. Its deployment by individual lecturing staff can be enriched by observing the innovations, experiences and adaptations of colleagues, as indeed happened during the survey.

Mason (1998) identified three models that describe online courses:

- content + support;

- wrap around;

- integrated.

We would like to suggest that none of the above models is entirely sufficient to describe electronic interaction in an integrated electronic learning environment. Because of their powerful interface, electronic learning environments such as WebCT can be used to create a model *with* students and *for* students while they are being used, and the beneficial ripples of the learning curve can cascade from one cohort of students to another. It appears that the more successful uses of the online learning environment were linked to a constructivist approach to its deployment. Students' motivation was higher when students were actively involved in the creation of the learning environment, and in the negotiation of the 'new electronic literacy'.

Finally, we have used the outcomes of this survey, together with our reflections, to assemble some guidelines which will hopefully assist other teachers who are new to ICT (particularly in a campus-based environment).

- Integrate your electronic learning environment within a clear structure and tailor the use of the electronic learning environment to your module (course). Explain to students why you are using it and manage expectations.

- Use it to support assessment (formative assessment, questions relating to lecture notes, samples of good work with attached comments or marking schemes). Make it clear to your students how they can use all the learning resources to maximize their chances of success.

- If you give lectures, regularly upload electronic versions of your lecture notes/slides. Encourage students to recognize their own preferred learning styles and work with the lecture notes accordingly.

- Avoid using the online environment like a textbook: exploit the dimensions of hypertext and multimedia which allow material to be broken into smaller and more appealing units of learning.

- Be prepared to build your learning resources incrementally. Attach useful relevant links and encourage students to contribute links. Building interactive links, tasks, activities and tests within or around them can enhance even lecture and topic outlines.

- Seed the discussion forum with interesting and unthreatening topics before embarking on serious academic topics. Encourage the students to do likewise.

- Do not be afraid to use discussion facilities for mundane purposes such as answering queries as well as academic discussion. (Consider multiple discussion fora).

- Tailor 'compulsory' online discussion activities to the likely availability of computers. Encourage students to plan how they will work as a 'virtual group', before embarking on crucial learning tasks.

- Do not underestimate some of your students' fear of computers.

- Organize surgeries and workshops early in the year to encourage engagement and to brainstorm technical problems. A brief generic induction may be sufficient only for the most confident and IT literate students.

- Minimize access problems, by directing students to all locations where they can access computers. Ensure that students are aware they can access the resources off campus.

- Liaise with your local staff development, technical support and other colleagues in developing electronic resources. If you develop mutual access arrangements with colleagues, it allows virtual peer observation which can be a powerful tool for spreading good practice *and* solving or avoiding problems.

ACKNOWLEDGEMENTS

The authors would like to thank colleagues Christine Broughan, Orla Dunn, Richard Gatward, David Grantham, Simon Igo and Jennifer Marchbank for their cooperation in carrying out the student survey, and for their helpful advice and insight.

REFERENCES

Assisting Small-group Teaching through Electronic Resources (Aster) (1999) *The Use of ICT to Support Small-group Teaching Activities in Selected Disciplines*, Aster [online] http://cti-psy.york.ac.uk/aster/resources/publications/aster-ts.pdf [accessed 28 January 2002]
Biggs, J (1999) *Teaching for Quality Learning at University*, Society for Research in Higher Education (SRHE)/Open University Press, Buckingham
De Corte, E (1995) Fostering cognitive growth: A perspective from research on mathematics, *Educational Psychologist*, **30**, pp 37–46
De Corte, E (2000) Marrying theory building and the improvement of school practice, *Learning and Instruction*
Jones, C R (2000) *Understanding Students' Experiences of Collaborative Networked Learning*, Networked Learning Conference, Lancaster, April [online] http://collaborate.shef.ac.uk/nlpapers/C.R.Jones1.htm [accessed 28 January 2002]
Mason, R (1998) *Models of Online Courses* [online] http://www.aln.org/alnweb/magazine/vol2_issue2/Masonfinal.htm [accessed 28 January 2002]
Murray, D E (1995) *Knowledge Machine*, Longman, New York
National Statistics (2000) *Omnibus Survey: Internet access* [online] http://www.statistics.gov.uk/pdfdir/inter0900.pdf [accessed 28 January 2002]

Orsini-Jones, M and Davidson, A (1999) From reflective learners to reflective lecturers via WebCT, *Active Learning*, **10**, pp 32–38

Papert, S (1996) A word for learning, in *Constructionism in Practice: Designing, thinking and learning in a digital world*, ed Y Kasai and M Resnick, Lawrence Erlbaum, Mahwah, NJ, pp 9–24

Travis, A (1999) Poll points to lift off for Internet, *Guardian*, 11 January

Warschauer, M and Kern, R (2000) *Network-based Language Teaching: Concepts and practice*, Cambridge University Press, Cambridge

8

Computer mediated communication: impact on learning

Maggie Hutchings

SUMMARY

Computer mediated communication (CMC) offers distinct features, which can be used to enhance learning, but its success is dependent upon a number of pedagogical, social, and environmental factors which can assist or impede its contribution to deep learning.

This chapter seeks to examine the complexity of factors and relationships operating in a CMC environment, by analysing the features of the medium, the variety of teaching methods possible, student conceptions and approaches to learning, and the situational context in which the medium is functioning. Key findings from research on student experiences and perceptions of CMC are used to construct a set of principles for consideration in the design of teaching strategies for effective integration of CMC within the curriculum.

INTRODUCTION

Drivers to widen participation and manage increasing student numbers within a limited resource base are encouraging staff in higher education to examine the potential of information and communications technologies to support learning and teaching. Computer mediated communication (CMC) is one of the technologies being used to increase accessibility and offer more flexible modes of delivery.

Studies of the literature, which compare online with conventional delivery, highlight no significant differences in impacts on learning between the different modes (Russell, 1999) though with some notable exceptions (Harasim, 1999; Marttunen, 1997). Though each medium has strengths and weaknesses, writers on learning technologies confirm that learning outcomes are related more to how a particular medium is used than to the intrinsic characteristics of the medium (Ehrmann, 1995; Hiltz, 1994: 20; Laurillard, 1993).

CMC offers distinct features which can be used to enhance learning. Its success is dependent upon a number of pedagogical, social, and environmental factors, which can assist or impede its contribution to deep learning. Hiltz points out that some courses are more successful than others. She argues that it is not that 'media do not make a difference', but that other factors interact with the communication medium to affect learning outcomes (1994: 20). The context in which learning takes place will play a significant part in the success or failure of CMC.

This chapter will examine the complexity of factors and relationships operating in a CMC environment, by analysing the features of the medium, the variety of teaching methods possible, student conceptions and approaches to learning, and the situational context in which the medium is functioning. Findings from recent research into the use of CMC within a campus based undergraduate course will be used to illuminate the impact of CMC on learning. The features of the technology and how they can contribute to the learning process will be examined first.

CMC TECHNOLOGY

Paulsen defines CMC as the 'transmission and reception of messages using computers as input, storage, output, and routing devices'(1995). E-mail, computer conferencing, bulletin boards, and information retrieval are included within this definition. These technologies share common features of being *asynchronous*, *text-based* and *interactive*.

CMC AS AN ASYNCHRONOUS MEDIUM

Students and teachers can log on at any time or any place provided they have access to a networked computer. Although some e-mail and computer conferencing systems offer online chat facilities, the main mode of communication is asynchronous. This means the receipt of messages is not dependent upon recipients being online at the same time as the sender of the message. Recipients can access new messages or review earlier messages stored in the computer at any time. In this respect CMC differs from teleconferencing and video conferencing where participants, though geographically dispersed, need to be co-present online in order to be able to communicate with each other. The key feature of time–place independence provides the potential for increasing accessibility and offering more flexible modes of delivery using CMC.

CMC AS A WRITING MEDIUM

CMC operates largely in text-based mode though graphics, moving images and sound can be incorporated. The written word, both received and sent, acts as the main mode of communication. This has implications for the kinds of learning that can take place within the medium. Kaye provides a sound pedagogical argument for using CMC by suggesting that 'the discipline of being obliged to formulate one's ideas, thoughts, reactions, and opinions in writing in such a way that their meaning is clear to other people who are not physically present, is of key importance in the majority of educational programmes' (1989: 10).

This is particularly significant because of the ways we assess our students. 'Most universities and colleges evaluate their students' progress and achievement to a large extent on the basis of the written materials (essays, term papers, reports) that they produce for their coursework or examinations' (Kaye 1989: 10).

Hence the benefits of CMC as a writing medium can be realized. The asynchronous text-based nature of the medium offers students opportunities for debate and discussion, reflection, and the development of academic writing skills outside the conventional classroom and in advance of the examination room.

CMC AS AN INTERACTIVE MEDIUM

The degree of interactivity is closely related to choices made in how the medium is used by both teacher and student. The teacher can adopt particular teaching methods to encourage particular kinds of interaction with and among students. The level of engagement of the potential learners with the medium is influenced by their approach to learning, their motivation and the demands of assessment. The degree of interaction in CMC is fundamental to its impact on learning, and the teaching methods adopted play a key part in promoting levels of interactivity.

TEACHING METHODS IN CMC

Paulsen juxtaposes his definition of CMC with a definition of pedagogical technique as 'a manner of accomplishing teaching objectives' (1995). Pedagogical techniques are classified under four headings, according to the way they prescribe student interaction with learning opportunities. These classifications coincide with his four CMC paradigms to form a framework of CMC pedagogical techniques:

- *One alone techniques: the online resource paradigm*, including online databases, journals, applications

- *One to one techniques: the e-mail paradigm*, including learning contracts, apprenticeships, internships, correspondence studies

- *One to many techniques: the bulletin board paradigm*, including e-lectures, symposiums

- *Many to many techniques: the conferencing paradigm*, including debates, role plays, case studies, discussion and project groups.

Paulsen's framework supports the argument that it is the teaching methods adopted within CMC, rather than the system itself, which can have a beneficial impact on learning. Different approaches to using CMC can encourage different kinds of learning. A teacher, considering if the CMC medium can assist learning, would need to examine the intended learning outcomes before being in a position to identify how the CMC medium could be used to deliver specific kinds of learning.

CMC AND LEARNING

CMC can be used in a wide variety of ways as indicated by Paulsen's framework (1995). So what kinds of learning can take place within the CMC environment and what is the breadth and depth of learning that can take place? Paulsen's four classifications can be linked to different kinds of learning as represented by Table 8.1.

The *online resource* paradigm sees the student working alone with a variety of learning resources from online journals to computer assisted instruction in an *independent learning* mode. The *e-mail* paradigm sees the student interacting with the lecturer, perhaps to ask questions or receive feedback, or interacting with individual students, perhaps to arrange a meeting. Here the student is operating in a *personalized learning* mode. The *bulletin board* paradigm sees the lecturer presenting information to students in the form of an e-lecture or

Table 8.1   *CMC paradigms and learning experiences*

Paradigm	Online resource	E-mail	Bulletin board	Conferencing
Interaction	One alone Student > resource	One-to-one Teacher > student Student > teacher Student > student	One-to-many Teacher > students Student > students	Many-to-many Students > students
Communi- cation sphere	With material	With individual	With many	Within groups
Learning resource	Online journals, Computer assisted learning packages	Learning contracts, Apprenticeships	E-lectures, Assignment guidelines	Peer group
Learning method	Self study	Supported study	Knowledge presentation	Teamwork
Learning mode	Independent learning	Personalized learning	Transmissive learning	Collaborative learning

providing assignment information in a *transmissive learning* mode. The *conferencing* paradigm sees small groups of students working together on specified tasks in a *collaborative learning* mode (Keisler, 1992).

Each of these kinds of learning, independent, personalized, transmissive and collaborative, have a part to play in student learning. The question is whether there are qualitative differences in the learning that takes place when using methods selected from each of Paulsen's four paradigms. Laurillard analyses the learning effectiveness of different teaching media through her model of a conversational framework, which describes the activities – discussion, adaptation, interaction, and reflection of conceptions and experiences – necessary by student and teacher in the learning process (1993: 103). Lectures and print material are similar in that they support only the description of the teacher's conception. The students have to put considerable effort into adapting and reflecting on the material, and without direct feedback on their attempts to interact with the resource, whether in lecture or print form. Print, like other educational media, has the advantage of being controllable by the student (Laurillard, 1993). The lecture may be considered analogous with the *bulletin board* paradigm and print and other educational media with the *online resource* paradigm. If this is the case, distinct and qualitative differences between the kinds of learning that can take place in the *online resource* and *bulletin board* paradigms, on the one hand, and the *e-mail* and *conferencing* paradigms, on the other, can be anticipated.

The *e-mail* paradigm may be considered like the tutorial, operating in one-to-one interactions, and hence can be viewed as a potentially powerful medium because learning can be personalized. The many-to-many group communication facility, the *conferencing* paradigm, can be used to promote collaborative learning. Abercrombie identified the importance of small group work in encouraging critical thinking, describing how students could be released from 'the security of thinking in well-defined given channels' and enabled 'to find a new kind of stability based on recognition and acceptance of ambiguity, uncertainty and open choice' (1969).

Text-based conferencing has advantages over e-mail. It can provide shared working and learning spaces, operating with varying degrees of formality (Kaye, 1992). Features of text-based conferencing, making it particularly well adapted to support collaborative learning, are identified in Table 8.2, alongside the learning opportunities they support.

The creation of group environments in which students can interact by means of written communication enables them to externalize their ideas as knowledge representations. They can reflect on their externalized ideas and those of others as objects. The objects can be students' comments, statements and critiques, selected readings, or the intervention of the tutor. As public text-based representations, they are available to be constructed and reconstructed. CMC would seem to offer the potential of a powerful learning medium for this process of knowledge construction and reflection, when students are actively engaged in the process. CMC may prove more beneficial in promoting knowledge construction when compared to the conventional classroom where opportunities to apply theory and externalize knowledge can be lacking

Table 8.2   *Key features of CMC and related learning opportunities*

Distinctive features of CMC	Learning opportunities in CMC
Many-to-many communication	Groupwork
Shared spaces	Knowledge representation
Message threading	Knowledge construction
Message organization	Critical thinking
Public archive	Reflection
Message history	Feedback identification
Text-based	Written communication, academic writing development
Asynchronous	Access Flexibility

(Dehler and Porras-Hernandez, 1998: 52), perhaps due to time constraints, teaching styles, or the dominance of some students.

However creating group environments for students in CMC does not necessarily lead to effective learning. CMC environments can be more effective when students are required to do something rather than just talk about it. Students need to work together as a team to produce academic outputs (Klemm and Snell, 1996). This process of constructivism enables students to build their own knowledge and develop understanding by getting involved in activities and reflecting on their own experiences.

Kolb's experiential learning model, represented in Figure 8.1, supports this constructivist approach (1984). Kolb's work is based on the sound premise that much of what we learn, we learn by doing, but that students need to experience all stages of the learning cycle in order to learn effectively. CMC can be used to provide students with opportunities to apply knowledge and test theories in a reciprocal relationship with their fellow students and lecturers as co-learners. Honey and Mumford used Kolb's model to classify learners according to their learning styles, identifying activists, reflectors, theorists and pragmatists (1992).

The reality of all learning is that it is an individual enterprise. Students go about their learning by using different strategies, with corresponding learning outcomes and levels of success. Learning is about changing the ways in which learners understand, experience or conceptualize the world around them as a result of a variety of learning experiences (Ramsden, 1992). The teaching methods adopted within CMC are likely to have different impacts on learning outcomes just as they might within a conventional learning environment (Tynjala, 1998). At the heart of the matter, it is not what we teach but what we enable students to learn. Ramsden proposes that: 'We, the teachers, need to reflect on what we do that influences the relation between the students and what they learn' (1989: 158).

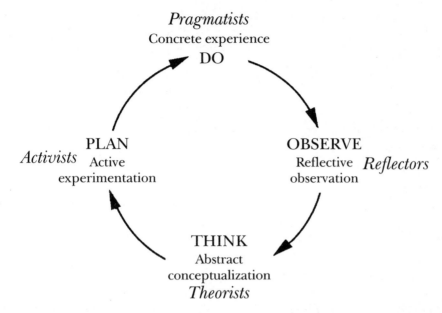

Figure 8.1 *Kolb's experiential learning cycle (1984) and Honey and Mumford's learning styles (1992)*

The educational context and the teacher's and students' conceptions of what learning and teaching is about, are key to answering the question of how CMC can impact on learning. CMC can offer a variety of learning experiences but its potential as a powerful learning medium lies in the ways the teacher chooses to use it to stimulate student learning. This depends on the teacher's conceptions of learning and teaching (Marton, Beaty and Dall'Alba, 1993; Knowles, 1988). The emphasis and underlying philosophy of CMC is a student-centred approach with the locus of control moving from the teacher to the students. Following Laurillard's model (1993), the tutor continues to play a pivotal role in the learning process but students are encouraged to discuss, adapt, interact and reflect on their conceptions and experiences with a variety of others – peers, resources, and tutors – as co-learners.

Given the significance placed on how the medium is used, over and above its distinct features, in influencing learning, findings from a case study will be used to situate CMC within a specific educational context and to develop and expand on the key themes identified above.

CASE STUDY RESEARCH FINDINGS

The case study is based on the student experience of using CMC within an undergraduate campus based course in leisure marketing (BALM). CMC was introduced to add value to the curriculum. It was intended to contribute to the development of student learning by providing active and collaborative learning opportunities outside the classroom.

Student perceptions of CMC were explored by means of focus group interviews. Students' learning styles and study orientations were analysed by means of the Approaches to Studying Questionnaire (Entwistle, 1981; Entwistle and Ramsden, 1983) and the Learning Styles Questionnaire (Honey and Mumford, 1992). The research (currently in publication) revealed a number of illuminative themes and some key findings are reported here.

Learning mode

Students saw the benefits of CMC as a collaborative learning medium. They appreciated the significance of knowledge construction and the value of peer group learning within CMC.

> You can feed off other people. You can get other people's opinions and maybe change the way you looked at something and change your ideas.

They identified advantages of the conferencing mode over the conventional classroom in that it allowed less confident individuals to put forward their ideas.

Students valued the archiving features of CMC as a resource, which enabled them to review and reflect on knowledge representations from other students. However the availability of this public record had a significant downside in that students' perceptions of CMC led them to feel their ideas were being judged by all.

> It's quite nerve racking putting your work on it when you can have 40–50 people judging how you react.

Developing capabilities

Students described the development of e-writing and argumentation skills:

> It's good because you can read the question you've written and you can actually clarify an argument in your head, which was helpful because when you're doing it in a group you tend to say something and then think 'Oh, no that's wrong.' When you're writing it you can change it a bit and then put it through.

But they also identified difficulties in developing e-writing and online social skills. The significance of small group size in building confidence and encouraging participation was clearly identified.

> I think if the conferencing was just a small group, I feel I could say more because it's a smaller group and I don't want to let people down.

Student approaches to learning

Students demonstrated a strategic approach to their learning, acknowledging the role assessment could play in encouraging interaction in CMC. Strategic choices were being made about use of time when marked assignments were taking priority over interaction in CMC. Assessment can act as a key motivator to more active participation in the CMC environment.

Analysis of learning styles and studying orientations revealed a strong preference for the *activist* learning style across each year of the course, together with a negative correlation between number of postings and the *activist* learning style. This could mean the majority of BALM students would not perform well in a CMC environment. But further analysis identified a pattern of well-balanced profiles across the studying orientations and learning styles for 'high performers', students with average grades of 60-plus per cent and five or more conference postings. This balanced profile seems to be a key contributory factor in achieving active participation in the CMC medium.

Management of learning

Students saw the value of CMC as a tutor-constructed resource in which the tutor provides knowledge and information for them. They appeared less comfortable with the idea of constructing knowledge among themselves, identifying the tutor's role in authenticating knowledge representation. This would suggest difficulties, at least in the initial stages, of promoting CMC as a student centred approach with the locus of control moving from the tutor to the students.

> When I was reading what people were saying, you could tell when they were just writing it on because they had to. They were just either waffling or they couldn't really understand it. It would be better coming from the lecturer, which is like having notes and talking about it rather than just leaving it up to us to read.

Students saw the advantages of an integrated course-wide strategy for the use of CMC. They felt other tutors could put information content, like lecture notes, on the system. Although these suggestions reinforce Paulsen's *online resource* paradigm as opposed to the *conferencing* paradigm, establishing a critical mass of course tutors operating with a variety of purposes within the CMC environment would act as an incentive, and could lead to more widespread use and valuing of CMC by the students.

CONCLUSIONS

The development of CMC environments requires careful thought and planning on the part of the tutor. The complexity and multi-layered potential of CMC and its impact on learning begin to emerge from what might initially be viewed as a rather simple and undifferentiated communication space where students can be placed to fend for themselves.

One of the most significant findings was the degree of discomfort felt by students engaging with CMC. The students made distinct comparisons between the comfort and familiarity of e-mailing friends and the discomfort and unfamiliarity of communicating within the conferencing environment.

> The stuff you put in the café, it doesn't matter, it's just a friendly talk. People aren't going to read it and think about it, they'll just read and write back. But with work stuff you're supposed to think about, criticize or not criticize, and understand, and if you get it wrong, it's not just some big joke or something.

Students appreciated the value of CMC as an online resource but were less happy about constructing knowledge for themselves. Figure 8.2 presents these findings in a model, which plots student experiences of the learning environment, both conventional and online, along two axes, one specifying degrees of *familiarity* and one specifying degrees of *structure*.

The model suggests students are comfortable in lectures and seminars where these are structured by the tutor. Where these learning environments follow a particular structure and pattern, they can also become very familiar to the students along the same familiarity axis as chatting to friends, though chatting to friends will be unstructured. These experiences sit on the left-hand side of the model, in what is termed the *comfort learning zone*. Learning environments can become more uncomfortable and less familiar as students have to engage more actively, as in presentations, student-led seminars, assignments and collaborative projects. This right-hand side of the model is termed the *challenge learning zone*. It is where students learn by doing, taking risks and making mistakes. The model is applicable in face to face and online environments. By adding in the associated learning technologies it is possible to see the impact of CMC environments.

Learning technologies associated with these learning environments have been placed in the four quadrants of the model. Web pages providing lecture and seminar material are structured though less familiar than face to face environments for both students and staff. E-mail may also be less familiar than face to face encounters and is unstructured. Students may be asked to design a Web site for a presentation or assignment. This is certainly likely to prove less familiar and perhaps less structured, in terms of accepted guidelines, than conventional assignments. However, it is the *conferencing* paradigm which is potentially the most unfamiliar and unstructured learning environment for students and tutors. It can be used to deliver e-lectures, online resources and seminars, or to set assignments, or for student-led debates and discussions, or for group work tasks as exemplified by Paulsen's extensive list of pedagogical techniques (1995).

In this sense CMC may be a victim of its own vast potential if its use is not carefully structured to overcome students' feelings of discomfort and to move them gradually from the *comfort* to the *challenge learning zone*. Although this model is a simplification of a far more complex reality, it may help us understand more about learning and teaching strategies within conventional as well as online learning environments.

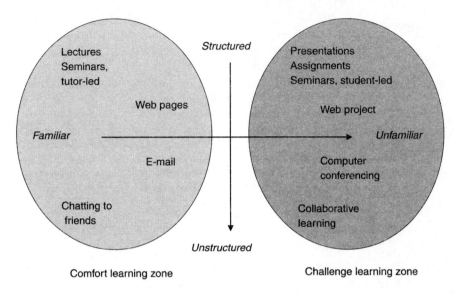

Figure 8.2   *Comfort and challenge learning zones*

Gibbs demonstrates that innovations are risky even in conventional settings of face to face lectures and seminars (1992). Students' reactions to unfamiliar approaches can be negative. Staff prepared to experiment with innovations, hoping to improve the quality of student learning, are faced with many challenges, including the risk of failure. For CMC to have an impact on the quality of student learning, it needs to be:

- Contextualized. The tutor needs to:
  - work with students' *comfort zones,* carefully considering *group sizes* and providing opportunities for *small group work* especially in the initial stages of working in the conferencing environment;
  - provide *social as well as work spaces,* eg student cafés;
  - include *essential information resources as incentives* to engage in the conferencing environment.
- Structured.
  - *Learning activities* need to be carefully planned and linked to *learning outcomes, assessment strategies* and *student and staff workloads (course design issues).*
  - Confidence building activities in small groups in the early stages of conferencing are important for developing *IT, social and e-writing and argumentation skills* and should be *fun.*

- Integrated.
  - Efforts need to be made to ensure the innovation is *shared by the course team* and not just seen as the work of a lone champion.
  - Consideration needs to be given to the creation of an *integrated learning environment* which contains information resources (lecture notes, Web resources, notices) as well as a focus for communication and group interaction.
- Valued.
  - By students, through linking it more closely to *assessment*, and giving primacy to the role of *feedback* in the early stages of discussions.
  - By staff, through ensuring it is *owned* by all the course team.
- Acknowledged.
  - Although CMC is a new and different learning environment, the *good pedagogic techniques* used in conventional settings can be applied in the CMC environment.
  - We are in a *transitional and developmental phase*, possibly unsure whether CMC should *supplement* or *replace* aspects of conventional teaching and constrained by *resourcing issues* (numbers of networked computers and proportions of students with Internet access from home) which act as powerful levers.
  - We will need to continue to address the issue of whether *the student goes to the learning* or *the learning goes to the student*.

CMC offers great potential as a learning medium but its implementation needs to be creatively managed within the context and structure of the course curriculum.

REFERENCES

Abercrombie, J (1969) *Anatomy of Judgement*, Penguin, Harmondsworth

Dehler, C and Porras-Hernandez, L H (1998) Using computer mediated communication (CMC) to promote experiential learning in graduate studies, *Educational Technology*, May/June, pp 52–55

Ehrmann, S (1995) Asking the right question: what does research tell us about technology and higher learning? *Change: The Magazine of Higher Learning*, 27 Mar/Apr [online] http://www.learner.org/edtech/rscheval/rightquestion.html [accessed 28 January 2002]

Entwistle, N (1981) *Styles of Learning and Teaching*, Wiley, Chichester

Entwistle, N and Ramsden, P (1983) *Understanding Student Learning*, Croom Helm, London

Gibbs, G (1992) *Improving the Quality of Student Learning*, Technical and Education Services, Bristol

Harasim, L (1999) *What Are We Learning About Teaching and Learning Online: An analysis of the Virtual-U field trials*, TeleLearning Network of Centres of Excellence, British Columbia [online] http://www.telelearn.ca/g_access/research_projects/news/vufieldtrials.pdf [accessed 28 January 2002]

Hiltz, S R (1994) *The Virtual Classroom: Learning without limits via computer networks*, Ablex, Norwood, NJ

Honey, P and Mumford, A (1992) *Manual of Learning Styles*, Peter Honey, Maidenhead

Kaye, A R (1989) Computer-mediated communication and distance education, in *Mindweave: Communication, computers and distance education*, ed R Mason and A R Kaye, Pergamon, Oxford

Kaye, A R (1992) Learning together apart, in *Collaborative Learning Through Computer Conferencing: The Najaden papers*, ed A R Kaye, Springer-Verlag

Keisler, S (1992) Talking, teaching, and learning in network groups: lessons from research, in *Collaborative Learning Through Computer Conferencing: The Najaden papers*, ed A R Kaye, Springer-Verlag

Klemm, W R and Snell, J R (1996) Enriching computer-mediated group learning by coupling constructivism with collaborative learning, *Journal of Instructional Science and Technology*, **1** (2), March [online] http://www.usq.edu.au/electpub/e-jist/docs/old/vol1no2/article1.htm [accessed 28 January 2002]

Knowles, M S (1988) *The Modern Practice of Adult Education: From pedagogy to andragogy*, Cambridge Adult Education, Englewood Cliffs, NJ

Kolb, D A (1984) *Experiential Learning*, Prentice Hall, London

Laurillard, D (1993) *Rethinking University Teaching: A framework for the effective use of educational technologies*, Routledge, London

Marton, F, Beaty, E and Dall'Alba, G (1993) Conceptions of learning, *International Journal of Educational Research*, **19**, pp 277–300

Marttunen, M (1997) Teaching argumentation skills in an electronic mail environment, *Innovations in Education and Training International*, **34** (3), pp 208–18

Paulsen, M F (1995) *The Online Report on Pedagogical Techniques for Computer-Mediated Communication*, Oslo, Norway [online] http://www.nettskolen.com/forskning/19/cmcped.html [accessed 28 January 2002]

Ramsden, P (1989) Perceptions of courses and approaches to studying: an encounter between two paradigms, *Studies in Higher Education*, **15** (2), pp 155–68

Ramsden, P (1992) *Learning to Teach in Higher Education*, Routledge, London

Russell, T L (1999) *The No Significant Difference Phenomenon*, North Carolina State University, NC

Tynjala, P (1998) Traditional studying for examination versus constructivist learning tasks: do learning outcomes differ? *Studies in Higher Education*, **23** (2), pp 173–89

9

ICT for worldwide collaborative professional development

Gillian Jordan

SUMMARY

This chapter examines the development and implementation of a Masters programme in continuing professional development for health professionals, delivered through asynchronous computer conferencing. The use of computer mediated communication (CMC) as a tool for collaboration, reflection, critical thinking and research will be discussed. Current issues around continuing professional development (CPD) in the health professions will be considered, particularly in relation to the worldwide cohorts of students who access the programme.

   The programme is now in its fifth year of delivery and, as a result of feedback from students, staff and external examiners, the programme team has implemented some modifications during this time. The pedagogical thinking underlying these changes will be examined and further improvements will be considered.

INTRODUCTION

Increasing numbers of undergraduate students and almost all postgraduate students are employed during their studies, and the University of Greenwich has responded to this demographic change of combining study with work by increasing the range of part-time and flexible study routes. For several years an increasing number of programmes and courses have been delivered electronically, but this has always been innovation-driven. The MSc Continuing Professional Development (Health) offered by the School of Health is one example of such a programme. The university is now engaged in making the organization fit for purpose in this arena through its current E-University project.

THE MSC CONTINUING PROFESSIONAL DEVELOPMENT (HEALTH)

The MSc CPD (Health) (Collaborative Learning through Reflective Practice and Computer-mediated Communications) was developed after extensive market research which revealed a clear need for health professionals to have opportunities for continuing professional development. However, today many of these health professionals face a dilemma; ongoing evidence of professional development is an essential part of working life, yet study leave, paid or unpaid, is increasingly difficult to obtain in the present climate of economic constraint. Therefore a programme that leads to a recognized award but does not require attendance at an institution, with the additional time, travelling and costs that implies, is an attractive option. Within a part-time structure students are able to fit in their studies in a more flexible way in their own time and in their own home or workplace.

The programme was conceived as a generic model and although we are using it only with health professionals, it has the potential to be used for many other disciplines, particularly where there is a requirement for evidence of CPD activity.

The programme began in October 1996 and in 1999 it was successfully revalidated for a further five years. The fifth annual cohort of students started their studies in September 2000. To participate, students must be qualified and practising health professionals. A wide range of professions are represented in the student cohorts, including medicine, physiotherapy, occupational therapy, podiatry, speech and language therapy, orthoptics, nursing, midwifery and osteopathy. The programme is international and students are based in the UK, Canada, USA, New Zealand, Malaysia, South Africa, Malta, Greece, France, Italy, Switzerland and Austria.

HOW INFORMATION AND COMMUNICATIONS TECHNOLOGY (ICT) IS USED

Information and communications technology is used at a relatively unsophisticated level. Our experience indicates that this simple technology enables us to fulfil the learning outcomes of the programme without expecting students to have more than a basic level of computing skills. However, even at this level, it is important that technical support is provided for both staff and students to ensure the programme runs smoothly by resolving problems as they arise and implementing developments. ICTs, as used in the MSc CPD (Health), are essentially providing a means of communicating in writing by supporting the background structures that enable this to take place: conferences, databases, common rooms and resource centres.

In deciding the most appropriate software for the programme, several alternatives were considered. Important factors determining the final decision included cost, reliability, ease of use and flexibility. The chosen platform, Lotus Notes, has proved reliable and popular with both tutors and students, as confirmed by this student' s comment:

I agree about the technology being a transparent tool. It simply acts as a sort of facilitator and enables the process to occur.

Participants are expected to log in at least two or three times a week in order to replicate: that is, while they are connected to the university server for a very short time, information is sent and received. The new material can then be responded to off line, giving time to reflect and access other resources, before being transmitted back to the host computer by another logging on. This provides great flexibility for busy professionals. In reality most students log on more frequently, sometimes several times a day when they are deeply involved in the development of a discussion. One student described it as:

like face to face really but it is conversation on paper.

Another student suggested that:

with computer mediated communication there are a lot more advantages than with other distance learning because you have the support of your peers and their instant availability.

As all discussion is both archived and searchable this is an added resource.

Course tutors are responsible for setting up a timetable and a series of tasks, with any associated resources, such as reading lists, being included. Tutors provide feedback to individual entries to keep the momentum of the discussion on track and at the end of each activity. There is evidence that this asynchronous conferencing medium facilitates high quality thinking, as one tutor commented in an evaluative interview of her experiences:

The quality is very high... their written skills are good... I think one student was quite insulted when I pointed that out: 'I've done a BSc, of course I can write.' That wasn't what I meant, it's fluency and the ability to communicate in writing which often doesn't exist at very high levels, you only have to look at some of the textbooks academics turn out. What our students are doing is learning to communicate in more subtle ways of writing, which is a useful skill for everybody to learn. I think that is one of the main benefits of the medium.

Tutors and students each have separate common rooms which provide opportunities for confidential discussion and information sharing. The resource centre provides access to documents that are needed on the programme. Lotus Notes is a dynamic system and enables new resources to be added quickly and easily as needs arise.

All tutors involved in the programme have undertaken professional development in online tutoring skills through undertaking appropriate courses. This has been an essential part of the programme's success and several of the tutors have subsequently been involved in working with staff in other departments of the university and outside bodies to share their skills and experiences.

UNDERPINNING PHILOSOPHY

Continuing professional development (CPD)

CPD is an umbrella term for a wide range of activities relating to professional competence, some practice or clinically based and occurring in the workplace, and others more academically based, and initiated and run in higher education institutions (HEIs). The profile of CPD has, in recent years, risen substantially across all professions as the demands for quality, efficacy and accountability require that professional practitioners must be able to demonstrate how they are maintaining and developing their skills, knowledge, competence and expertise.

CPD is at the core of what being a professional means, and recognition of professional status brings with it responsibilities and obligations to demonstrate continuing professional development. This is particularly true in the health professions where, in the current climate of accountability, promoting excellence and ensuring safe practice, it is essential for all the health professions to ensure that their members have in place mechanisms and structures for both CPD and competence. Among the drivers leading to this focus on CPD are greater consumer awareness, an increased body of research evidence, an emphasis on evidence-based practice, the implications of clinical governance and risk management, and individual responsibility.

In the context of CPD, learning is a process that, if it is to be relevant, must be located within the framework of the workplace, and the interaction and cooperation of those in an active community of practice clearly provide opportunities for ongoing learning and development. As our students engage in their studies while continuing their practice, this facilitates the development of a community of practice through the computer conferences where they can share their knowledge, skills and experiences.

Continued competence to practise demands that professionals engage in regular, relevant and appropriate learning activities applicable to their areas of expertise so that they can initiate and respond to the changing requirements of the work environment. It has been suggested (Grant, 1994) that professional knowledge has a half-life of five years and that obsolescence will occur if no new knowledge is assimilated and incorporated into practice within that time. What is at issue is not agreement by the professionals themselves, or their regulatory and professional bodies, on the importance of CPD, but clarity and accord concerning the range of learning activities which contribute to it and, importantly, how such professional learning is recorded, monitored and assessed. It is these aspects of continuing professional development that many of the professional organizations and regulatory and licensing bodies are currently addressing, and which was at the forefront of the MSc CPD development team's thinking.

Student-as-resource/collaboration

The development team holds a strong philosophy that professionals, such as the ones for whom the programme was developed, have much to offer their fellow students from their previous learning and experience. It was agreed from the start that learning processes selected for the programme would have to acknowledge and make the most of this knowledge: 'the richest resources for learning lie in the adult learners themselves' (Knowles, 1990).

In an asynchronous CMC environment everyone in a multi-professional group of students is, at different times, colleague, peer, learner and expert, and it was considered that significant deep-level learning could result from the discussion, conversation, debate and argument between these groups which CMC would facilitate. Evidence that this approach was what health professionals themselves wanted is borne out by this entry from a student:

> I have always held near to my heart the potential that peer to peer collaboration has for individual and multi-professional continuing professional development.

For the students to see themselves as an important and crucial resource ensures that the content and context of every course is relevant for each and every participant and also that the group processes that are fostered result in an atmosphere of collaboration and cooperation. We think we are achieving this; one student recently wrote in a conference area:

> May we continue to bounce our ideas off each other like light and reflect images in a mirror or window in our world in our efforts to illuminate the subject from all angles.

However although another student succinctly summarized what we hope to achieve when she said:

> The essence of collaboration is this safe environment in which we have contracted to operate in a non-judgemental mode

Her view was not shared by quite everyone. Since the programme began, two students have withdrawn precisely because they found the collaborative and inter-professional way of working threatening and stressful. Although it is made quite clear in all programme information and publicity that engagement in collaborative and inter-professional working is key, it would appear that occasionally some will find the reality of collaboration harder than merely believing it to be a worthwhile approach to learning.

Flexibility

Distance learning is attractive to the autonomous, self-directed, intrinsically motivated participants at whom this programme is aimed, but traditional distance learning courses often result in a sense of isolation and reduced motivation. The increased accessibility and flexibility which the use of ICTs offers helps to address these problems, and enables the participants to combine their studies for a higher degree while remaining in their own workplace. The asynchronous nature of CMC enables the students to participate at times to suit themselves. This enables worldwide registration of students, as different time zones become irrelevant to their ability to participate in discussions. One student wrote:

> The major strength, as I see it, must be in the flexibility of the programme which allows communication to take place at any time of the day or night, and there is inbuilt in this flexibility the opportunity to respond to activities according to individual time preferences.

The flexibility needs to be maintained within a defined structure and have boundaries imposed to ensure that the learning adheres to an academic framework. Deadlines for the submission of assessed work are also adhered to, but the use of electronic submission affords some flexibility. Students are expected to interact and contribute at prescribed intervals; it is the time of the week or day that students and staff choose to access the system that gives the flexibility. Even so the adaptability of the system itself is demonstrated in this comment from a student:

> One of the strengths of CMC is that a conversation can continue after a point has been raised and everyone has gone on to another topic.

Currency

It would be overstating the case to suggest that what we developed for this programme was a content-free curriculum, but nevertheless it was important to our philosophy that the curriculum should be process-orientated and able to be modified to respond to immediate needs. In the health arena change is a constant, both in the UK and throughout the world. The immediate nature of ICT enables tutors and students alike to address policy changes, political imperatives and professional and consumer developments as they arise. The details of recent health policies and relevant health issues can be highlighted immediately by tutors and students, and discussion topics in the conference areas can be modified to incorporate their impact, while at the same time the participants are developing strategies in their workplaces for implementing them. A programme dependent on written materials is less likely to be able to adapt to change so readily.

Conferences are influenced by students' contributions, which may take the discussion in different directions from those anticipated. This is one of the advantages of working with professionals from a range of disciplines. The tutor then has a responsibility to ensure that the discussion will lead ultimately to a fulfilment of the learning outcomes for that part of the course. The learning outcomes are however worded in broad terms to facilitate this.

An added facility of tutoring at a distance using CMC is the potential for team teaching. Specialists can contribute to a CMC programme while it is operating, and current materials and topics can be introduced much more readily than in a traditional distance mode. Our experience also reveals that tutors themselves benefit considerably from being able to collaborate with their peers while their course or topic is running.

Multi-professional and worldwide

The intention of a multi-professional approach was to give the participants a deeper understanding of theoretical and practical concepts in the full context of the diverse social, economic and political health environments in which they work. As the participants come from a wide range of the medical, nursing, midwifery and therapy professions, practising in the UK and worldwide, such diverse groups, working in an equally diverse range of health care situations, have much to offer each other in terms of their own professional expertise and experience. A student commented,

> The benefit of it is that you are in a privileged position of sharing your work with fellow professionals so you can actually learn a lot more.

While another said:

> People from other professions have brought ideas which I haven't discussed with my own colleagues because we are all from the same profession – you get more from other people.

Research

A series of reports published in the early 1990s about developing different aspects of the UK National Health Service had emphasized the importance of the contributions that research and development make to improvements in health practice and patient care. These reports also highlighted the need for health professionals to have opportunities for postgraduate research, training and development. The MSc (CPD) was designed to respond to this need in a flexible and accessible way.

THE PROGRAMME CONTENT

There are five courses in the programme, which are followed sequentially. In the interests of developing a learning community, a decision was made at the start that there would be no option courses so that a cohort of students would be able to work together and collaborate throughout the programme. However inevitably some students interrupt their studies and return to join another cohort, and several students on other Masters' programmes have used courses on the MSc CPD (Health) as option courses for their own programmes. This has not resulted in any loss of group cohesion or impaired the student experience. So a future development of the programme will be to introduce some option courses which will add further flexibility and relevance.

The first course is Collaboration and Computer Mediated Communication. In this course the participants begin to explore the meaning of collaboration, both uni-professionally and inter-professionally, and critically examine the place and future of collaboration within the context of professional development.

In the second course, The Reflective Practitioner, participants explore the practice of reflection as an essential part of professional development and build on their knowledge and experience to improve the theoretical and clinical bases for their own practice.

Reflective practice does not come easily to everyone, but to facilitate this process the students first of all consider theoretical perspectives underlying models of reflection, then select a model to apply to their own practice and report back on this experience to the conference. One student responded to this by writing:

> For me it was the collaborative/shared learning experiences [in the conference] which helped me to at last begin to unravel the reflective process at an academic level rather than from what the majority of us would, I suspect, claim to have already been doing within our professional practice.

Another said:

> Reflection in/on action since beginning the MSc has influenced any tendency to be prescriptive.

These quotes, and other comments in course evaluations, suggest that the collaborative ICT environment provides useful opportunities for the development of and implementation of reflective practice. However the actual practice of reflection is very much an individual activity, and it is not unusual for it to reveal hitherto unarticulated concerns and anxieties. The course tutor therefore engages in individual e-mail dialogue with each student throughout the course so that such problems can be dealt with.

In the third course, Reflection in Context, participants explore the epistemology of professional practice through political, economic, historical, sociological and cultural perspectives while discussing the use of reflection as an organizational change agent.

The advantages of ICTs as the delivery medium are again clearly revealed in this course. As the students represent so many health professions and countries, the exploration of healthcare systems is much more wide-ranging than if the students came only from one profession or one country. The CMC discussions inevitably provide a rich and diverse panoply of information and opinions and ensure that students examine their own work environments and practice in a more informed and critical way.

The Research Methods course gives participants opportunities to consider the theoretical perspectives and methods of qualitative and quantitative research and statistics in the context of modern health care. One student thought:

> This critical thinking and analysing of findings is vital for healthcare professionals to stake out our own professional autonomy.

Using small group work through ICTs to learn about research methodologies gives students both greater depth and breadth of coverage, as a more extensive range of material and research examples from many areas of practice is available for consideration than might otherwise be possible within the time frame. The course tutor is able to follow each student's progress much more carefully than is usually possible in a conventional course, and problems or difficulties are identified and dealt with quickly. Students themselves frequently take on a tutoring role to explain the complexities of a particular methodology or introduce a research example from their own practice. This is not something that usually happens in a face to face course and is a distinct advantage of the ICT environment.

The Research Project is the culmination of the programme and enables each student to explore in depth an area relevant to his or her own practice. The final product is an individual piece of work, but the use of ICTs gives students the advantage of being able to discuss the development of their ideas in the conference area before starting the actual research. That this is a valuable opportunity is indicated by this comment by a student:

> In the unusual nature of CMC classrooms, it is fascinating to watch the evolution of students' research ideas from first thoughts to the final version of the research project. It is unusual because, following a tradi-tional degree pathway, students and tutors would not have intimate insight into the development of each of our research projects. In effect we are baring our souls for all to see and opening ourselves up to constructive criticism. The evolution and the shaping of our research ideas gives us, students and tutors, an extremely rich source of infor-mation: indeed this information is privileged, would students and tutors on other degree pathways have this opportunity to share such infor-mation? I doubt this very much.

ASSESSMENT

It has been suggested (Morgan and O'Reilly, 1999) that the assessment schemes on some distance programmes fall into the trap of harnessing new technologies as a medium for presenting old assessment methodologies in which the students are set on a burdensome treadmill of essay writing. Clearly there are important considerations around ensuring standards and consistency, assuring proof of ownership and avoiding plagiarism, while acknowledging the extra time that tutors must spend marking individualized learning activities.

The assessment activities on the MSc CPD (Health) have been modified and developed in response to feedback from students, tutors and external assessors. We hope that we are able to give the students a consistent pedagogical approach through a range of authentic and timely tasks which are aligned with both the objectives of each course and the overall philosophy of the programme. Each course requires submission (electronically) of an individual piece of work, and these include a report, a reflective diary, an essay and a critical review of research literature. In two of the courses collaborative summative assignments have been incorporated, at the request of students. Considerable time, thought, discussion and negotiation with students, institutional quality assurance monitors and validators and external assessors have resulted in what we feel are authentic tasks with fair assessment criteria.

One example of this innovative assessment is demonstrated in the first course, Collaboration and CMC. About halfway through the course the students form themselves into groups, not always easy in an asynchronous environment, in order to write collaborative papers focused on a critical evaluation of the role of collaboration in professional practice or continuing professional development. This contributes 30 per cent to the total marks for the course. Fifteen per cent of these marks are awarded for the process itself – evidence of collaboration, organization and development – and 15 per cent for the product: content, style and resources. The markers award a group mark, which applies to each member of that group, for the academic quality of the paper, and this mark is not open for discussion. The markers' overall marks awarded for the process are discussed by the student group who decide among themselves on how to distribute them. It was felt that this process of peer assessment will ensure that students who have played greater or lesser roles are rewarded most equitably. Interestingly almost always the students divide the process marks equally within the group, despite evidence that some group members have made greater contributions than others. Feedback from students confirms strongly that they approve of this way of marking and the opportunity for peer assessment.

EVALUATION OF THE PROGRAMME

The panel who initially approved the validation of the MSc CPD (Health) requested that an evaluation over and above the university's statutory requirement for quality monitoring be undertaken. The panel decided that this would be an opportunity to learn as much as possible about the effectiveness of an innovative development that had the potential for wider application.

In line with the programme's integral theme of collaboration, staff and students worked together to plan the scope, methodology and process of the study. The process involved the creation of a questionnaire based on the key issues that had been identified through an evaluation conference discussion database. These key issues were:

- The effectiveness of Lotus Notes as a curriculum support tool.
- The MSc CPD (Health) as a distance learning experience for learners.
- The MSc CPD (Health) as a distance learning experience for tutors.
- The multi-disciplinary nature of the programme.

The questionnaire was distributed and returned electronically and anonymously. Analysis of the responses resulted in the development of an interview schedule. Interviews were then conducted online asynchronously, by telephone or face to face, with staff and students being both interviewers and interviewees. Some of the main findings from this evaluative study were:

- 91 per cent found that CMC made studying at a distance an enjoyable experience and 77 per cent of respondents confirmed that without CMC they would not have been able to undertake Masters level study. 73 per cent agreed that CMC was a 'student centred' means of studying.

- Only 5 per cent of the students' employers were supportive in ensuring that they had the requisite technology to undertake the programme, and 35 per cent said they had experienced financial hardship in order to obtain the necessary equipment.

- 91 per cent agreed that an important outcome of the programme was the positive impact it had on their professional practice.

- 86 per cent stated they had benefited from the collaborative aspects of the programme but 18 per cent felt that the expectation for collaboration could at times impinge on an autonomous and individual pace of working.

- All the tutors agreed that the demand on their time was higher than anticipated, and they had not been timetabled for enough hours to cover the work they actually did on the programme.

- All the tutors said that the quality of student contributions was higher in the CMC environment than in their experience of similar level face to face situations.

The evaluation study has clearly identified a number of important areas for future research including:

- Why do students choose an ICT-delivered programme in the first place, do they do so because they have needs which are different from those choosing a conventional programme, and are these needs met?

- Is the level of competence and ability in using ICTs a limiting factor in student achievement or tutor performance?

- Is it possible to a) identify a pattern of development in language and style in CMC discussions and b) devise a methodology and staff development programme to nurture consistent student progression?

- Can the evidence be found (from the archived conference entries) to substantiate the perception that this ICT environment enhances the development of critical thinking skills?

- To what extent is CMC collaboration and participation influenced by face to face meeting or voice to voice contacts?

- Can methodologies be identified that facilitate CMC group discussions, enable CMC group tutoring and enhance collaboration?

- Why did a minority of participants not find the collaborative aspects of the programme beneficial?
- Should contributions to the virtual classroom be assessed and how could this be done?

IN CONCLUSION

The last words in this brief chapter come from the interview transcripts that were part of the recent programme evaluation. One student stated:

> I feel that this is one of the best programmes I have seen that any working professional could want to do that would offer them support and advice and opportunity to study.

Another, then nearing the end of her studies, said:

> It's very easy to get used to and when it is all finished I shall miss it.

REFERENCES

Grant, R (1994) Continuing education: does it make a more competent practitioner?, *Australian Physiotherapy,* **40** (1), pp 33–37

Knowles, M (1990) *The Adult Learner: A neglected species,* 4th edn, Gulf Publishing, Houston

Morgan, C and O' Reilly, M (1999) *Assessing Open and Distance Learners,* Kogan Page, London

University of Greenwich Centre for Learning and Teaching (2000) *An Exploratory Study of the Perceptions of Students and Tutors Using CMC as a Curriculum Support Tool in the MSc CPD (Health),* University of Greenwich, London

10

Use of the intranet to develop students' key skills

Sue Drew

SUMMARY

From 1998 to 2000 the Key to Key Skills project was funded by the Teaching and Learning Technology Programme (TLTP3) of the Higher Education Funding Council for England (HEFCE). This project aimed to make a Web based system developed at Leeds Metropolitan University (LMU) portable to other institutions. The project partners were LMU, Sheffield Hallam University (SHU), and the University of Plymouth.

The project products were made available to higher education (HE) in the UK in May 2000. These products are either downloadable free from the project Web site (Key to Key Skills Project, 2000) or at a small cost on CD ROM from SHU. In addition contents for the system developed and funded by SHU are purchasable on a licensing basis (Drew and Thorpe, 2000).

FOCUS FOR THIS CHAPTER

During the project itself there were two main foci for the development work at SHU: the portability of the system, and the contents for the system. The main project is now complete and the 'continuation' phase is in progress. In this continuation phase the portability issues continue, as do issues relating to updating the content, but there is also an additional focus relating to the integration of the system into the curriculum. This chapter looks not at the Web based system itself and at how useful it might be in supporting students' learning, but at development issues relating to:

- portability of the system;
- content;
- integration into the curriculum.

DEVELOPING THE PORTABILITY OF THE SYSTEM

This section considers the portability of the system in relation to the development process and development issues, rather than in relation to the actual technicalities. The key points are:

- the importance of acknowledging and valuing the critical role of technical team members and of encouraging team building;

- the need to identify baseline computing infrastructure provision where a system or package is to be generally available across HE;

- the possibility of having a development and evaluation process which is not only effective and rigorous but also efficient, and which can then be rolled out to the wider HE community (that is, trialling a development in one institution, using that experience to inform the trial at a further institution, then confirming efficacy by a further small scale trial);

- the need for reassurance and personal contact by those in the wider community installing such a system, even where there is full and adequate written/electronic support.

LMU and SHU are located only 40 miles apart, and the project teams from each institution met monthly to review progress and plan actions. These teams included academic, technical, research and administrative staff, some of whom (the author included!) had difficulty in grasping the technical issues. It is perhaps to be expected that teams including both technical and non-technical members might have difficulties in communication and understanding, yet for projects such as this effective collaboration between members is critical. The technical team members themselves had regular meetings, were in frequent communication, and shared a common understanding and concerns. Their common interests and mutual respect were a large contributor to reducing the 'us' and 'them' possible in cross-institutional projects (indeed, sometimes the 'us' was all the technical members and the 'them' those struggling to get to grips with the issues involved – regardless of institution!). Plymouth is located 300 miles away, and funding and time did not permit frequent face to face contact. However the LMU/SHU technical team visited there twice, once at the beginning of the installation and then afterwards to review what had happened. When communicating by phone or e-mail the staff therefore knew each other personally and, again, the Plymouth technical team were part of the common shared understanding.

At the start of the project the team attempted to identify general norms for software and hardware within HE, but this proved difficult. There is an annual survey of computing provision carried out by the University and Colleges Information Systems Association (UCISA) but this did not provide the information needed. The best the team could do was to identify software and hardware provision at the three partner institutions, to also gather information from those attending dissemination workshops along the way, and to use the 'general knowledge' of the technical members of the team.

The development process was:

- The LMU team rewrote the script for their system to make it portable to SHU and produced full draft technical documentation.

- SHU then installed the system, using the documentation, identified needs for amendment and carried them out, and produced a short installation guide.

- Plymouth then installed the system, identifying further issues for the LMU/SHU team to address, and also used and provided valuable feedback on the Technical Guidance Notes, which were subsequently amended (the Plymouth team contributing an additional guidance note).

Before 'rolling out' the product to the HE community we wanted to feel confident about the portability, given the diversity in computing infrastructures. Two further institutions agreed to collaborate with us. They received no project funding, but they did get the draft SHU contents to use (and subsequently received the final contents free for a three-year period). The institutions were chosen partly by happenstance: the faculty of Crewe and Alsager of Manchester Metropolitan University contacted SHU for advice in the Key Skills area and the new principal of the College of Ripon and York St John had been the chair of the project steering group. As small campuses they provided a very different environment from those of the three large partner institutions, and this made them attractive as collaborators. They found the system easy to install and the guidance notes easy to follow, which suggests that the development process of 'porting' a system from one institution to another and then to a second is sufficient to iron out most portability problems and is therefore quite efficient. Their experience contributed to the management and editorial guidance notes produced by the project, for example providing information about estimated times to install the system.

A final issue is the support needed by others to install the system. Once the project ended there would be no further funding for the team to provide installation support, so we aimed to ensure that no further support would be needed. All the technical guidance needed was provided in the form of the evaluated technical guidance notes. These, and the system files, could be downloaded from the project Web site by all HE institutions by merely typing in an HE e-mail address. Where there were installation difficulties, institutions could have telephone support at cost (currently £30 for 30 minutes or a part thereof). We would create a frequently asked questions (FAQ) facility on the project Web site for common queries.

All very thorough? Unfortunately it does not quite work like that. Individuals phone SHU with small queries which it is hard in all conscience to charge them for. They do not look at all the guidance notes (there are management and editorial guidance notes, technical guidance notes and user notes) but only at some of them, and then phone with a question to which the answer is in another note. Non-technical or semi-technical people misunderstand or are unaware of installation issues and telephone with their misunderstandings. There are a few, but very few, issues that arise which are real installation difficulties. It seems, however, as if individuals want a reassuring voice and that time/allowance needs to be built in for this. This interestingly reflects our evaluation findings about students' use of the system, which is that human contact is important in encouraging usage and that the system cannot stand completely alone.

DEVELOPMENT OF THE CONTENT

The key points in developing the content for the system include:

- a close relationship between the content and the technology: the one impinges on the other;
- tension between 'not invented here' and the resources needed to produce home-grown material;
- the need for all the materials in a system to 'hang together';
- whether the contents should be written by one person or by several people;
- the importance of small scale piloting;
- the need to make updating easy.

The following section reviews a series of emergent issues that link to the above key points.

Part of the project to make the system portable was to explore how far an institution could create and insert its own content. HE staff in general seem to dislike material which is 'not invented here', so the project aimed to make it easy for institutions to insert content by using templates. The project also produced details of published resources to be inserted into the system, each one in a template which can be amended (for example, to include location information such as library classifications in a particular institution). This aim to allow flexibility affected the technical aspects of the project. It would be possible to produce a ready-made system (say, on a CD ROM) but if institutions are to be able to customize it and insert their own content the system must be more like a self-assembly kit, and that, in turn, requires computer staff to put it together. The project attempted compromise by producing a 'self-assembly kit' which made it as easy as possible to install and customize. Decisions about the content, therefore, had knock-on effects for the technical aspects of the project.

SHU funded the development of its own contents, based partly on existing materials (Drew and Bingham, 1997; Pettigrew and Elliott, 1999; Bingham and Drew, 1999). The contents consist of a number of themes (such as Working with Others). Each theme starts with a Skill Check, a self-assessment which helps students identify their strengths and needs for development and leads them to guidance in the system. Most of the Skill Checks are at two levels, 'starter' based on the Qualifications and Curriculum Authority (QCA) Key Skill level 3 and 'development' based on QCA Key Skill level 4 (QCA 2000). Each theme is divided into topics (such as Group Work), most of which have guidance at two levels, again based on the QCA Key Skill levels, and also a 'Resources You Can Use' section with details of further resources outside the system. During the project SHU evaluated all its draft contents, Plymouth evaluated the SHU Writing Skills theme only and LMU slotted the draft Skill Checks into their existing contents and evaluated them.

Given the theme of this chapter, it is not appropriate to go into more detail about the SHU contents. However it is important to note that they are based on well thought through pedagogic principles, underpinned by research (such as the research on skill transfer) and that the final version of the contents were based on a thorough project evaluation. What is more to the point here are the following development issues.

The first is that the SHU contents, even given that many topics were based on existing material, took a considerable time to produce. Including drafting and making amendments based on the evaluation it probably took one person year. QCA published new Key Skill specifications during the course of the project, and before any final amendments could be done of either Skill Checks or content, new learning outcomes had to be written for each topic based on those new specifications. This in itself was a time-consuming and difficult task. There was a considerable technical investment required. In particular the evaluation findings led to a complete rewriting, redesign and reprogramming of the Skill Checks.

The second issue is that the nature of the content relied heavily upon what the technology could do and on the attitude of the courseware developer (a technical role), and the relationship between the writers and the courseware developer was critical. For a non-technical person it is hard to know what is or is not possible. Tasks that seem small are long and time-consuming and tasks that seem large can be surprisingly quick and easy. It is hard to visualize what a screen will look like until it has been created, and then amending it can be time-consuming. Courseware developers can sometimes be more concerned with pushing the technology to its limits than what will actually run on the average university infrastructure, and the project leader needs to keep a constant check on this (difficult, if the project leader has limited technical knowledge!).

An early project experience was the production of a prototype Skill Check using a plug-in, which proved to be not generally available. The pedagogic underpinning for the SHU materials is that students do not develop skills by being given a list of handy hints but rather are encouraged to think about what works for them in a particular context. They are also given suggestions and ideas to try for themselves. The initial information giving only drafts were not in keeping with this approach. When we came to amend the contents the courseware developer had a 'can do' approach which allowed us to insert interactions (within the limits of what was feasible for the 'bottom line' infrastructure which might be expected), and this was much more in line with the pedagogic underpinning.

The third issue is that the system needs to hang together. For example, feedback is a common issue for many topics covered in the system (such as using feedback to improve presentations or written work) as are plagiarism and referencing. It would become tedious for such items to be repeated each time for different topics, and the advantage of an integrated system is that cross-referencing is possible. The evaluation indicated clearly that the Skill Checks had to be integrated with the guidance. They were originally conceived as flexible instruments which could be inserted into systems containing other material (for example, the LMU contents for their system are different from those at SHU), with a link at the end to slightly different guidance. For example, both LMU and SHU have guidance on essay writing, and the idea was that the Writing Skill Check could link to either. The evaluation indicated very clearly that this was not possible and reinforced one of our guiding principles, namely that any form of diagnosis must lead to help in the system. It was clear that it not only needed to lead to help but that it needed to lead to help which was closely related to questions in the Skill Check. So students did not just want guiding to 'essay writing', but, in order to make their effort in completing the Skill Check worthwhile, to a relevant section within the 'essay writing' guidance. When the SHU contents were amended, therefore, the Skill Check for a theme had to be amended alongside the topics in that theme to ensure compatibility.

This leads to the issue of amending the contents following piloting and evaluation. The project consortium had bid for three years of funding but this was reduced by HEFCE to two years, to allow them to fund a further Key Skills project. A major effect of this was to reduce the time available for piloting. Instead of the small scale pilot envisaged, followed by a large scale field trial, we had to move directly to the field trial. Had we been able to carry out a pilot of a small part of the system this would have revealed major amendments required which could then have been incorporated from scratch in the remaining contents. Following trials of the full system some further amendments would have been expected, but perhaps not of a fundamental nature. In reality we piloted the whole contents and then had to amend the whole contents. This was a valuable learning experience.

At LMU the contents (which already existed at the start of the project) had been written by staff from across the university with the aim of therefore encouraging ownership, and had been accumulated over a five-year period. At SHU we had a very limited timescale in which to produce the contents, and found that commissioning writers and chivvying them to produce the material to a deadline sometimes presented difficulties, especially where the person did not have a strong vested interest in the system. For the system to look coherent and to 'hang together' there was also often a considerable amount of editing required. Through the project and its evaluation we learnt a considerable amount about the sort of layout, length of sentence, and type of language which seemed most appropriate for the Web, and also identified the need for interactions. The two main writers became very experienced in this particular type of writing, and the 'guest' writers were not operating from a similar experience base. The experience from the SHU perspective and the context of a limited timescale was that it seemed best to base the main writing in a small number of people, to use 'guest' writers with a vested interest in the system, to build leeway into deadlines for them and to allow for editing time.

A further and ongoing issue is that the need for updating needs to be reduced and made simple. We have linked into other Web pages which are regularly updated by those responsible for them (for example a list of skills workshops run by a central department) and our information specialists (librarians) have agreed, on a yearly basis, to update the resource details. We are planning to revise the contents once a year to avoid a never-ending tinkering with the system. The reduced timescale of the project, however, gave little opportunity to thoroughly try out such procedures.

Finally, in practice colleagues in other universities seemed less interested in inserting their own content than anticipated. Most seem to have a sense of the time involved in producing such material and do not want to start from scratch. It was realized through the various project dissemination workshops that staff wanted not only a starting point but for the bulk of the contents to be provided, although they also wanted the freedom to be able to customize them and add to them. The project collaborated with a publisher who is now selling the contents on a licensing basis (Drew and Thorpe, 2000). This means that institutions can: either insert their own material; use the SHU content; use the SHU content and also add in their own; or use parts of their own instead.

However feedback from early purchasers of the content is that, while they like the idea of being able to customize the system, in reality they find it difficult to find the resources to do so (for example, to insert their own classification numbers into the resource details) and are wary of customizing, certainly until they have got to grips with and have had experience of using the content.

INTEGRATION INTO THE CURRICULUM

The project team expected perceptions of usefulness to vary across subject disciplines, but in fact variations were related not to discipline but to the model of use. The evaluation of the project suggested there were four models of usage by staff.

- *Optional*: students are told of the system and that it will be helpful to them (students in this model tend not to use the system).

- *Directed*: students are introduced to the system in class and directed to a particular part of it which might help them (some students in this model use the system).

- *Partially integrated*: students are introduced to the system in class and are required to use part of it, for example for an assessed task (students in this and the following model use the system and may go on to use further aspects of it independently).

- *Fully integrated*: students use the system in class and the whole unit or module draws on it.

The developer has two main concerns. At SHU there is a considerable amount of good practice in integrating skills development into the curriculum. The first concern is that staff may remove skills support from the curriculum if they see this as an 'add-on' which can replace it. The evaluation shows clearly this will not work (see 'Optional model' above). There is already some indication that staff are directing students to the system rather than using other sources of support, when those other sources are valuable for different but complementary purposes (for example, the paper based Skill Packs on which part of the system is based: many students prefer the resources on paper and they can be used in classes or other situations where there are no computing facilities).

The second, and related concern, is how to encourage staff to use the system in ways that will be most effective. In a large university dissemination and communication are major issues. Strategies being used at SHU include:

- e-mail to all staff with the user notes as attachments;
- e-mail to all learning, teaching and assessment coordinators in schools offering to run school based workshops;
- inputs about the system at school away-days;
- encouraging enthusiasts to 'spread the word';
- providing information for course planning teams;
- a mini-conference: a one day event advertised to all staff which will focus on the integration issue.

The contents of the system are extensive. One issue is simply the time it will take staff to familiarize themselves with it, so that they can identify topics of use to their students. Our current advice is to locate one topic they think meets a particular need and to consider first how that can be used with students before doing a more general exploration. This leads to further questions which we have not yet addressed: is it, for example, better to have a comprehensive system where staff need time for familiarization or a small system where it is easy to locate a much more limited number of items?

SUMMARY AND CONCLUSIONS

The project identified a number of issues for developers in relation both to making a computer based (specifically a Web based) system portable to other institutions and to producing the content for such a system. It is identifying issues around updating such a system, customizing it and integrating it into the curriculum. It is expected that these latter issues will become much clearer over the coming year, well after the funding for the project has ceased, and this in itself raises a further issue. This project is probably not unusual in that the 'real' usage of its products in a 'real setting' (that is, one not supported by extra staff or funding) becomes apparent only when the extra staff and funding which could monitor that usage have disappeared. In the case of this particular project this effect is mitigated by the fact that it was led from an educational development department which continues to exist and continues to have a lively interest in it. However often when project teams disband there is no such 'home base'.

There are many additional and highly beneficial spin-offs for developers from such project work, in terms of expertise gained which transfers to related, although not identical, contexts: for example writing for the Web, and effective working practices between technical and non-technical members of staff. Above all, perhaps, this project has indicated some of the key points for developers in producing a system which can be useful and effective not only within, but across institutions.

REFERENCES

Bingham, R and Drew, S (1999) *Key Work Skills*, Gower, Aldershot

Drew, S and Bingham, R (1997) *The Student Skills Guide*, Gower, Aldershot

Drew, S and Thorpe, L (2000) *Key Skills Online: Intranet support for students* [CD ROM] Gower, Aldershot

Key to Key Skills Project (2000) Key Skills Project Web site [online] http://www.shu.ac.uk/keytokey/ [accessed 28 January 2002]

Pettigrew, M and Elliott, D (1999) *Student IT Skills*, Gower, Aldershot

Qualifications and Curriculum Authority (2000) *Key Skill Units*, QCA, London

11

Student assessment using ICT

Christine Steven and Stan Zakrzewski

SUMMARY

At the University of Luton the computer based assessment (CBA) system is centred on Question Mark Designer for Windows. In the academic year 2000/2001 over 10,000 students sat summative and 3,000 formative computer based assessments. This chapter describes the introduction and successful use of ICT student assessment from both the institutional and individual lecturer perspective. It suggests reasons for the introduction of both summative and formative CBA into the undergraduate experience, and puts forward a number of critical success factors for its implementation. It further maintains that a sound pedagogic umbrella that utilizes a team approach based on a well formulated staff development programme is essential.

INTRODUCTION

Computer based assessment at the University of Luton was piloted in the department of psychology in the academic year 1993/1994, with 150 comparative psychology students taking a summative examination using Question Mark Designer for Windows (Pritchet and Zakrzewski, 1996). Within five years the summative system had become university-wide (Zakrzewski and Bull, 1998). Summative assessment in subjects, which include accounting, business, economics, politics, leisure, psychology, the applied sciences, mathematics, design, languages, linguistics, media and social science, were delivered in a central information technology (IT) suite comprising over 200 workstations. In 1998 the University of Luton was awarded a grant from the Teaching and Learning Technology Programme (TLTP) for a three-year project whose aims were to disseminate good practice guidelines, models of implementation and evaluation, and to assist institutions to implement computer assisted assessment (CAA). The CAA centre was thus established (www.caacentre.ac.uk). By the academic year 1999/2000 over 10,000 student sittings of summative examinations were undertaken. Formative assessment grew quite naturally from the summative system. The main areas of growth using formative assessment were accounting, biology, law, nursing/midwifery and computing, with some 3,000 student sittings each year since 1998.

From the academic year 2000/2001 'Perception', which is Question Mark's Web based assessment engine, has been piloted with students from biology and linguistics. The move to a Web based system has offered flexibility in delivery and full integration with virtual learning environments (VLEs).

THE CASE FOR CBA ASSESSMENT: AN INSTITUTIONAL PERSPECTIVE

Students, as stakeholders in the 21st century, demand from higher education (HE) high quality learning environments which help to deliver the knowledge and skills required in a volatile jobs market. They expect in their assessment methodology reliability and validity with fast feedback on performance. The appropriateness of content and balance (are the right knowledge and skills being assessed?) is therefore critical. CBA systems meet student expectations through their ability to offer a wide range of question types covering many topics that test both lower and higher cognitive skills (Heard, Nicol and Heath, 1997), and with the emergence of artificially intelligent engines, through their increasing ability to mark essay type questions.

- Fast feedback in formative systems guides students to explore and search for the right answers, developing in them more autonomous learning that is student centred.

- Summative CBA examinations enable fast feedback to academic staff, and with exam results and statistics available instantaneously, the institution can plan its academic year more efficiently and effectively.

- Automatic marking and the production of exam statistics result in cost savings in academic staff time for the institution.

In 1998 a study was conducted across the University of Luton that compared the time taken to design examinations, mark, second mark and produce statistics for the exam boards for those modules whose end of module examinations in the previous academic year were assessed using traditional methods but were, in 1998, assessed using CBA. With an average class size of 140, and objective tests which average 60 questions, the average academic staff time saved was 50 per cent. This release of time enables academic staff to further pursue academic areas of interest, and more importantly their research. More realistic research targets can therefore be set and agreed within the institution.

The ability of formative Web based CBA systems to enable students to work at their own pace and as often as they like alleviates the pressures of using central resources and reduces the costs of travelling to campus. In many institutions the development of such systems will support both the widening participation and social inclusion agendas. The University of Luton is committed to further increase its part-time provision. The attractiveness of modules to part-time students must be reflected, not only in content, but also in their ability to offer both flexibility and negotiation in their assessment method. Web based formative assessment systems are responsive to the needs of part-time students who increasingly require learning environments that are sensitive to their individual needs and help them to achieve their goals. Additionally both summative and formative Web based assessment systems bring together regional and international teaching and learning communities with similar interests and identical examinations all over the world, as HE institutions in the United Kingdom (UK) seek both national and international collaboration in an increasingly global market.

THE CASE FOR CBA ASSESSMENT: AN INDIVIDUAL LECTURER PERSPECTIVE

At the beginning of the academic year 1993/94 many lecturers in UK higher education were suddenly faced with teaching and assessing larger numbers of students than ever before. For instance, the average size for a first year undergraduate core (compulsory) subject at the University of Luton was well in excess of 100. Among the questions most lecturers asked were, 'How do we test them effectively?', and 'How do we give feedback quickly enough to be useful?' One of the solutions proposed to those questions was to use ICT, and this led to the consideration of CBA as a possible instrument for assessment.

When the idea of using CBA became a definite possibility, individual lecturers then began to consider the wider implications of their proposed actions. It made them rethink not only the purposes of assessment but also the problems that using this type of assessment could bring.

What is the purpose of assessment? In its simplest form it is to check on how much information the students have retained from the lectures and tutorials and to establish what they can now achieve. It was decided by many lecturers, as a result of the above, that the initial use of CBA should be for first year undergraduate students where 'knowledge gained' could be assessed using fairly straightforward procedures. As lecturers became more experienced with the chosen assessment package (Question Mark Designer for Windows) so the complexity of the questions was increased, thus enabling the assessment of higher order skills. The effectiveness of assessments is always difficult to establish but some believe (Perkins, 1999), that the use of computers can help in many areas because of their flexibility.

Another potential problem was that of computer phobia. Just because computers are used so widely it is no guarantee that all the students will be happy to use them. If a case arose where an individual student was worried or even fearful at the prospect of using a computer for an assessment exercise, this would surely invalidate the results. How could we, as lecturers, guard against this happening? It was decided that students could be given some initial training in the use of the CBA package, and that if there were any students who still felt unable to undertake the assessments using an electronic format they could use it in its paper based form instead. Against this there were statements by others (Lens, 1994) suggesting that where there is no computer anxiety, computer assisted assessment enhanced motivation. If this were so then surely the students would prefer to do their assessments utilizing computers.

Some lecturers felt not only that they needed to give faster feedback to students but that it should be more detailed. These two requirements appeared to be in direct opposition to each other. Could CBA assist in this dilemma? If it could, it would then help the students to study more effectively and ultimately lead to an increase in the responsibility they displayed for their own learning (Steven and Hesketh, 1999).

The major questions asked by lecturers when confronted with the possibility of using CBA were 'How will it affect me?' and 'What will the students think of it?' The former question was answered quickly. This would initially increase the workload for all the academic staff. The training to use the system, the initial preparation of questions and answers, and the familiarization of students with the system would all take time and effort. The second question required more consideration. It could be that students would consider this type of assessment as 'easier' than the more traditional approaches and therefore put less effort into their work. It could be, as previously stated, that they would be reluctant to use the technology. It was therefore decided to canvass the opinions of the students throughout their exposure to the use of ICT. It was however felt that this would all be worthwhile for the long-term benefits that would be forthcoming.

CRITICAL SUCCESS FACTORS

Staff development

Computer based assessment has always been open to criticism as not providing sufficient challenging in depth questions that can test a whole range of cognitive skills. Effective creation of objective questions that test, not only knowledge, but also comprehension, application, analysis, synthesis and evaluation involves an effective CBA staff development programme. Experience has shown that such a programme of staff development must also describe the system under which the tests are designed and implemented, and is critical to the success of the system. The aim and objectives of the programme at the University of Luton are shown in the box opposite. The staff development programme at the University of Luton is integrated into the annual staff development events directory. All academic staff are invited to attend the programme as an essential prerequisite to test design and implementation. Such a programme is best delivered on a departmental basis. In the initial stages the following are identified:

● Who is being tested?
● What is the purpose of the test?

● What abilities and knowledge are to be tested?

● The suitability of objective testing for the purpose intended.

The assessment system is described to the academic staff. They are able to familiarize themselves with the information technology (IT) suite where the tests are delivered and are given documentation outlining system policies and procedures. Academic staff are shown the functions and capabilities of the software used for test design and delivery and the range of question types available. Examples of effective question design are available on the CAA Centre Web site.

During the latter stages of the programme academic staff are split into small groups and encouraged to design objective questions that test the full range of Bloom's taxonomy (Bloom *et al*, 1956). Their designs are then discussed within the whole group. Ongoing support and advice is always available at the CAA Centre. The staff development programme acts as a springboard to test creation and implementation.

CBA staff development programme

Aim

The aim of the programme is to describe CBA and explore the pedagogic issues surrounding the construction and use of objective tests.

Specific objectives

● To introduce summative and formative approaches to CBA.
● To describe the roles and responsibilities of academic and support staff.
● To describe the operations and procedures of the university-wide CBA system.
● To outline specific question types that can be used.
● To explore the benefits and drawbacks of objective testing.
● To explore the suitability of using objective testing at levels 1, 2 and 3 with reference to testing both low and high order cognitive skills.
● To outline a structured approach to effective design of objective tests.
● To consider both student and academic staff reactions to using objective tests.
● To list the main outcomes of the CBA system that has evolved at the University of Luton.

Team approach

Institutions wishing to embark on implementing CBA require a solid framework (Zakrzewski and Steven, 2000), which suggests a team approach to ensure pedagogic, technical, operational and financial feasibility. So what constitutes a team and who should be involved? Perhaps this is best answered by describing the roles and responsibilities of staff involved with CBA at the University of Luton.

At the centre of the system are the academic staff who are responsible for setting the examination papers. At the beginning of each semester academic staff new to the system attend the staff development programme coordinated centrally by the staff development unit. CAA Centre staff concentrate on effective question design, while specialist staff in Learning Resources outline the systems procedures and university policy on CBA implementation.

When appropriate, guest speakers and consultants are invited to further enhance the staff development programme and a 'Question Mark' user group at the university encourages the exchange of views and ideas on a regular basis.

Once the examination papers have been designed they are converted by Learning Resources staff into 'Question Mark' format and those at levels 2 and 3 (which count towards the final degree award) are sent to an external assessment adviser, an assessment specialist as opposed to a subject specialist, for comment. The assessment adviser's role is to offer advice on the structure and format of the examination, the range of skills that the examination tests and the relationship to module learning outcomes.

Academic staff have the papers returned to them so that they may reflect upon the comments. Only after this is the examination paper sent to an external examiner who is a subject specialist. The external examiner's role is to ensure that justice is done to all students, that the standard of the university's awards is maintained, that regulations are complied with and that the programme objectives are met. Once the external moderation process is completed the examination is ready for an official pre-test in Learning Resources. Academic staff and Learning Resources staff pre-test the examination together under real examination conditions to ensure the reliability and technical integrity of the user front-end, to ensure that answer files are stored on the server and that a 100 per cent score is achievable. After a successful pre-test the examination is forwarded to the Examinations Office in both electronic and hard copy format.

It is the responsibility of the Computer Services Department to ensure the technical integrity of the system. The networking infrastructure must be tested for both performance and security. A technical audit of workstations (of which there are 200 in the central IT suite) is conducted by the Computer Services Department prior to the examination weeks and all workstations are prepared ready to host the examinations.

The Examination Office is responsible for timetabling all examinations during the last two weeks of each semester. The only difference between traditional examinations and those utilizing ICT is that the Examination Office assigns both academic invigilators and technical support staff to the suite where the examinations are held. During exam weeks an independent auditor is asked to monitor the system.

Students are not just passive takers of the examinations but are actively involved in the evaluation of the current system and in testing any upgrades or new software platforms that may be introduced. Their views on system operations and procedures are fed to a computer based assessment steering group.

The computer based assessment steering group consisting of academic staff, support staff and the external assessment adviser are responsible for the compilation of an annual monitoring report with recommendations for future action that coincides with the university annual monitoring cycle. The report is sent to the University Teaching and Learning Committee and finally to the University Academic Standards Committee for discussion and endorsement of any future action. Without senior management commitment and involvement the CBA system at the University of Luton would not be able to evolve but would remain in the hands of a few dedicated enthusiasts.

Management commitment

Senior management commitment embraces both investment and integration. Investment in CBA systems requires both capital expenditure and the release of staff time to initially pilot and then expand the system. Capital expenditure can be broken down into three major areas, the software platform, computer workstations and privacy screens. Institutions can now obtain a test development licence on a single workstation with an unlimited test presentation licence for approximately £1,000. In most universities the issue of computer workstation investment is one of availability and not additional expenditure, although approximately 200 workstations are required for a university-wide examinations system.

At the University of Luton a central IT suite is made available for summative end of module examinations. For two weeks in January at the end of semester one, two weeks in June at the end of semester two and during referral week in September the central IT suite is totally dedicated to the delivery of end of module examinations. It needs senior management commitment and university policy to dedicate resources for such use, as this affects other students not taking computer based end of module examinations. At the University of Luton all students are aware of the issues concerning the availability of the central IT facility as this is well publicized, and they plan their work accordingly.

Formative tests are also made available in the IT suite throughout the academic year but these are taken on a drop-in basis. Investment in privacy screens is essential to ensure appropriate student conduct in a formal examination setting. Most IT suites are not designed with formal objective testing in mind. Usually workstations are set too close together, contravening examination regulations. Privacy screens are an effective deterrent as they shield the work conducted on a workstation from its neighbours. The investment in 200 privacy screens is approximately £10,000 (UK 2000 prices).

The investment in academic staff time is primarily for staff development in effective test design and in the time taken to design the test itself. This may involve an initial investment in a series of workshops undertaken by specialist external consultants before in-house staff development can take place. Support staff also require development in managing the technical integrity of the system, and additional invigilation costs will have to include the support staff as they need to be present during formal examinations.

For a CBA system to be effective it needs to be integrated into the systems and procedures of the university. This cannot be done without a clear commitment and support from senior managers. Integration can also be broken down into three major areas. The involvement of key central systems, the production of documentation and compliance with the annual monitoring cycle are essential. The operation of CBA is not isolated and will interact with other systems in the institution. It needs to be integrated with the examination timetabling system, the staff development system, the financial system of the institution, the networking infrastructure and the quality assurance system, all of which are headed by senior managers. CBA documentation must be integrated with an overall learning technology strategy that in turn must be integrated with the institution's teaching and learning strategy.

Only in such a way can deliverable goals and targets be set and supported in the short, medium and long term. Procedural documentation for CBA implementation must also be accepted by the institution and made available to both academic and support staff. Validation documents will require changes as the assessment vehicle in the degree programme changes. The annual monitoring cycle should include a report on CBA activity with recommendations for the coming academic year.

At the University of Luton the Dean of Quality Assurance receives a report from the CBA steering group which is then presented to the University Academic Standards Committee and finally to the Academic Board for final approval. Each year, the report includes a comparative evaluation of CBA achievement against traditional assessment formats, the review of the effectiveness of staff development, the evaluation of CBA procedures and administration, staff and student comments on CBA delivery and recommendations for future improvements.

Student involvement

After extensive discussions involving teaching, administrative and technical support staff it was determined that the student body should be involved in the new venture of implementing computer based assessment as much as possible. All students who are new to the university are given training in the use of the current IT equipment as part of their course. This is now extended to encompass the use of the CBA software. Students are usually introduced to the software in a tutorial/practical session where they are encouraged to work at their own pace.

When the use of CBA was in its infancy at the University of Luton, students were given questionnaires to complete regarding their familiarity with and attitude to CBA. Their comments were studied and these informed the way in which students were introduced to the concept of CBA. The involvement of the student body has been encouraged at all levels; their comments are sought concerning the systems currently being used and their opinions canvassed as to how the questions and particularly feedback could be further improved. The views of the students are also invaluable regarding the operation of the examinations themselves, whether as formative or summative assessments. It is the feedback from students that has encouraged many staff to widen the use they now make of CBA.

Research generation

Among the many roles to be played by university lecturers is that of researcher. Lecturers need to show that they are, at worst, keeping abreast and at best ahead of developments within their field of subject expertise. When this role manifests itself in the production of papers within their subject area this has for many years been considered valid research. But what of those lecturers who are interested in the development of pedagogic issues? The emergence of the use of ICT as an aid to teaching has enriched this area of research. The use of ICT and CBA has provided an area for debate that shows no indication of being resolved. Many books and papers have been written on the subject, and there are always those who will expound the virtues whilst others will explain why it is not a good thing.

Whatever the point of view, it has provided the front-line lecturers with an abundance of research material. Those who employ ICT within their assessment regime usually have a large data set on which to base their findings and a group of subjects willing to express their views on the acceptability of the assessment and teaching techniques used. There have long been debates about the suitability of differing types of assessment materials. Lecturers are constantly trying to find better and more effective ways of assessing students' knowledge and understanding. For those lecturers whose primary concern is teaching, the use of ICT and the myriad of approaches to it have opened up innumerable research ideas and opportunities.

CONCLUDING REMARKS

This chapter has attempted to give an insight into some of the dilemmas facing both the institution as a whole and the individuals within that organization. The problems are diverse and compromise must always be made to resolve them. A team approach must be fostered, with team members drawn from all levels of the organization. The student who is experiencing at first hand the use of ICT based assessment is as important as the senior management who are providing resources for the programme. The lecturers who are developing the questions and providing pedagogic input would be less effective without the help of technicians and experts in the use of the chosen packages. The main lessons learnt by this institution were first, that it is inadequate to rely on a handful of enthusiasts: the programme will fail, and it is necessary to have a team of people involved from the beginning. Second, no one should be expected to use, or be subjected to, a new form of assessment technique without adequate training. If the use of ICT based assessment is to be effective it must be accompanied by intense and rigorous training.

The University of Luton believes that it has been successful in its introduction and widespread use of ICT based student assessment. As described in the chapter, the staff, both academic and administrative, have gained from the experience. The students' experience has been enriched because of the innovative and varied use that has been made of ICT based assessment within their subjects.

REFERENCES

Bloom, B S, Englehart, M D, Furst, E J and Krethwohl, D R (1956) *Taxonomy of Educational Objectives: 1. Cognitive domain*, David McKay, New York

Heard, S, Nicol, J and Heath, S (1997) *Setting Effective Objective Tests*, University of Aberdeen, MERTal Publications

Lens, W (1994) Personal computers in the learning environment and student motivation, *Scandinavian Journal of Educational Research*, **38** (3/4), pp 219–30

Perkins, M (1999) Validating formative and summative assessment, in *Computer-assisted Assessment in Higher Education*, ed P Race, S Brown and J Bull, pp 55–63, Kogan Page, London

Pritchet, N and Zakrzewski, S (1996) Interactive computer assessment of large groups: student responses, *Innovations in Education and Training International*, **33** (3), pp 242–47

Steven, C and Hesketh, I (1999) Increasing learner responsibility and support with the aid of adaptive formative assessment using QM designer software, in *Computer-assisted Assessment in Higher Education*, ed P Race, S Brown and J Bull, pp 103–12, Kogan Page, London

Zakrzewski, S and Bull, J (1998) The mass implementation and evaluation of computer-based assessments, *Assessment and Evaluation in Higher Education*, **23** (2), pp 141–52

Zakrzewski, S and Steven, C (2000) A model for computer-based assessment: the Catherine wheel principle, *Assessment and Evaluation in Higher Education*, **25** (2), pp 201–15

12

The use of ICT in education for research and development

Paul Blackmore, Mick Roach and Jacqueline Dempster

SUMMARY

The Technology-Enhanced Learning in Research-Led Institutions (TELRI) project was established at the Universities of Warwick and Oxford, funded by a Teaching and Learning Technology Project (TLTP) award from the Higher Education Funding Council for England (HEFCE). The project sought to tackle two interrelated issues. The first is that in many universities the two main activities of research and teaching are not closely linked, and the former has higher status than the latter. The second is that the wider availability of powerful ICT tools brings with it the need to make sure that the tools are used in ways that best support students' learning. The project aimed to tackle both of these issues by assisting academic staff to develop research-based approaches to teaching, through the effective use of learning technologies.

INTRODUCTION

The project team was aware of the intense debate about supposed links between research and teaching, and aware also that, despite the generally inconclusive research evidence (see Hattie and Marsh, 1996 for a meta-analysis of 58 studies), a belief that research informs teaching persists. The team believed that research and teaching could beneficially be linked, with one enriching the other, if this was planned for. The alternative situation, in which students receive no direct benefit from lecturers' research, whilst academics feel pulled between two competing demands for their time, is obviously undesirable. Although the improvements in students' learning that the project sought to bring about do not require a research-led environment, it was believed that certain environments, of which research-led institutions are an example, offered particular opportunities for bringing research and teaching together in a productive relationship. The point was trenchantly made in the USA by the Boyer Commission report that criticized research-led universities for failing to make use of their natural advantages and urging that research and teaching should be brought closer together (Boyer Commission, 1996).

Several possible forms of linkage between research and teaching were identified. The content argument supposes that researchers can bring their own leading edge research into the curriculum, although it is also widely suggested that this can be problematic, particularly in the sciences (Feldman, 1987). Others, more pragmatically, take a resources approach, pointing out that research brings better libraries, better research tools and higher levels of resourcing generally. A third main area is in learning processes, since undergraduates and researchers are both engaged in learning.

In considering the potential value of ICT in these forms of linkage, the project team could see the usefulness of supporting staff to make more and earlier use of research tools, many of which are, of course, technology based. Certainly the early introduction of research tools – for simulations and textual analysis for example – offers another large area for development. However, the area of learning processes was thought to be a much more valuable – and challenging – area to work in, since it addresses such a central educational issue.

The focus of the TELRI project was therefore on what, ideally, researchers and undergraduates share: a culture of personal inquiry, the process of inquiry and learning (Light, 1999). It is reasonable to suppose that experienced researchers and others who apply a discipline professionally will have developed a range of higher-level cognitive skills. Their intellectual processes and methods of working provide a useful model for their students' own learning. It would be of immense benefit to students if they could be helped to develop those skills through an appropriately delivered curriculum, so that the skills would then be available for further work both in the discipline and in other fields. The TELRI team was not claiming to have discovered a new idea. Clearly in all disciplines there are many existing examples of research and student learning being linked in this way. However, it was believed that without careful planning the benefits of academics' research expertise would not be fully realized. TELRI could be a prompt to thought and a source of guidance on appropriate tools and their use.

WHAT RESEARCH CAPABILITIES ARE

Attempting to link research and teaching immediately suggests problems of the definition of those terms (Elton, 1986), and these may be discipline-related (Hattie and Marsh, 1996). However, across all disciplines one would expect a number of broad capabilities of a proficient researcher, including:

- being innovative;
- working independently;
- setting and solving problems;
- analysing critically;

- handling large quantities of information in a wide range of media.

What these might mean in practice would clearly be very different from one discipline to another. Nevertheless they seem to be a reasonably robust set of terms which academic staff in any discipline would agree are desirable attributes, and this probably explains their repeated appearance in published lists of skills from many sources.

These capabilities require the presence of:

- a body of disciplinary knowledge;
- techniques used within the discipline;
- higher order cognitive skills.

A FOCUS ON HIGHER ORDER COGNITIVE SKILLS

TELRI sought to identify and develop those aspects of expertise that have widest applicability within and beyond the discipline. For this reason the team's interest was at two levels: the broad research capabilities listed above and, more fundamentally, the cognitive skills that inform them. It was believed that, while disciplinary knowledge and techniques are vital and must be taken into consideration, they did not need reinforcement through the work of the project, since they are self-evidently important and are explicitly taught. In contrast, cognitive skills are rarely developed explicitly. The TELRI team therefore chose to focus on higher order cognitive skills. These skills include the abilities to:

- make meaning, by interpreting information, forming and applying concepts and principles, critical analysis, synthesis into coherent wholes;
- generate ideas, using innovative thought, creativity;
- take decisions, using procedures, algorithms, strategies, heuristics and judgements about applicability;
- reflect on one's own purposes and processes, including justifications for judgements and decisions, and possibilities of transferability.

Crucially for this discussion, the project team identified two essentially comple-mentary and mutually supportive learning methods. The first of them, adoptive learning, is a reproductive process and occurs when a situation has already been defined. It requires the application of well understood knowledge, techniques and procedures. Adoptive learning is very useful: a great deal of any person's learning will be adoptive. However, there may be difficulties in transferability to new situations. Adaptive learning, on the other hand, is a generative process in which originality and creativity are involved and which requires higher cognitive skills. An accomplished researcher will be skilled in adaptive learning and potentially may be well placed to help others to develop similar expertise.

THE IMPORTANCE OF TRANSFER

There has been much debate about the importance of skills, termed variously core, key and transferable skills. Throughout the discussion there is a concern to identify those central capabilities that are of use in many areas of life, whether vocational or otherwise, and to ensure that curricula enable students to develop them. Cognitive skills, it might be argued, are vitally important in transfer because they are not as context-dependent as other abilities and because they are themselves used to effect the transfer. Because of this they have been termed 'skills of transfer' (Bridges, 1994).

Much discussion of skills is conceptually thin, as has been pointed out (Hyland, 1994), and there is an interesting tension between the clearly vocational drive of much skills development work and the fact that it restates what many have taken to be higher education's 'traditional ideas of autonomy and breadth' (Barnett, 1994). However, as Barnett also points out, higher education has not always been particularly attentive to this mission, and has certainly not been in the habit of articulating its purposes.

The project team saw the opportunity of using the project to encourage academic staff to pause and to analyse their teaching purposes in terms of the capabilities they were intending to develop, and the processes (rather than content) that would be likely to being these capabilities about. They saw the link with research as a strong motivator to engage with this really rather challenging area. Further, they sought at that point to invite staff to consider the ICT tools that were available to them and to consider which of them might be useful in developing those capabilities and how the tools could best be employed.

WHAT THIS MEANS FOR THE CURRICULUM

A curriculum should develop not only disciplinary knowledge and techniques but also the higher level cognitive skills that are essential for their development and use. The potential for the latter may be maximized if the curriculum is designed to provide appropriate course processes and assessment approaches that emulate the research environment.

The following were considered to be useful guides for the design of a curriculum to encourage the development of broad research capabilities and of cognitive skills:

- Activities should prompt the concentrated development and use of cognitive skills.

- Expertness, as distinct from competence, derives from the capacity to engage in novel thinking in complex and uncertain situations. Therefore:

- – Students should be encouraged to set as well as solve problems.

- – Open tasks are better than closed tasks

- – Problem based learning is more beneficial if the student has a part in defining the problem.

- Students should be encouraged to reflect on their learning processes.

Assessment is of central importance. Assignments that require the presentation of well established knowledge are adoptive in nature and will encourage students to take an adoptive approach to their learning. Instead, assignments should require more than a procedural or learned response. They should require judgements of value, likelihood and probability, together with innovation and creativity.

Reflection is also very important, since it is by reflecting on work in progress and learning to make judgements about its quality that students will gain insights into the nature of expertise in the field.

Again, there is nothing novel in TELRI approaches, which borrow from ideas about autonomy in learning (Boud, 1988), the creation of form (Kuhn, 1981), 'deep' and 'surface' learning (Marton and Saljo, 1976), transformative learning (Mezirow, 1997) and competence and expertise (Dreyfus and Dreyfus, 1986). The strength of the TELRI approach is believed to be that it bases its work on the research expertise of academics and that it encourages a more thoughtful use of ICT tools within that context.

WHAT LEARNING TECHNOLOGIES CAN CONTRIBUTE

It is easy to find examples of the use of learning technologies to make research tools, data and information available, thus contributing to students' disciplinary knowledge and techniques. However, learning technologies are less often used deliberately to develop higher cognitive skills, although they have considerable potential to do so. The Boyer Commission report makes this point strongly, asking for ICT that 'enriches teaching rather than substitutes for it', and wanting students to have tools 'with which they can discriminate, analyse and create rather than simply accumulate' (Boyer Commission, 1996).

There are many possible contributions. Creativity and originality are highly valued in researchers. Both are difficult to define, but it can safely be said that those who work in open situations, with the greatest autonomy, who are required to identify and set as well as solve problems, are most likely to be encouraged to be creative because of what they are required to bring to the situation themselves. Therefore TELRI was concerned with the integration of ICT tools to support learning that takes place in 'open' settings.

Researchers characteristically deal with large amounts of complex information, and require the skills of analysis, the ability to make and discern structure. Therefore ICT tools that require learners to give meaning and value to information are particularly useful. Research requires considerable precision. ICT tools that demand a high degree of focus, particularly on meaning, are therefore valuable. Finally, the ability critically to reflect on working processes is vital, and so tools that make apparent the processes of learning are useful. All of these tools are more effective when they offer immediate feedback to the learner. These links may be summarized as shown in Table 12.1.

WHAT THIS MEANS ACROSS THE DISCIPLINES

Discussion and debate enable the exploration of ideas and generation of meaning and are central to the development of research capabilities in the arts and humanities. ICT tools may assist these processes by making it possible to improve the amount and timeliness of tutorial support, particularly as group sizes increase. Where they enable students to submit, to view and to comment on their own and others' work, they may help them to develop skills of critical analysis, to explore matters of form and style and to learn from seeing – and perhaps participating collaboratively in – work in progress. Modern languages tutors have found Web publishing particularly useful in moving beyond basic skill acquisition and into critical thinking and understanding of related issues.

Discussion is equally important in the social sciences, where students must gather, evaluate and present evidence and construct arguments. The application and testing of theories and concepts is also central. Tutorial and small group work are very important in development of students' capabilities and, once again, ICT tools can offer the opportunity of more effective support. Case studies are very commonly used throughout the social sciences. ICT tools may enable the sharing of scarce case study material and offer access to 'real' primary source materials that are more akin to the materials used by researchers. Indeed the work of researchers – including that of the tutor – may be more readily made available.

In the sciences, curricula may develop problem solving and reasoning skills. Activities may require that students identify, evaluate and make use of sources of data, employing a range of methods to reach reasoned conclusions and solve

Table 12.1   *Links between ICT tools and research capabilities*

Desired research capability	What ICT should offer
Ability to be original, creative, innovative	Tools that present and offer resources for open situations
Ability to deal with complexity	Tools that support the learner in evaluating, analysing, selecting and structuring
Ability to work with precision	Tools that permit a high degree of focus on a particular skill
Ability to reflect on working processes	Tools that make working purpose and processes transparent
Ability to form justified discipline-based judgements	Tools that enable discussion of reasoning, judgements and decisions

problems. Problems classes are a staple item in many science curricula, where prompt feedback is vital if learning is to be effective. Once again the potentially collaborative nature of ICT-based working can be useful, mirroring the ways in which scientists customarily work.

CHOOSING TOOLS

TELRI approaches do not require the use of particular software. What is important is the nature of the task and the assessment that is designed: the tool is incidental. Any virtual learning environment that enables the sharing of documents and discussion – WebCT, Learning Space or COSE – may be used as a means of structuring case studies and encouraging student–student and staff–student interaction. Conferencing software such as FirstClass or WebBoard might also be appropriate.

Web publishing was seen to be particularly useful as a means of enabling students to see and contribute to work in progress and to evaluate it, thus offering them insights into approaches to and criteria for assessment. Early on in the project it was realized that many academic staff did not have ready access to the tools that were needed, so a simple Web publishing tool was designed that enabled students to publish to the Web and to comment on others' work. The tool is simple to use and free and has, therefore, been very attractive to staff who wanted to work in this way without a requirement that either they or their students should develop sophisticated Web publishing skills.

SUPPORT FOR STAFF

Working with TELRI did not necessarily mean changing one's educational purposes or, necessarily, one's approaches to teaching and assessing. The team offered a process of curriculum review (Roach, Blackmore and Dempster, 2000) that was intended to assist in translating the course's purpose into a transparent form. The process supports staff in being more analytical about what they are seeking to achieve through their teaching, and more deliberate about how they set about it, making use of educational technologies where they can provide a clear benefit. The process includes clarification of the capabilities and cognitive skills that are to be the focus of attention; a review of existing approaches; development, in conjunction with the staff involved, of appropriate approaches to teaching and assessment; and the establishment and use of a means of evaluating the effectiveness of the intervention.

TELRI has employed this approach to support staff in 13 departments within the universities of Warwick and Oxford in implementing technology enhanced learning. The team produced case studies detailing the context, the technological tool and the capabilities and skills developed. A second phase extended the approach to further departments in several other research-led universities, including Durham, Birmingham and Southampton. A third phase provided staff development workshops and consultancy across the HE sector.

CONCLUSIONS

The work described here offers a means of bringing together research and teaching, by focusing on the process of learning, which is common to both. Part of the purpose is to ensure that research is not seen as an activity remote from other forms of learning. There are a number of potential benefits for, as has already been suggested, we believe that learners may thus become more capable in a range of activities in later life, including research. We believe also that academic staff find this linking of the two activities to be stimulating.

It is believed that making use of ICT tools to make links between research and student learning makes good sense. The substantial investment made in ICT in higher education, and the increasing use of ICT tools in undergraduate curricula, make it vital that we are able to analyse the costs and benefits. If ICT tools are used unreflectively, delivering packaged learning to passive recipients, higher education may be considerably damaged. However, if ICT can be a means of engaging more closely with the development of those capabilities and cognitive skills that have traditionally been the concern of higher education, even though they have not always been articulated, the benefits will be immense.

REFERENCES

Barnett, R (1994) *The Limits of Competence: Knowledge, higher education and society*, Open University Press, Buckingham

Boud, D (1988) *Developing Student Autonomy in Learning*, Kogan Page, London

Boyer Commission (1996) *Reinventing Undergraduate Education: A blueprint for America's research universities*, Carnegie Foundation for the Advancement of Teaching, New York

Bridges, D (1994) *Transferable Skills in Higher Education*, University of East Anglia, Norwich

Dreyfus, L and Dreyfus, S E (1986) *Mind over Machine: The power of human intuition and expertise in the era of the computer*, Blackwell, Oxford

Elton, L (1986) Research and teaching: symbiosis or conflict, *Higher Education*, **15**: 299–304

Feldman, (1987)

Hattie, J and Marsh, H W (1996) The relationship between research and teaching: a meta-analysis, *Review of Educational Research*, **66** (4), 507–42

Hyland, T (1994) *Competence, Education and NVQs*, Cassell, London

Kuhn, D (1981) The role of self-directed activity in cognitive development, in *New Directions in Piagetian Theory and Practice*, ed I E Segel, D Brodzinsky and R M Golinkoff, Lawrence Erlbaum Associates, Hillsdale, NJ

Light, G (1999) *Integrating Research and Practice*, SRHE/SEDA Educational Development Research Network Meeting, 29 June

Marton, F and Saljo, R (1976) On qualitative differences in learning: I. Outcome and process, *British Journal of Educational Psychology*, **46**: 4–11

Mezirow, J (1997) Cognitive processes: contemporary paradigms of learning, in *Adult Learning: A reader*, ed P Sutherland, Kogan Page, London

Roach, M P, Blackmore, P and Dempster, J A (2000) *Supporting high level learning through research-based methods: Guidelines for course design*, TELRI Project Publication [online] http://www.telri.ac.uk/staffpack/ [accessed 28 January 2002]

13

ICT in support of projects and dissertations

Mike Fuller

SUMMARY

Many subjects require or encourage students to carry out a substantial project or dissertation as part of their degree level studies. This can be seen as an opportunity to do work that is preparatory to research or professional practice. ICT resources can play a major role in supporting both generic and subject specific aspects of such work. However there is scope for further development of the use of such resources to support the likely expansion of project work in higher education more efficiently and effectively.

INTRODUCTION

Many degrees in a wide range of subjects require or encourage a substantial project or dissertation as part of their programmes. One telling piece of evidence for this is provided by the subject benchmarking exercise of the Quality Assurance Agency (QAA, 2000a). In 20 of the first 22 subject benchmark statements of the Quality Assurance Agency, projects or dissertations are mentioned explicitly or indirectly as suitable or expected forms of assessed work within a first degree. The two exceptions are accounting and education. In the case of education this may reflect the authors' expressed intention not to 'set out any specific or detailed requirements for course content, methods of learning, teaching, or assessment' (QAA, 2000c: 5). In accounting a Web search reveals that there are certainly examples of departments that use such approaches, even if they are not mentioned in the benchmark statement.

In addition to their use in undergraduate study, most taught Master's degrees include a dissertation or project element. Here the emphasis on research and the need for contextualization of the topic investigated in relation to the literature of the discipline are likely to be more substantial than in a final year undergraduate project. In both undergraduate and postgraduate taught programmes the role of a major project near the end of the degree has the character of an integrative academic 'capstone' in the metaphor used in her editorial by Fincher (1999).

Why do so many subjects, as diverse as architecture and philosophy, or chemistry and politics, see projects and dissertations as important? The subject benchmark statement for classics and ancient history (QAA, 2000b: 12) puts the case briefly and well. They are 'considered particularly valuable in encouraging self-direction and intellectual independence and initiative, as well as in requiring students to acquire research skills'.

This shows that there are many aspects of project work that are generic in character, cutting across disciplines. The next two sections look at these generic features, using a key skills approach. Later sections of the chapter then focus on the support that ICT can give to both generic and subject specific aspects of project work in HE. This is followed by a proposal for developing the usefulness of ICT in supporting project work.

Before moving on, however, it is important to consider the resource costs of project work, which because of reliance on individual supervision has traditionally had high marginal costs for additional students. Appendix 2 of the Dearing Report (NCIHE, 1997) identified the pressures on UK HE to replace individual or small group teaching by work in larger groups and by lectures. The authors of the appendix said that:

> it seems that the most efficient combination of teaching methods sustainable for increasing student numbers, will fulfil the following criteria:
>
> - improve rather than diminish students' learning experience;
> - increase the use of fixed cost rather than variable cost methods;
> - increase RBL (resource based learning) developed externally rather than in-house.

Projects and dissertations are generally seen as enhancing the learning experience. However the financial background means that they must be delivered in a way that makes effective use of learning resources developed for the sector as a whole, rather than just for an individual department or institution.

KEY SKILLS IN PROJECTS

As previously suggested, there are a number of common features of projects across disciplines, in particular, the development of key skills. The English Qualifications and Curriculum Authority (QCA) has a brief that extends from schools into further education (FE) and higher education (HE). Its description of key skills for the HE levels on this scheme (levels 4 and 5) identifies six key skills: communication; application of number; information technology; working with others; improving own learning and performance; problem solving (QCA, 2000). Projects are, by their nature, very likely to develop almost all these skills.

At the highest level (level 5) on the QCA scheme of work is a unit entitled Personal Skills Development that is 'about building on your current capabilities and applying your skills in an integrated way, in order to manage dynamically complex work'. As evidence of this skill, learners are required to:

- Explore the demands of the work and formulate viable proposals for meeting these demands.

- Plan to manage the work, and meet your own skill-development needs, and gain the necessary commitment from others.

- Manage the work, adapting your strategy as necessary to resolve at least two complex problems and achieve the quality of outcomes required. Formally review, with an appropriate person, your use of skills in: communication, problem solving, working with others.

- Evaluate your overall performance and present the outcomes, including at least:

  - one formal, oral presentation of the outcomes from the work;

  - one written evaluation of your overall approach and application of skills.

(QCA, 2000: 4–5)

The guidelines, activities and assessment criteria typically used for projects and dissertations enable many, if not all, of these high level activities to be demonstrated. Given the nature of level 5 work, projects can be seen as a bridge from study to professional practice.

GENERIC CHARACTERISTICS OF PROJECTS AND DISSERTATIONS

In degrees with one or more major projects they have a number of features that crop up frequently. One is scale, with a project (where it exists) typically being regarded as the single major item of the final year of an undergraduate programme, often worth 25 per cent or more of the marks for the year. Other aspects are grouped here in relation to the six key skills headings of the QCA scheme, but reordered for this purpose:

Working with others

Projects can be individual or group, with some degrees providing both styles, generally with a group project preceding an individual project. Group projects clearly provide direct experience of working in teams, but in an individual project there will still be a relationship with the supervisor and with gatekeepers controlling access to data. In particular in the directly professional disciplines which favour such links, projects may be based on work done with an employer or a 'research client' who will be interested in the findings. A striking interdisciplinary example of a university linking student projects to meet the needs of local employers and community groups is the CRISP project at the University of Leeds (CRISP, 2000). In working with others in these various ways, participants' influencing and negotiating skills will be enhanced.

Problem solving

Many project modules provide an opportunity to choose a topic for research, either from a menu of projects suggested by staff based on their own interests, or in some cases as an example of independent study. In either context, there will be an element of problem formulation and structuring, followed by the development of a strategy for collecting relevant evidence. The methodology of the project will require extensions of the participant's research skills. Inevitably in carrying out the project, particularly one involving primary data collection or links with an employer or external client, problems requiring solutions are likely to emerge in practice.

Improving own learning and performance

To carry out a project and deliver it on time, considerable skills of time management and personal organization are required. Mapping out a project requires skills of scheduling – effectively project management skills in much the sense used in many business and management degrees. In a very real sense, because of the independence and level of work involved, projects also enhance skills of learning how to learn.

Application of number

Extension of skills in the application of number is not absolutely guaranteed in the carrying out of a project or dissertation, but it is very likely to be a feature of most projects. It is almost invariably present to some extent in successful science and social science projects. In some subject areas the project provides a major opportunity to show how quantitative methods may be applied to a 'real' problem.

Communication

Projects and dissertations require the completion of a substantial report, significantly longer than coursework essays, laboratory practical reports and other written output on degree courses. As well as this written communication, which is likely to provide most of the marks for the module, many project courses require a presentation to an audience of staff and peers, either at or towards the end of the project. This might take the form of a short talk using presentation aids, followed by questions, or perhaps a poster session, or an interview by the examiners of the project report. (The earlier this takes place, the more useful it can be for providing formative feedback for use in preparing the final report.)

Information technology

Information technology has a clear role to play in helping deliver a successful project. Since this is the focus of this chapter, it clearly merits more than a paragraph. The next section briefly considers specific aspects of projects. Then the following section outlines ways in which ICT can contribute to the work of a project or dissertation. Useful resources and some gaps in resources are identified.

SUBJECT SPECIFIC ASPECTS OF PROJECTS

Projects on a degree programme must clearly draw on the domains of knowledge of the subject(s) involved. They should deepen the learner's under-standing of the subject, and often provide an opportunity to link topics covered in several taught modules to enable an integrated approach to the investi-gation of a problem. Such ideas are present in a number of the subject benchmark statements referred to at the start of this chapter. In judging the quality of a project, the extent to which it shows a grasp of the discipline(s) to which it relates and of relevant methodologies will be major factors.

Project work can also be seen as providing students with an opportunity to enter in the community and culture of the discipline. In the view of Seely Brown, Collins and Duguid (1989: 3) 'learning is… a process of enculturation'. Projects provide the student, like an apprentice, with the opportunity to use the tools of the trade in their subject. Clark and Boyle (1999) see this 'authentic activity' as important for learners and teachers in computer science. Similarly Ryder and Leach (1997) see science projects providing opportunities for students to apply subject skills working with the guidance of an expert practitioner.

In disciplines where project work is thoroughly embedded, such as computer science, reviews of practice can be of value to those outside the field as well as inside it. The recent collection of papers gathered by Sally Fincher (1999) certainly falls into this category. Details are given of research and resources relevant to project work in the subject. Computer science also provides an excellent example of a project Web site, at School of Computing, Information Systems and Mathematics at South Bank University, which is distinctive in giving prominence to details of students' projects as well as to the advice and resources provided by the staff (Inman, 2000).

ICT AND PROJECT WORK

In assessing the current role and potential for development of ICT in project work the Internet provides the dominant but not the only form of support. It has become a vital research tool for searching academic, professional and general media. It provides electronic means of communication. It also provides access to resources for developing research skills, and for supporting report writing and presentations. These features are considered in turn below.

USING THE INTERNET FOR RESEARCH PURPOSES

Students undertaking projects are generally expected to set their work in context by undertaking a literature review. Indeed, for projects that are largely library based, reviewing the literature to produce a synthesis may be the major component of their work. Learners need ways of searching the academic literature.

Links to the Institute for Scientific Information (ISI) Citation Databases provide international access to the literature of academic research in many fields (ISI, 2000a). British higher education has negotiated favourable access to the Web of Science (WoS) (ISI, 2000c) and to ISI's Index to Scientific and Technical Proceedings (ISTP) (ISI, 2000b) to which most institutions subscribe. These form part of the services funded centrally through the Joint Information Systems Committee (JISC, 2000) at Manchester Information and Associated Services (MIMAS, 2000).

Students can access academic literature effectively using these specialist databases. They are also likely to find more general guides to their subjects of value. One wide ranging source of selected Internet resources across all major disciplines is the BUBL Information Service (2000), again funded by JISC. In a limited but growing range of fields, the Resource Discovery Network (2000) provides access to a cooperative network of subject gateways to online resources. A North American site with broad scope is the Internet Scout Project (2000). Its Signpost service provides access to its past reports. Access to selected high quality sources of information is clearly of considerable importance to learners working in each discipline.

Academic journals increasingly have online editions to complement hard copy, or even entirely replace it. BUBL provides access to the contents pages or full articles for some 200 journals, and information about similar services.

Internet search engines provide the means of discovering a wider range of professional and general media available online. There are now many different search engines. Fuller (2000) provides further details and an example of searching for materials about population issues. One of the potential advantages of Internet resources is that the use of hyperlinks can enable data to be linked to metadata providing commentary and analysis about them.

There are, however, clearly quality issues in a medium where most of the material is self-published. One of the skills that those doing Internet searches must develop is a critical awareness and sound judgement of what is encountered. In addition there are issues of the cost of access to some sources of data, where charging is applied, just as it would be for equivalent hard copy sources. Except when an external client is involved, the typical student project has no funds for purchasing resources.

ELECTRONIC COMMUNICATION

Electronic communication has a vital role to play for both student and supervisor in a project. While face to face supervision will continue to be important, teachers can encourage learners to provide a brief e-mail note of what they have agreed to do between one supervision and the next. Any differences of interpretation then have some chance of being corrected promptly.

E-mail can also provide access to other expertise. In the early days of the Web, enquiries to e-mail discussion lists often received a sympathetic response. For some purposes this culture survives, for example on the statistical consulting list, <stat-L@lists.mcgill.ca>, or sci.stat.consult, its newsgroup counterpart. As usual though, the enquirer must realize that the respondent is not necessarily a fully-fledged expert – the buyer must beware.

On group projects, electronic communication, either simply as e-mail or through a bulletin board, would enable a log of the project to grow organically. This would be a feature of project work based in a virtual learning environment (VLE), such as WebCT and TopClass. These provide controlled access to course materials and other searchable resources, assessment tools and the tracking of student progress, timetabling facilities for pacing learning, communications facilities and file storage facilities for participants.

Lee and Thompson (1999) report on the creation of a VLE to support a MSc in Computer Based Learning taught in part at a distance. This made heavy use of video conferencing. For those looking to use the structuring that a VLE provides, but to do so with an 'off the shelf' product, the collection of resources by the Learning Technology Support Service (LTSS, 2000) provides a suitable starting point.

For projects where data is to be collected from a population whose members have Internet access, direct electronic data collection is possible, and short surveys can then be effective in terms of response in relation to time and cost.

DEVELOPING RESEARCH SKILLS, INCLUDING REPORT WRITING AND PRESENTATIONS

Web searches suggest a very patchy pattern of provision across disciplines of resources for developing subject specific research skills needed for project work. This seems to be a significant gap in what is available to support their use in degree level work.

The subject specific aspects of supporting projects and dissertations in UK HE are probably best met by asking the 24 subject centres of the Learning and Teaching Support Network (LTSN, 2000) recently established to look at the needs of their disciplines and to work in conjunction with similar institutions elsewhere.

Generically, more could be done to encourage better use of the structuring tools already available within word processing software, to provide a coherent framework for reports and dissertations, and to take advantage of biblio-graphic software for organizing references.

Web searches reveal that there are many UK HE sites providing resources for developing presentation skills, and departments from a number of subjects that have guides to writing a project or dissertation online. The need here is to fill any gaps in the provision and to ensure that students have access to the best available resources, so that departments do not have to devote staff time to the creation of their own guides to project work for local use only.

A COLLABORATIVE INTERDISCIPLINARY PROJECT WEB SITE?

Although there are quality resources available to support project work in HE, there are also gaps in provision. Many aspects of projects are subject specific, but other aspects (particularly project management, report writing, presentation skills) are largely generic. The role of projects within UK HE is increasing as institutions reduce their reliance on traditional examinations and look for an appropriate mix of methods of assessment related to programme aims and objectives.

Against this background, and the cost pressures identified in the introduction, there would seem to be considerable merit in creating an interdisciplinary Web site to support student project work, providing a guide to resources and using a collaborative approach to fill any gaps. This could be a potential major project for the LTSN's Generic Learning and Teaching Centre (GLTC), which is based together with JISC's new Technology Integration Centre (TIC) in the Institute for Learning and Teaching's offices in York.

CONCLUSION

Student projects and dissertations are widely seen as valid forms of work within degree programmes, providing an integrative experience that provides a bridge between study and professional work of a graduate level. ICT has a substantial role to play in enabling the benefits of this approach, with the enhanced learning experience project work is seen as providing, to be provided cost effectively. In the UK context, gaps in what is readily and conveniently available to support subject specific and generic needs in project work should be major concerns of the Learning and Teaching Support Network's subject centres, and particularly of its Generic Learning and Teaching Centre.

REFERENCES

BUBL Information Service (2000) http://bubl.ac.uk/ [accessed 28 January 2002]
Clark, M A C and Boyle, R D (1999) A personal theory of teaching computing through final year projects, *Computer Science Education*, **9** (3) (December), pp 200–14
CRISP (City and Regional Initiative on Student Projects) (2000) http://www.leeds.ac.uk/ services-to-business/crisp.htm [accessed 28 January 2002]
Fincher, S (ed) (1999). Special issue: project work in computer science education, *Computer Science Education*, **9** (3) (December), pp 181–280
Fuller, M F (2000) Net benefits: six billion characters in search of an author, *Teaching Statistics*, **22** (2) (Summer), pp 49–52

Inman, D (2000). *Project Guide 2000/2001* [online] http://www.scism.sbu.ac.uk/
inmandw/projects/past/0001/index.html [accessed 28 January 2002]

Internet Scout Project (2000) http://scout.cs.wisc.edu/index.html [accessed 28 January
2002]

ISI (Institute for Scientific Information) (2000a) http://www.isinet.com/

ISI (2000b) ISTP (Index to Scientific and Technical Proceedings) available at http://
wos.mimas.ac.uk/

ISI (2000c) WoS (Web of Science) available at http://wos.mimas.ac.uk/ or demonstration
available at http://www.isinet.com/isi/demos/webofscience/demo

JISC (Joint Information Systems Committee) (2000) http://www.jisc.ac.uk/

Lee, M and Thompson, R (1999) *Teaching at a Distance: Building a virtual learning environment*
[online] http://www.jtap.ac.uk/reports/htm/jtap-033.html [accessed 28 January 2002]

LTSN (Learning and Teaching Support Network) (2000) http://www.ltsn.ac.uk

LTSS (Learning Technology Support Service) (2000) *Virtual Learning Environments*
[online] http://www.ltss.bris.ac.uk/resources_vle.htm [accessed 28 January 2002]

MIMAS (Manchester Information and Associated Services) (2000) http://www.mimas.ac.uk/

NCIHE (National Committee of Inquiry into Higher Education) (1997) *Higher Education
in the Learning Society* [online] http://www.leeds.ac.uk/educol/ncihe/ [accessed 28
January 2002]

QAA (Quality Assurance Agency for Higher Education) (2000a) *Benchmarking
Academic Standards – April 2000* [online] http://www.qaa.ac.uk/crntwork/benchmark/
benchmarking.htm [accessed 28 January 2002]

QAA (2000b) *Classics and Ancient History* (Subject Benchmark Statement) [online]
http://www.qaa.ac.uk/crntwork/benchmark/classics.pdf [accessed 28 January 2002]

QAA (2000c) *Education Studies* (Subject Benchmark Statement) [online] http://
www.qaa.ac.uk/crntwork/benchmark/education.pdf [accessed 28 January 2002]

QCA (Qualifications and Curriculum Authority) (2000) *Key Skills Units Levels 4 and 5,*
QCA/99/455, QCA, London

Resource Discovery Network (2000) http://www.rdn.ac.uk/

Ryder, J and Leach, J (1997) Research projects in the undergraduate science course:
students learning about science through enculturation, in *Proceedings of the 4th
Improving Student Learning Symposium, Bath, 1996*, ed G Gibbs

Seely Brown, J, Collins, A and Duguid, P (1989) *Situated Cognition and the Culture of
Learning* [online] http://www.ilt.columbia.edu/ilt/papers/JohnBrown.html [accessed
28 January 2002]

14

From chalkface to interface (absolute novices to ICT enter university)

Marina Möller

SUMMARY

This chapter presents material from studies conducted at Vista University in South Africa. This university serves a disadvantaged urban population, many of whom continue to live in informal settlements without modern amenities. The students arrive at their university studies with the absolute minimum of prior experience of electronic technologies. Furthermore, their pre-university education has been focused on rote learning rather than exploratory. The chapter focuses on a cohort of student teachers as they take their first steps towards use of computer based education materials and the quite different approach to learning that this demands.

INTRODUCTION

A century of thinking about education has left us with a much richer understanding of the processes involved in teaching and learning. More recently, the development of computers and digital media has exploded, offering us previously unavailable opportunities to improve our craft as educators. Today's student teachers will teach tomorrow as they are taught today. As technology moves to the centre in schools and classrooms, it should also by now form an integral part of all student teacher programmes. Teacher education should always be one step ahead, not only to cater for the changing needs in the schools, but also to equip new teachers in such a way that they become much sought after in the growing competitive market.

RELOCATION OF BLACK SOUTH AFRICANS

The early 1990s marked the start of an important period of change in South African education. The government finally allowed its racially segregated schools to begin admitting children of all colours. By the end of this decade the South African school system had already changed enormously. Different groups had different reasons for supporting the opening of schools. The white population was getting smaller, and one way of preventing many white schools from closing was to admit learners from all races.

Many Africans moved from rural areas to the cities where they could not afford any housing. They became squatters in informal settlements. Housing is erected by the occupants themselves, generally with unorthodox building materials which may comprise anything from tin shacks, cardboard shacks, tents and old cars to empty drums. These areas are often densely populated and generally poorly serviced. The areas lack sport and recreational facilities. As a result, the children have nothing constructive to do and are therefore idle (Platzky and Walker, 1985).

In the last few years the government started to build houses and more schools in these black townships. The schools are provided with water and electricity but most of the time electricity is not available in the classrooms. The cables are either stolen or the wall sockets, windows and doors are broken and not fixed.

Despite South Africa's success in opening all schools to all races, the majority of children have not experienced racial integration. Many African, Indian and coloured families moved into former white areas but most Africans still live in the townships, squatter camps or high density areas and in the rural areas. Most of the children still attend schools that have only African students. For a range of different reasons, for instance unemployment and poverty, many of the schools in the townships are still not as well equipped as those in the former white areas.

African, Indian and coloured learners believed their schools were inferior and their facilities not as good as those in the white schools. Businesses want to expand the country's skilled workforce by demanding better education and training to more people of all races. One of the obvious results of these trends is that teacher education had to change: one reason being the demand from businesses for better and more hands-on education for learners to fulfil changing needs, and another to assist government in uplifting standards in the so-called 'black' schools. More and more learners from races other than white had the opportunity to share in the 'advantages' of the historically so-called white schools and there is still a constant move to these so-called 'white' schools.

MEDIUM OF INSTRUCTION

Language is of major importance for effective teaching, communication and learning in education. Effective learning and teaching depend upon a learner's ability to comprehend what is communicated (Mkabela and Luthuli, 1997).

Black learners in township schools are instructed through mother-tongue medium only during the lower primary phase. The onset of the higher primary phase marks a sudden and abrupt transition to English as medium of instruction for the entire primary curriculum. This transition causes many problems in the education of the black learner. Foremost is the disparity between the English proficiency of these learners and the proficiency required of them in order to master all school subjects through the medium of English (Van Rooyen, 1990).

Moreover, teachers in black schools themselves often lack the English proficiency that is necessary for effective teaching. Teachers do not have the knowledge and skills to support English language learning and to teach literacy skills across the entire curriculum. The problem is compounded by a lack of suitable textbooks and other resources. The teachers therefore fall back on writing notes on the chalkboard for the learners to copy down in their books. Other activities do not take place, only the copying down of notes. In the classrooms of many disadvantaged communities the chalkboard has been for long the only technology that is used to try to enhance learning. The grade12 pass rate is very low, especially in the township schools. This can be ascribed to the fact that the learners and teachers have not mastered the language of instruction because it is their second or sometimes even third language. Therefore the learners rely on rote learning and are not able to show insight and understanding.

USE OF TECHNOLOGY

The majority of the students at Vista University are drawn from these township schools. The obvious implication is that many of them have never been exposed to the variety of technology that forms part of the life-world of learners in the more advantaged areas.

Vista University is not only the youngest, but also the largest historically black university in South Africa. There are eight Vista campuses located all over South Africa within urban areas near black townships. The major reason for the establishment of the different campuses of Vista University in 1982 was to bring higher education closer to the people in the then so-called 'black' areas. Its multi-campus nature marks the institution as different from single historically black universities in the rural areas such as the University of Fort Hare in the Eastern Cape.

In most of the schools in the townships, the use of technology is limited to the chalkboard. When learners arrive at university, they are for the first time in their lives exposed to technology such as overhead projectors, videos and computers.

With the availability of all the different technology in the 21st century, the face of the classroom is now changing from chalkface to interface. The interface can be described in different facets. It developed from drills, tutorials, simulations and games (Alessi and Trollip, 1991) to hypermedia programmes and Web based instruction on the Internet.

To determine how the changes in education have influenced and effected student teachers at Vista University, and to illustrate how the face of the classroom has changed from chalkface to interface, the following experiment was conducted using a hypermedia programme as interface.

STRUCTURING OF THE EXPERIMENT

Preamble to the experiment

In the curriculum of student teachers at Vista University, students have an elective course, School Librarianship. Students taking this course at the Sebokeng campus participated in this experiment. These students did not have any background of the organization of a school library or school media centre because most of the time the schools in the black townships either do not have libraries, or the libraries are poorly equipped with mainly outdated reading material. The 34 students in the group were divided into an experimental group and a control group, by using a table of random numbers (Borg, Gall and Gall, 1993). Then all the students were exposed to a pre-test, consisting of 20 general questions concerning the organization of the school media centre. Only 28 students turned up to write the pre-test, 15 from the control group and 13 from the experimental group. No matter how carefully the subjects of a study are selected, it is common to lose some as the study progresses. Experimental mortality is the loss of subjects during the period of the experiment (Borg, Gall and Gall, 1993). The reason for the mortality in this experiment could be that four of the students repeated the course and it was not compulsory for them to attend classes. The other two absences may be due to normal circumstances like illness or transport problems.

From the pre-test it was determined that the highest score for the control group was 75 per cent and the lowest score was 35 per cent. Of the 15 students in this group, 40 per cent failed the test. The mean score for this group was 49 per cent.

The highest score in the experimental group was 65 per cent and the lowest score was 20 per cent. Of the 14 students in this group 53.8 per cent failed the test. The mean score for this group was 46.5 per cent. (See Table 14.1.)

Table 14.1   *Pre-test results distribution*

Score %	20	25	30	35	40	45	50	55	60	65	70	75
Control group				3	2	1	3	4	1			1
Experimental group	1			3	2	1		2	4	1		

These results proved what was anticipated, namely that the students did not know much about the organization of the school media centre. When the data of these two groups was compared, it appeared that the experimental group started the research with a lower pre-knowledge (46.5 per cent) than the control group (49 per cent).

Implementation of the experiment

Two lessons were presented, one for each research group. During the exposition of content however, different technology and teaching approaches were used.

Control group
A video was used in the lesson of the control group: Resource Centre, VEIA007, available from the Centre for Education Technology and Distance Education (CETDE) in Pretoria. This 10-minute video gives an explanation of the nature, use, purpose, arrangement, and where applicable, the classification and cataloguing of the most important material in the school media centre. To ensure that the video programme was integrated effectively in the lesson, suggestions according to Heinich, Molenda and Russell (1989) were followed. In preparing for the lesson, objectives were identified. To prepare the students for the video to be viewed, the objectives were mentioned to them. Their attention was drawn to important aspects in the video. A worksheet was given to them to complete during and after the viewing of the video programme. While the video was shown, the students had to be attentive viewers and they had to refer to the worksheet. The video was stopped and questions were asked. The video was viewed for a second time. The follow-up activity was to complete the worksheet.

Experimental group
The experimental group was exposed to the hypermedia programme that was developed for this study by the School Media Centre.

The 13 students in this group worked together in pairs at the computers. At one computer three students worked together. This was done not only because not enough multimedia computers were available at the time of conducting the experiment, but also to include cooperative learning. Computer assisted education lends itself to cooperative learning and group work (Kennedy, 1993). The students were told to take turns to operate the programme by using the mouse. This hypermedia programme lends itself to a heuristic learning experience. According to Snyman and Kühn (1993), heuristic means to master contents by experimenting and self-discovery. The students, for example, had to move the cursor over the screen to look for active areas. Clicking on 'hot spots', gave them more information, or they could be taken to other screens. They decided themselves which topic to do next or to go back to a previous screen if they did not understand something. They also completed the same worksheet as the control group.

End of the experiment

The evaluation phase of the lessons for both groups consisted of a post-test which was exactly the same as the pre-test. This was necessary to determine how much impact the interventions had on the knowledge acquisition of the students.

The highest score of the post-test for the control group was 70 per cent and the lowest score was 35 per cent, with the mean 54.7 per cent. Of the 15 students in this group, 26.7 per cent still failed the post-test.

The highest score of the post-test for the experimental group was 85 per cent and the lowest score was 25 per cent, with the mean 61.5 per cent. Of the 14 students in this group, only one student still failed the post-test, in contrast with the control group. (See Table 14.2.)

The knowledge acquisition of the control group improved by 5.7 per cent and that of the experimental group by 15 per cent. This means that the experimental group participating in the hypermedia programme gained more knowledge than the control group, following the video programme. (See Table 14.3.) This can probably be ascribed to the fact that during the development of the hypermedia programme, certain pertinent aspects such as motivation, interaction, control, questions, feedback and hypermedia were built in to reinforce learning as is suggested by Alessi and Trollip (1991), Erickson and Vonk (1994) and Trieschmann (1990).

EXPERIENCING THE USE OF THE HYPERMEDIA PROGRAMME

To determine how students experienced the use of the hypermedia programme, a questionnaire was given to them for completion. The questions in the questionnaire can be divided into three categories: questions concerning the affective domain, psycho-motor domain and cognitive domain.

Table 14.2   *Post-test results distribution*

Score %	25	30	35	40	45	50	55	60	65	70	75	80	85
Control group			2	1	1	1	3	2	4	1			
Experimentzal group	2					2	1	1	4	2	1		1

Table 14.3   *Pre and post-test mean scores*

	Pre-test	Post-test
Control group	49	55
Experimental group	47	62

Affective domain

Questions on this domain are concerned with emotions or attitudes. Table 14.4 shows the experiences of the students on the affective domain.

All the students would like to do the programme again and all of them were satisfied with what they learnt. Of the students, 92.3 per cent would recommend it to a friend. Of the students, 84.6 per cent liked the graphics and drawings. Doing the programme with a friend was preferred by 76.9 per cent of the students, and only 38.4 per cent would like to do the programme alone. This indicated that the computer, for this programme, might lend itself to cooperative learning, and correlates with research done by Kennedy (1993), concerning cooperative learning with computers. Only 30.7 per cent of the students thought that the drawings and graphics were too childish, which showed that it correlates with the target group for which the programme was developed.

Table 14.4   *Statements on the affective domain*

No	Statement	% Yes
1	I would like to use the programme again	100
15	I was satisfied with what I learnt	100
3	I would recommend the programme to a friend	92.3
18	I liked the graphics and drawings	84.6
12	I liked doing the programme with a friend	76.9
6	I would like to do this programme alone	38.4

Psycho-motor domain

Questions on this domain are concerned with movement or motion skills. Table 14.5 shows the experience of the students on the psycho-motor domain.

Of the students, 62 per cent indicated that they found it easy to navigate through the programme, although it was the first experience with a computer for 46 per cent of the students. Only 31 per cent had difficulty in using the mouse. This shows that the mouse was not an obstacle for the majority of students to continue doing the programme.

Cognitive domain

Questions on this domain are concerned with the intellect. Table 14.6 displays the experience of the students on the cognitive domain.

Learning assisted by computer seems better than classroom instruction for 92 per cent of the students and only 23 per cent indicated that they would have learnt more from a lecturer than from this programme. The feedback in the programme helped all of them to learn from their mistakes. This is why it is important that questions asked must always be followed by answers and feedback (Bitter, 1989; Schimmel, 1988). Of the students, 92 per cent were concerned that they might not understand the material but 77 per cent of the students found the presentation of the course material easy and only 23 per cent of the students found the questions difficult. Although only 23 per cent of the students knew what they were expected to do, 62 per cent could easily navigate through the programme. It is evident that the students experienced the hypermedia programme positively on all three domains.

Table 14.5   *Statements on the psycho-motor domain*

No	Statement	% Yes
11	It was easy to navigate through the programme	62
5	This is the first time I have ever used a computer	46
19	I had difficulty in using the mouse	31

Table 14.6   *Statements on the cognitive domain*

No	Statement	% Yes
14	The feedback helped me learn from my mistakes	100
4	This way of learning seems better than classroom instruction	92
2	I was concerned that I might not understand the material	92
16	I found the presentation of the course material easy	77
7	I had to think to get the right answer	69
13	I found most questions too easy	46
8	I knew what I was expected to do	23
9	I found it difficult to understand the questions	23
17	I would have learnt more from a lecturer than from this programme	23

ANECDOTAL RECORD

According to Fraenkel and Wallen (1993), an anecdotal record is a record of observed behaviours written down in the form of anecdotes by the researcher as observer. Some of them will now be given.

- The students had difficulty in using the mouse in the beginning. They held the mouse in the strangest positions. They soon got used to holding and handling it.

- They discussed the contents of the programme with each other and when they had to answer a question, they decided on the answer together.

- After they had clicked with the mouse, and something unusual had happened on the screen, they screamed or laughed.

- They pointed with their fingers at the screen and sometimes touched it.

- When they answered a question incorrectly, they liked to discuss the answer with each other.

- After they had finished with a topic, they consulted the worksheet to see which topic came next.

- After they had finished a topic, they first completed that part of the worksheet before going on to the next topic.

- Some of the students constantly moved the mouse around and clicked on every picture on the screen to see whether something was going to happen.

THE IMPORTANCE OF THE EXPERIMENT FOR TEACHER EDUCATION

This experiment, although on a small scale, proved that although most of the students attending our university come from disadvantaged areas where the schools have only the chalkface as technology, they adapt fairly easily to the interface. They have the advantage that they are extremely eager to experiment with technology and are also eager to learn. However, the interface that is used must be specially developed or adapted or presented with support. Programmes that are used must have lots of interaction, questions, feedback and the language difficulty must be on the level of the students.

CONCLUSION

Teacher education institutions must prepare their students to teach in tomorrow's classrooms. Yesterday the face in the classroom was the chalkface. Today it is the interface. We must all work together to help ensure that tomorrow's teachers are educated and prepared to meet the challenges, demands and faces of teaching in the new millennium.

Similar sentiments apply to all university students regardless of discipline, and the material presented here illustrates that no matter how disadvantaged the students' pre-university educational experience, they appear to be immediately able to take full advantage of computer based instruction.

REFERENCES

Alessi, S M and Trollip, S R (1991) *Computer-based Instruction: Methods and development*, Prentice-Hall, Englewood Cliffs, NJ
Bitter, G G (1989) *Microcomputers in Education Today*, Mitchell Publishing, Watsonville
Borg, W R, Gall, J P and Gall, M D (1993) *Applying Educational Research: A practical guide*, Longman, New York
Erickson, F J and Vonk, J A (1994) *Computer Essentials in Education*, McGraw-Hill, New York
Fraenkel, J R and Wallen, N E (1993) *How to Design and Evaluate Research in Education*, McGraw-Hill, New York
Heinich, R, Molenda, M and Russell, J (1989) *Instructional Media and the New Technologies of Instruction*, Macmillan, New York
Kennedy, I M (1993) *Cooperative Learning with Computers: Three model lessons*, unpublished MEd dissertation, University of Pretoria
Mkabela, N Q and Luthuli, P C (1997) *Towards an African Philosophy of Education*, Kagiso, Pretoria
Platzky, L and Walker, C (1985) *The Surplus People: Forced removals in South Africa*, Ravan, Johannesburg
Schimmel, B J (1988) Providing meaningful feedback in courseware, in *Instructional Design for Microcomputer Courseware*, ed D H Jonassen, Lawrence Erlbaum, Hillsdale, NJ

Snyman, R and Kühn, M J (1993) Structured teaching and learning, in *Classroom Practice: An orientation*, ed W J Louw, Academica, Pretoria

Trieschmann, M (1990) Drill and practice software: What is appropriate feedback?, *The Computing Teacher*, **17** (5), pp 53–55

Van Rooyen, H (1990) *The Disparity Between English as a Subject and English as the Medium of Learning*, HSRC, Pretoria

15

Introducing instructional technologies into the classroom: the 'Möbius metaphor'

Estelle Paget and Susan Chandler

SUMMARY

This chapter discusses the methodologies through which a new university with a focus on distance learning has introduced ICT-based teaching to both students and faculty. Both groups may be many thousands of kilometres from the institution. The authors utilize the metaphor of the Möbius strip to illustrate their 'seamless' approach which places great emphasis on reflection with peer analysis and support.

INTRODUCTION

*Möbius strip = one-sided surface formed by joining the ends of a rectangle after twisting one end through 180 degrees. (Feel free to try this at home.) German mathematician in 1868 (*Oxford English Dictionary*.)

When the German mathematician, Möbius, created his strip (see Figure 15.1) in 1868, little could he have guessed the metaphoric value of his discovery for describing best instructional practice in the 21st century.

For us, the Möbius strip symbolizes two things: the continuous exchange of lessons learned about effective teaching, between face to face and virtual instruction, and the way we have chosen to work at Royal Roads University (RRU) in Victoria, BC, Canada.

For several months, two units at RRU have been working together in an informal partnership to enhance student learning. The Distributed Learning Unit works with faculty to create and deliver online courses. The Office of Learning Facilitation Programs (LFP) provides pedagogical coaching to faculty taking the Certificate Program in Learning Facilitation. This chapter describes the collaboration between these units and outlines our philosophic and institutional context, the rationale behind our decision to join forces, some of the projects and strategies we have jointly developed and the resulting institutional

Figure 15.1   *The Möbius metaphor*

advantages. Our experience illustrates the Möbius metaphor in action. The authors hope readers will enter into our Möbius metaphor and find strategies they can apply to their institutional contexts, and opportunities to work collaboratively with colleagues.

The Learning Facilitator Certificate Program mirrors the format used for the university's mainstream Master's programmes at Royal Roads, in a much-condensed way. (For the Master's programmes the students (mostly mid-career professionals) take a three to five week hiatus from their regular work to participate in a 'residency' on site at the university. When their residency is over, the learners return to their homes and continue their studies online.) Faculty members participate in a three-day workshop known as the Instructional Skills Workshop. Several aspects of the workshop have been modified to meet RRU needs. However, all faculty who participate in this peer-based workshop are expected to teach and be videotaped three times. After each lesson, their peers provide them with feedback. This format works well for faculty who are on site. The majority of RRU faculty are associate faculty, who may live in Victoria, the city where RRU is located, but more likely live hundreds or thousands of kilometres away. A challenge has been to remain faithful to the three-day workshop outcomes, yet achieve them with faculty members online.

The Möbius metaphor moves to the forefront of this exercise. We have taken the decision not to stream a video of someone teaching – quite feasible with the technology at hand. Instead, because we want to encourage learner centred approaches to teaching, we have decided to avoid promoting a virtual 'stand and deliver' philosophy. In other words, we have taken what we have learnt about best instructional practice and transferred it to an online environment. We have developed online scenarios which resemble authentic online classes. Participants (faculty) respond to the scenario, using the words and approaches they would use in a similar situation. Other participants provide the facilitator with feedback on their facilitation skills.

The following is our guiding principle for technology implementation in both face to face and virtual environments: technology should only be used because it contributes to best instructional practice, and not for its own sake.

By best instructional practice we mean sound pedagogical or andragogical practices that recognize how adults learn. We generally take a constructivist approach and encourage instructors to think of themselves as facilitators who enable their learners to 'construct' and take responsibility for their own learning. Having said this, we also recognize that good teaching can take many forms. Dan Pratt's extensive research on teaching perspectives substantiates this viewpoint (Daniel D Pratt and Associates, 1998). In fact, we have observed, in the online environment, that learners require some structure and clarity. Learner feedback suggests a completely constructivist approach can leave them feeling overwhelmed and like they are working in a vacuum. What seems to work best is an eclectic approach – what we call 'Situational Teaching' – that draws from a broad palette of techniques and learning theories. Learner-centredness and recent research on brain-based learning are also fundamental to our definition.

INSTITUTIONAL CONTEXT

The Möbius strip characterizes the learning community at Royal Roads University (RRU). This university was created in 1995 and was mandated to deliver its programmes using a distributed model. The university is meeting its mandate in all five of its graduate programmes. As a point of contrast, the two undergraduate programmes were originally delivered face to face in classrooms. They are now evolving into mixed models. The term 'mixed' for us refers to the inclusion of instructional technologies in more traditional settings. The new E-Business undergraduate programme combines an on campus residency programme with distance learning. The hitherto more traditional undergraduate programmes are introducing instructional technologies as a way to enhance student learning.

All RRU programmes enjoy an exceptionally high retention rate (98 per cent). We attribute this success to key elements that define RRU:

- core values that inform the culture of the university;
- dedicated and caring faculty;
- highly motivated student body;
- learner-centred and community based model;
- outcomes based programmes;
- the distributed nature of online learning.

It is this institutional context that informs our approach, implementation and partnership. When writing this chapter we experienced difficulty focusing specifically on classroom delivery, and realized that at RRU everything is integrated. However, to make this chapter useful to the reader, we describe a specific classroom example within the broader context of distributed learning.

Case study

Mickie Noble has been teaching undergraduate science courses in Applied and Environmental Microbiology and Ecotoxicology for several years, and will be teaching these courses again. Each course has about 50 students. Each course also has labs.

Mickie met with us to see how information technologies could be integrated into the courses to address some of the ongoing challenges.

Challenge

Both courses are organized around a building-block approach: in other words it is necessary for students to understand one concept before they move on to the next. Mickie often finds that class time is taken up reviewing concepts and readings, rather than focusing on applications for those concepts.

Mickie would like students to understand the readings and concepts before coming to class, so that the class time can be used more effectively.

Strategy

We hypothesized that one reason learners might not fully understand the concepts before coming to class was because they were studying and reading in relative isolation, if at all. Unless they informally worked with other learners, they would not have a place to discuss, reflect and review the content.

We decided to organize the learners into teams of five, with each team having an online discussion space. The space would be private (only accessible by the team and the instructor). Before class, readings would be assigned and students would be asked to work online with their team to come up with key questions (encouraging critical thought about the material). The questions generated by each of the teams would be posted to a public forum so they could be viewed by the entire class, and would form the basis of the classroom discussion.

To encourage students to consider each of the questions, they were randomly called upon to give a brief presentation on any one of the questions. The learners were also to be evaluated on how effectively they contributed to the online discussion. Effectiveness is defined in terms of how often the student contributes something of value, listens to the concerns of others, assumes the role of teacher as well as learner, and answers as well as asks questions.

Besides focusing the classroom time more effectively, it was hoped that the use of discussion groups would let Mickie identify those students who were having difficulty (not participating online, not asking appropriate questions, not supporting other learners) so that she could provide early intervention.

It was also hoped that if the students were encouraged to complete the readings ahead of time, they would come to class with a shared understanding, rather than some students being way ahead and others far behind. This was an ambitious – some might say unrealistic – goal but even if it could be achieved to some extent, the opportunity to use class time more effectively would be increased.

From the perspective of the learners, we hoped that this technique would provide them with useful technical skills, teach them how to work as part of a virtual team, and encourage them to take greater responsibility for their own learning.

We also talked about the need to work with learners ahead of time to help them to become familiar with the technology, understand how to converse online, and understand what is meant by constructive feedback. This training was to be provided during a laboratory period to allow it to be incorporated into the teaching plan for these courses.

Working with Mickie Noble (see the case study) illustrates the Möbius metaphor at work. It symbolizes for us the ideal exchange between face to face and online instruction. What we have learnt since 1995 is that distance delivery has advantages beyond efficiency and geographic reach. It forces us to look at models other than the traditional transmission perspective described by Pratt (1998). Moreover, combining distance delivery with the best of face to face ensures optimal learning.

Similarly, the Möbius strip metaphor applies to the way the DL and LFP units are working. It models the seamless and continuous exchange of knowledge, abilities and values we suggest should exist between colleagues and various forms of instruction. The following projects illustrate this synergistic relationship:

- *LFC Program Web site*. When the LFP needed a Web site, a meeting was held between members of that office and members of the larger technical group of which DL is a member. That lively exchange informed both groups of the needs of the other, and their preferred ways of working. Both sides came up with creative solutions normally considered to be the domain of the other group (Chandler and Paget, 2000). (More information on this transformative teaming can be viewed by scrolling the 'quick links' to 'Learning and Teaching' on the Royal Roads Web site (www.royalroads.ca).)

- *Creation of online evaluation tools*. We have taken what works well in the classroom and modified it for the online environment (peer evaluation and one-minute paper.) The DL unit has developed an electronic tool to measure peer participation in virtual teams.

- *Training for instructors*. We worked together to modify the Instructional Skills Workshop to include both face to face and online facilitation skills for all RRU faculty. The workshop focuses on best instructional practice in both learning environments.

- *Customized training for RRU faculty*. Some of the RRU instructors requiring training are on campus: others can be as far away as Hong Kong or Barbados. We needed a training tool that could be delivered both face to face and online. The Mickie Noble case study (see the box on page 166) illustrates how we work with instructors on an individual basis, sometimes to problem solve by introducing technology into the classroom; other times to increase their repertoire of instructional techniques.

ADVANTAGES TO ONLINE LEARNING

In the early 1990s distance delivery was seen as a way to provide flexible, cost-effective and geographically dispersed programmes. It has proven to be convenient for many learners, especially those in their mid-career, as it allows them to continue working and participating in their community while studying. Distance delivery has also allowed some institutions to expand their geographic reach. However, given the cost of technical infrastructure, the jury is still out on cost effectiveness.

The challenge that online delivery presented was that traditional models of teaching did not necessarily translate to the virtual classroom. (Professors who read their lecture notes at the front of their class were never terribly inspiring, but at least students could concentrate on their teacher's facial or other mannerisms. In the online environment students have no distractions and such poor instructional practices become soporific.) As stated earlier, distance delivery has taught us that there are values beyond convenience and geography. In the online environment, it becomes even more critical for instructors to engage their learners. Successful online instructors, whether consciously or not, adopt a learner centred approach. It generally includes key elements.

SUCCESSFUL ONLINE INSTRUCTORS

It is our observation that successful online instructors:

- make an emotional connection with their learners (an example would be phoning students individually prior to beginning a distance course);
- create a learning community (build an expectation into the course that learners will work with each other collaboratively and engage socially);
- respect individual learning preferences;
- encourage inclusivity (they make an expectation that everyone will participate, and use examples that are welcoming to all learners);
- facilitate rather than teach (help learners to construct their own learning and experience transformative teaming);
- model outstanding organization by providing course outlines, readings, expectations, learning outcomes;
- encourage students to expand their repertoire of skills;
- recognize that learning is not bound by time and place.

Many of these elements also characterize effective face to face learning. The face to face learning environment has advantages that are sometimes difficult to transpose to the online environment. These include:

- Immediacy:
  - In the traditional classroom, instructors constantly receive feedback when they read the facial expressions and body language of their learners. They experience learners' energy (or lack thereof) in the classroom. The effective instructor responds to these cues immediately.
  - Learners and instructors can share – at the same time – an emotional connection, be it humour or pathos.
  - Flexibility: instructors can spontaneously adjust their method of instruction or content to meet learner needs.
- Learner centredness:
  - Similarly, classroom instructors can respond immediately to questions.
  - They can change their examples to increase the relevance of the lesson to their learners.
- Social context:
  - Learners can easily develop a social bond between them. Research on brain-based learning suggests learning is enhanced in a social context.
  - Similarly, learners often learn more easily from their peers than from their instructors.
  - When learners instruct each other they tend to learn more effectively.

Recognizing the elements of effective classroom teaching informs some of the decisions we have taken when introducing technology into the classroom.

EDUCATIONAL/INSTRUCTIONAL STRATEGIES

Information technologies can be incorporated into the classroom in a variety of ways; and can run the gamut from sensational multimedia extravaganzas to overhead projectors.

When contemplating introducing instructional technologies it is important to consider:

- the comfort level of the instructor with technology;
- how instructional technologies can be used to enhance student learning.

These questions are used as the starting point when we are working with Royal Roads instructors who wish to introduce technology into their classrooms. Our experience has taught us that information technologies, when used wisely, can build learning communities, can provide flexible learning (that is, any time, any place), can encourage a more egalitarian classroom, and can encourage transformative learning (when learners become teachers and vice versa).

The rhythm of online learning is also different from that which takes place in the classroom. Classroom learning is usually time and space delineated in nature; students and teachers meet in a particular place at a particular time, and the time spent apart usually involves individual rather than collective learning.

In comparison, when learning at a distance, time and space become irrelevant, and while activity does increase prior to the due date for an assignment, the pace is generally more modulated and continuous. If a course is designed around the concept of a learning community, learners will work and support each other on an ongoing, rather than on an occasional, basis.

The next question becomes, how can we transfer some of the value of online learning into the classroom? A discussion started in class can be continued 'after the bell has rung' by using virtual discussion groups (also referred to as chat or newsgroups). Learners will be more likely to participate if: the questions are specific (controversial questions generate the most response); the discussion group is moderated; and (despite all our best intentions of encouraging students to learn for the joy of learning) participation contributes to marks. From an andragogical perspective, having students continue a discussion after the class has finished gives them a chance to reflect, refine and build upon what they have learned.

The convergence between classroom and distance modes of teaching also means that students are encouraged to be autonomous and independent learners. In this model 'teachers become mediators between learners and their access to information provided by various sources' (Trindade, Carmo and Bidara, 2000).

Another benefit of extending the discussion that takes place in the classroom to an online forum is the opportunity to hear from all learners, even the quiet ones who sit at the back of the classroom and who are usually too shy to make a comment. Once learners know how to use the technology, the online environment can be less intimidating than the classroom. Learners can prepare and think clearly about their contribution, and they do not have to have a loud voice or strong physical presence to be heard.

In other words, supplementing face to face learning with online learning adds a dimension of inclusivity to the learning environment. As indicated above, it enables learners with different learning preferences to work in their preferred style, and those unable or reluctant to speak in a large group to participate fully. At the same time, it encourages learners who tend not to express their thoughts in writing, or to reflect before speaking, to expand their learning abilities.

For those teaching in traditional classrooms, an abundant literature, developed by experienced teachers, is available. It supports new instructors and helps them develop strategies to increase their teaching effectiveness. Similarly, online teachers are learning from each other. For example, when designing a virtual discussion group, it is important to recognize that too many voices online can become overwhelming (quite simply there can be just too much to read and follow). With large classes it is useful to divide the learners into teams of between five to eight people, and then to create separate discussion spaces for each group. Not only does this manage the volume, it also encourages learners to get to know, and to converse, with students they might not usually associate with in the classroom.

TEAMWORK

Information technologies can also provide a way for teams to connect and work collaboratively. If learners are required to work as part of a team, providing some online collaborative tools can lubricate the process. Again, this gives learners flexible learning options and removes the barriers of time and place.

ASSESSMENT

The one-minute paper (whose origin is much debated, but whose value was promoted by the Harvard Assessment Seminars some years ago (Mosteller, 1989)) is a useful classroom technique, used to acquire feedback from learners on how well their learning is being facilitated. Conducting the process online is a valid option with its own advantages and disadvantages. For example, anecdotal evidence suggests that the feedback received when learners have had an opportunity to review and reflect on their learning is more considered and more valuable.

AUTOMATED APPLICATIONS

Automated applications provide another way to deal with the time constraints of the classroom. For example, if you like learners to work collaboratively in teams, but find it difficult and time consuming, there are other options. You can assess team dynamics, to verify that individual contributions have been equal and fair, by asking students to complete online peer evaluations referred to earlier.

PAIRING

Many a maths professor has modified her/his approach to reach the 'maths phobic' student. But what can you do when an otherwise reasonable and intelligent professor displays similar phobic tendencies at the mere suggestion of introducing technology? One of the writers of this chapter (not the head of Distributed Learning Technologies!) has experienced similar visceral reactions to using new technologies. Yet here she is, creating online programmes for faculty. Her stress level plummeted when she began to work with the other author of this article. In this non-threatening, professional partnership she was able to observe the advantages of technology, and appreciate the logical nature of various programmes.

From this personal experience came the idea of pairing faculty. We asked 'technologically savvy' faculty members to serve as resources for their less IT-inclined colleagues. We have termed these pairs CCs or complementary colleagues.

PORTFOLIO

The CCs are proving particularly helpful to faculty enrolled in the Certificate Program who use sophisticated technology to record their progress and reflections. Innovative and high quality educational experiences for learners are a major institutional priority at RRU. The President himself has been a driving force in developing the Certificate Program for all core faculty members, including deans. Given the distributed environment and electronic focus of the university, it seemed only natural that the Certificate Program for faculty (Learning Facilitators) reflect this trait. Thus, a developer in the IT department worked closely with the Director of Learning Facilitation Programs to create an Electronic 'Learning and Teaching Portfolio'. Designed to simplify the task of recording one's reflections and achievements, this electronic journal enables individual faculty members to consult the learning outcomes and the indicators or 'markers of success', of the programme as they write in their portfolio. This electronic document also allows users to muse and keep their musings private, in a special section of the portfolio!

Learning to use the portfolio is not difficult, but it can appear daunting to a 'technophobe'. Pairing is proving useful in introducing the tool to non-technologically inclined faculty. In a gentle and safe way, technologically averse faculty are working with trusted colleagues who explain, demonstrate and stand by, as they explore the tool and increase their proficiency in using it.

CHALLENGES

Working with people and working with technology inevitably leads to some challenges. Most faculty members at RRU are already over-extended in their roles. Some resent the top-down approach to the mandatory Learning Certificate Program or to introducing technology into their classes. We suspect there is a fear element and the need to save face in front of learners and peers.

TECHNOLOGY

Technology can be viewed as a double-edged sword. It offers its own challenges – usually at the worst possible time! Yet much of our success, we feel, is due to the distributed environment at Royal Roads, described earlier in this chapter. We are fortunate to have the necessary technical support and infrastructure in place, as well as experience on which to draw.

SUGGESTION

If you are working on your own, and have reservations about integrating instructional technologies, you may want to find a way to have the technical infrastructure in place before introducing them. Much of the fear (and loathing) around technology can be removed if you are working in an organization that provides you with support in the form of instructional designers (who can tell you what works from an educational perspective) and technicians (Web designers and developers, audio-visual support, programmers) who can tell you what is possible from a technical perspective. As well, an effective help desk that is available to both you and your learners will go a long way to increasing comfort levels and success rates.

CONCLUSION AND KEY MESSAGE

As we have tried to illustrate, technology is a wonderful tool, if it is used in a meaningful way and contributes to effective learning. The Möbius strip is a concrete reminder to maintain the link between different forms of effective teaching and collaborative working relationships.

Sadly, in many institutions of higher learning, the culture encourages academics to work competitively rather than collaboratively. Similarly, the tradition thus far has been to create a dichotomous relationship between face to face and virtual instruction. Hopefully, readers will feel inspired by our experience to support collaborative relationships, not only between colleagues, but also between instructional environments.

REFERENCES

Chandler, S and Paget, E (2000) *Moving Towards National On-line Learning Commons Where the Scholarship of Teaching Can be Celebrated*, paper to Conference of the Canadian Association of Distance Educators (CADE) Quebec

Daniel D Pratt and Associates (1998) *Five Perspectives on Teaching in Adult and Higher Education*, Krieger, Florida

Mosteller, F (1989) The 'muddiest point in the lecture' as a feedback device, *On Teaching and Learning*, **3**, Derek Bok Center for Teaching and Learning, Harvard University [online] http://www.fas.harvard.edu/ bok_cen/docs/mosteller.html [accessed 28 January 2002]

Trindade, A R, Carmo, H and Bidara, J (2000) Current developments and best practice, *Open and Distance Learning*, **1** (1) (June) [online] at http://irrodl.org.v1.1.html [accessed 28 January 2002]

16

Appropriate use of instructional design to maximize learning

Raja Maznah Raja Hussain

SUMMARY

Web based learning has been hailed as the delivery system of the new millennium. This chapter shares the experience of developing contents for the Web based Multimedia Learning System project at the Multimedia University, Malaysia. One of the important issues in integrating Web technology into classroom teaching is that the content needs to be created based upon some pedagogical principles. Instructional design principles need to be utilized in the development of Web sites for teaching and learning (Ritchie and Hoffman, 1996). The chapter describes the process of developing an instructional design guideline for use by lecturers to develop quality content to maximize online learning. It is hoped that with the guideline the process of developing courses online for the Multimedia University will be easier and more systematic. With the use of appropriate instructional design the online learning materials will be able to maximize student learning.

INTRODUCTION

Information and communication technology (ICT), especially the Internet, has made its presence felt in Malaysia. The Internet has become an important medium of communication, education and politics. One of the seven flagships of the Multimedia Super Corridor (MSC) project in Malaysia is the development of Smart Schools. In its Smart Schools pilot project, the Ministry of Education identified 90 schools to use highly interactive multi-media including the Internet in teaching and learning. This began in 1999 (Ministry of Education Malaysia, 1997). Higher education institutions (HEI) are also affected by the MSC project. Most HEI have changed their missions and corporate strategies to include the use of ICT in education. Two private universities were established in line with the MSC needs. These universities are at the forefront of the ICT application in education. Malaysia's first virtual university, Universiti Tun Abdul Razak (Unitar), was established in 1997 to showcase a virtual learning environment. The other private university is the Multimedia University (MMU) which was actually established in 1996 as Telekom University. In 1999 the name was changed and a new campus was built in the heart of Cyberjaya, where the MSC headquarter is located.

One of the Multimedia University's missions is to produce a workforce to meet the needs of the MSC project.

> Multimedia University aspires to achieve world class excellence in teaching, research and consultancies, in its quest to provide the necessary knowledge workers as required by the various local and multinational multimedia and IT companies, particularly located in the MSC. (Multimedia University, 1999a)

MMU offers academic programmes that focus on the development of information technology, engineering, creative multimedia, business and management. Currently, the university has 6,000 classroom based students. Being associated with the MSC, MMU has attracted a high number of potential students demanding entrance to a limited place in the university. A larger student body will limit both the physical and academic resources in MMU.

As one way to meet the needs of the growing student body, MMU is developing an alternative delivery system, known as the multimedia learning system (MMLS). MMLS is a computer managed learning platform that will enable learning to take place any time and anywhere using the Web. This chapter presents the development of the MMLS at the Multimedia University from the perspective of an instructional designer who is involved in the content development project for MMLS. The presentation is in two parts. The first part focuses on the MMLS development and the needs for instructional design intervention; the second part focuses on the programmes to enable lecturers to develop quality content for the MMLS project.

THE MULTIMEDIA LEARNING SYSTEM

The multimedia learning system (MMLS) is a Web based application for delivering and managing of learning online at MMU. The system is being developed by the Centre for Multimedia Education (CMED) and tested in-house as one of the research and development projects at the university. It is designed to meet the needs of the university and the nation, enabling teachers and students from all over the world to participate in virtual learning (Multimedia University, 1999b). MMU decided to develop MMLS after studying several computer managed learning systems (CMLS) from other parts of the world (such as WebCT, TopC, Learning Space and ToolBook). The decision was made in line with the spirit of homegrown innovation in the MSC. The development involves research work and high skill knowledge. MMLS features an integrated system consisting of:

- staff and student registration;
- file manager;
- intelligent navigation;
- short notes;
- e-mail, chat, and video conferencing;
- news group and bulletin board;
- a system to generate reports and monitoring of student progress.

MMLS consists of four modules:

- administration module;
- lecturer module;
- student module;
- miscellaneous module.

MMLS was expected to be ready for implementation in December 2000. In order to test the system, content was developed concurrently. MMU realized early that appropriate instructional design is crucial in the development of content for the MMLS.

THE NEED FOR APPROPRIATE INSTRUCTIONAL DESIGN

As a young private university, MMU has its strengths and limitations. The visionary leadership is steering the university to meet the aspiration of the nation to compete in the global knowledge economy. The young workforce (of about 300 academic staff) has the motivation to share the vision of the university leaders. The university had a plan to deliver at least 30–50 per cent of the course content online using MMLS by the end of the year 2000. Lecturers from different faculties were selected to develop MMLS contents from the beginning of the year. The pilot group worked on their own with minimum help from the programmers or instructional designers. As subject matter experts the lecturers found themselves in a difficult authoring system specialist role, a role that requires knowledge and experience in planning and putting together pedagogically sound technology based learning materials. They were performing the tasks required of instructional designers, graphic artists and programmers.

In preparation for the content development, lecturers were initially exposed in short training programmes to several authoring tools, such as graphics application software and Web development packages. Content development progress was slow and success was limited. Many of the courses developed did not meet the criteria of a good multimedia Web based learning product. Initial preview of the products by instructional designers found that many of the courses used a traditional lecture method to deliver the content online.

As observed by Parson (1997), much of the effort to use the Web for teaching and learning has merely resulted in using the Internet based structure to deliver content by merely transforming traditional text to electronic text. Being new to the teaching profession, many lecturers had little exposure to the technology based learning approaches. There was minimum interaction built into the pilot courses to allow for active participation from students. As commented by Peraya (1994), Web designers do not take into consideration the unique attributes of the Web in delivering instruction. The Internet will become a passive learning technology if it is used to deliver traditional instructional materials without realizing its capabilities of facilitating communication and collaboration (Doherty, 1998). Promoting effective learning becomes a challenge for instructional designers and content developers in the MMLS project.

It was observed that basic instructional design elements such as learning objectives, practice, guidance and feedback were missing from most of the pilot MMLS courses. The instructional designers recommended revisions before these courses are taken into the 'virtual classroom'.

THE INSTRUCTIONAL DESIGN COMMITTEE

Convinced that instructional design (ID) was the gap (need) in the MMLS content development process, a committee was formed in April 2000. Since there was no single recipe for courseware development which is either universally accepted or could be used in all circumstances (Bostock, 1998), the committee's task was to provide a guideline for instructional design. The guideline will have to be specific to the MMLS situation and needs. The second task was to develop a quality assurance procedure to ensure the quality of the Web based learning materials developed for MMLS.

The committee was chaired by a visiting professor who was on sabbatical at MMU. The team consisted of the head of department and three lecturers from the Centre for Modern Languages and Communication and one lecturer from the Faculty of Creative Multimedia. The team members had their basic training in education and some formal training and experience in instructional design.

The ID committee met in early May 2000 to develop a plan for action and set target dates and deliverables. The immediate task was to carry out a need assessment to determine possible weaknesses and confirm the problems, if any, that the lecturers were experiencing in developing courses for MMLS. Given that the content development project was well on its way to completion by some lecturers, the team had to plan the need assessment, just in time. The first data source was collected from the instructional design workshop conducted in March 2000. Subsequent data sources were obtained from the formative evaluation exercise (a product preview) in June 2000.

INSTRUCTIONAL DESIGN WORKSHOP

Prior to the formation of the committee, a two-day workshop on instructional design for Web based learning was conducted in March 2000. The workshop was initiated by the Centre for Modern Languages and Communication (CMLC) and supported by the Centre for Multimedia Education (CMED). Thirty lecturers from different faculties attended the programme. A quick audience analysis was carried out before the workshop proper. The purpose was to determine the group composition and their current knowledge and experience with Web based learning. It was determined that 30 per cent of the attendees had some form of training in teaching and learning, varying from a few days' workshop on teaching and learning to a Master's in Education degree. Fifty percent of the participants were new lecturers, with less than two years teaching experience in higher education.

The majority of the lecturers had had some experience in putting lecture materials online using Lotus Notes, but few had had experience of developing multimedia Web based learning materials. They were asked to list possible problems that they had experienced and that a novice developer would experience in developing content for Web based learning.

PROBLEMS

Since Web based learning is new, most lecturers indicated that being novices, they were not prepared to do the development. Time constraints and their lack of knowledge and skills in instructional design and development were the main reasons. Mastering the technique of authoring courseware using specialized software (such as Flash and Dreamweaver) was the other reason. Many lecturers were unhappy with their 'heavy' teaching load and that some of them were using their free time to develop the courses online. As reflected by a lecturer, 'I do not have enough time to think carefully with too many classes to attend.' Proper instructional design and development takes time.

Guidance on ID for lecturers was limited. From the comments given by the lecturers in the survey and the activities conducted during the workshop, it was clear that there was a gap in the knowledge of instructional design as a tool and a process for developing learning materials, as reflected in the following statements indicating problems:

I have ideas but don't know how to do it; I am too shy to ask other lecturers for help.
The course content (how to put them online).
How to structure and flow the information.
I am not creative.
To transfer content into the Web, to make it interactive.
To make sure the Web based instruction is pedagogically okay.
How to make Web based instruction interesting.
Integration of teaching elements.

I don't know what is the best design for students.
Don't know what my students' expectations are.
Don't know what a good Web is.
Understanding of architecture of the Web based materials, and what steps to adopt.
How to attract the students with the Web and make them come time and time again.

From these statements (each from practising lecturers), it was clear that there was a need for some form of structure and ID guidance to ensure that everyone has the same understanding of what multimedia Web based learning is all about and how to do it.

THE INSTRUCTIONAL DESIGN GUIDELINE

The ID Committee was pressed for time, since some of the departments had started developing the courses for the MMLS, and others were on the way. Lecturers were asking for guidance and help. Deadlines for the course development were changed several times. The guideline needed to be ready before the next batch of lecturers started work on the development. Training had to be planned for this group. The committee worked very closely with the MMLS team of programmers and graphic artists from CMED. They are the people who worked on the system and with the lecturers. Therefore, it was necessary that they understood the instructional designers' roles in the development of the MMLS content and the importance of the ID guideline.

The ID guideline is a 30-page guidebook consisting of main text and appendix. The purpose of the ID guideline is to provide lecturers with a tool or a job aid. The ID guidebook will also be used as training materials for the training of content developers, programmers and graphic artists when necessary. A draft guideline was ready in June 2000 and was presented to the MMLS committee. A draft copy of the electronic version of the ID guideline is also available online (password protected). The guideline was developed using a basic instructional design model, ADDIE (analysis, design, develop, implement and evaluate) as a framework. The framework was then expanded to include steps for each phase, purpose for each step, input for the step, activities or tasks to be performed and the output for the step.

The challenge was to ensure that everyone concerned agreed on the ID approach and understood why appropriate instructional design is desirable and possible in maximizing students' learning. Instructional design begins with a sound knowledge of the content and includes other areas, such as deciding what needs to be taught, planning of delivery and other learning activities, preparing materials and assessing student learning (Ayersman, 1999). Over the years the definition of ID has changed. The changes are brought about by the rapid development in the field of instructional technology. Merrill *et al* (1996) define instructional design as a technology for the development of learning experiences and environments that promotes the acquisition of specific knowledge and skill by students. Instructional design is a technique which incorporates known and verified learning strategies into instructional experiences which make the acquisition of knowledge and skill more efficient, effective and appealing.

ID QUESTIONS TO MAXIMIZE LEARNING

The ID team was guided by the following five questions. These questions are posed to the MMLS content developers in the ID guideline:

1. What part of your course should be delivered using MMLS?
2. What should your students be able to do after learning the course using MMLS?
3. How should you sequence the learning events to optimize the use of the MMLS?
4. How do you make sure that the students are actively learning when they are using MMLS?
5. How would you know if the course is achieving its aims?

Question 1: What part of your course should be delivered using MMLS?

The university has decided that at least 30–50 per cent of the course content is to be selected and developed for online delivery. Selection of the content is the lecturer's responsibility. Lecturers are to select the most appropriate content for delivery using MMLS.

Lecturers are to:

- perform an analysis of student needs, course content and tasks;
- decide on the content scope that can be 'surrendered' to the students;
- identify the part of the course content that can be learned by discovery or peer interaction, ie the part that can be constructed by the students.

Question 2: What should your students be able to do after learning the course using MMLS?

In most cases, it is important to let learners know early in a lesson what they will be responsible for at the end of the instruction (Ritchie and Hoffman, 1996). Once the lecturers have identified the content scope, they are to:

- identify the general goal of the course;
- transform the lesson content into specific learning outcomes, based on for example Gagne's categories of learning (Gagne, 1985);

- state learning outcomes in terms of observable, measurable and achievable performance according to Bloom's Taxonomy (Bloom *et al*, 1956);
- use the learning outcomes to write an outline;
- use the learning outcomes to write the learning assessment items.

Question 3: How should you sequence the learning events to optimize the use of the MMLS?

According to Dick and Reiser (1989), instructional sequences usually include at least seven common elements: motivating the students, explaining what is to be learnt, helping the learner to recall previous knowledge, providing instructional material, providing guidance and feedback, testing comprehension and providing enrichment and remediation. The lecturers will then have to decide on how to incorporate each of these events in the instruction designed for delivery on MMLS. Based on the learning outcomes and the content scope, the lecturers are to identify and sequence the learning experience by:

- selecting the types of teaching strategies to achieve the objectives;
- identifying learning activities which will give students control over their learning experience;
- identifying types of guidance that the students will need to process online information;
- selecting the sequence in which information is presented to the students.

Question 4: How do you make sure that the students are actively learning when they are using MMLS?

Generally speaking, a more active learner will integrate new knowledge more readily than a passive learner (Ritchie and Hoffman, 1996). Giving students control over their learning experience and providing appropriate learning activities will provide opportunities for active learning and student interaction in an online environment. Lecturers are to:

- identify learning activities that are appropriate for each topic and alternative activities to meet the needs of different students;
- decide on the assessment criteria for each activity;
- identify the forms of guidance and feedback for the learner response.

Question 5: How would you know if the course is achieving its aims?

To ensure students have integrated the desired knowledge, it is useful to assess their learning (Ritchie and Hoffman, 1996). Lecturers are to:

- identify opportunities for the students to demonstrate task performance and or exhibit retention of knowledge;

- select appropriate tools (tests and activities) to assess the student's performance;

- write pre-test, diagnostic test and post-test items and exercises;

- write practical activities and experiences to facilitate retention and transfer of learning;

- set standards and criteria for evaluation.

Detailed steps are given in the ID guidebook for each level of the analysis, design, developing, implementing and evaluation of the MMLS courses. The content experts worked closely with the ID team and graphic artists to translate the teaching strategies and learning activities into storyboards. Appropriate media elements were selected based on the types of content and activities identified earlier. As the project progressed, the MMLS project team was learning and discovering new ways to prepare, enable and motivate content developers.

ENABLING LECTURERS

What has been learnt so far is that developing instructional materials takes time and energy. Content developers for MMLS needed guidance and help. The formation of the ID committee was one of the strategies that the Multimedia University had taken to enable the lecturers. The lecturers should not be developing the content on their own any more. The content development procedure will be a team effort and conducted as follows:

1. The faculty will identify several courses for development and will also select the lecturers who are teaching the courses to be the content experts. Several lecturers will work on one course.

2. Lecturers will be trained to use the ID guideline. They will learn how to select and sequence content and produce the content storyboard. With the help of the ID team, lecturers will select activities and strategies for presenting the content so that students are actively engaged with the learning materials.

3. Lecturers will also be trained to use the graphic and Web development tools. This is to ensure that they know the limitations of the software and will be able to communicate with the graphic artists and the programmers.

4. Graphic artists will help lecturers to design the user interface and the screen layout. Lecturers will then use authoring tools to create the lessons.

5. The programmers will then help put together the course materials created by lecturers and integrate it into the MMLS for delivery.

Since the MMLS project is still in its infancy, it is too early to report the result of this change. Recently, 27 lecturers from different faculties were selected to be the new group of content developers. They were given the draft ID guidebook and access to the online version. Several links to good practices were also given in the guideline. Lecturers were trained to do ID and to develop storyboards. At the time of writing, the instructional designers have evaluated the storyboards. The next phase is to develop the prototypes.

The MMLS team is currently working on a project to automate the ID processes. The team is developing ID templates and 'wizards'. The templates will be incorporated into the MMLS engine under the lecturer's module. It is hoped that with the availability of the ID template the content developers will be able to create contents without having to know much about the decisions involved in doing instructional design. Basic design elements will be built into the template. Questions to guide the content developers will also be included. It is hoped that by automating instructional design for MMLS the process of content development will be made more efficient and effective.

ACKNOWLEDGEMENT

The author would like to express her gratitude to the Multimedia University for giving her the opportunity to spend a sabbatical at MMU, and the MMLS project team and the ID Committee, CMED and CMLC for all the help during her attachment at MMU. The author takes full responsibility for the content of this chapter which is solely the author's opinion and does not necessarily reflect the opinions of other ID Committee members and MMU.

REFERENCES

Ayersman, D (1999) *Creating Web-based Instructional Hypermedia Projects* [online] http://inte.mwc.edu/book/chapter02.html [accessed 28 January 2002]

Bloom, B S (ed), Englehart, M D, Furst, E J and Krathwohl, D R (1956) *Taxonomy of Educational Ojectives: Handbook I: Cognitive domain*, David McKay, New York

Bostock, S (1998) *Courseware Engineering: An overview of the courseware development process*, available at http://www.keele.ac.uk/depts/cs/StephenBostock/doc/atceng.htm (accessed 21 July 2000)

Dick, W and Reiser, R (1989) *Planning Effective Instruction*, Prentice Hall, Englewood Cliffs, NJ

Doherty, A (1998) The Internet: designed to become a passive surfing technology?, *Educational Technology*, **38** (5) pp 61–63

Gagne, R M (1985) *The Conditions of Learning* (4th edn), Holt, Rinehart and Winston, New York

Merrill, M D, Drake, L D, Lacy, M J, Pratt, J A and the ID2 Research Group (1996) Reclaiming instructional design, *Educational Technology*, **36** (5), pp 5–7

Ministry of Education Malaysia (1997) *Smart School Conceptual Blueprint*, Ministry of Education Malaysia, Kuala Lumpur

Multimedia University (1999a) President's Forward, *Research Report 1996–1999*, Multimedia University, Cyberjaya

Multimedia University (1999b) *Multimedia Learning System Concept Paper*, Centre for Multimedia Education, Cyberjaya
Parson, R (1997) *An Investigation into Instruction Available on the WWW* [online] http://www.osie.on.ca/ rparson/out1d.htm [accessed 13 January 2000]
Peraya, D (1994) *Distance Education and the WWW* [online] http://tecfa.unige.ch/edu-comp/ edu-ws94/contrib/peraya/fm.htm [accessed 28 January 2002]
Ritchie, D C and Hoffman, B (1996) *Using Instructional Design Principles to Amplify Learning on the World Wide Web* [online] http://edweb.sdsu.edu/clrit/learningtree/DCD/ WWWInstrdesign/WWWInstrDesign.html [accessed 28 January 2002]

17

Step-by-step approach to pedagogically based Web design

David Grantham

SUMMARY

This chapter begins from the assumption that electronic learning is here to stay and can be of great value to both students and tutors. It describes a developmental scheme for the design of Web based learning underpinned by what the author argues to be the first principle of meaningful development, sound but reflective pedagogy. Practitioners are invited to consider the pedagogy and to try out the scheme for themselves, at whatever point of entry is appropriate for them.

INTRODUCTION

Current technological progress, in the form of faster than ever information processing and almost immediate connection to pages of data, is here to stay. However, the reality of vast online stores of information has the ability to seduce both learners and teaching professionals into questionable beliefs. These can include the notion that information and communications technology (ICT) can provide answers to the increasing student/staff ratio, the practical difficulties of teaching large groups of students and increasing professional workloads. These pressures are unlikely to diminish, as the demand for higher education seems to show no signs of abating.

However, as more full-time students turn to part-time employment to make ends meet and as distance learning grows in popularity, the pattern of provision is likely to change over time. Increasingly, ICT is seen as the universal panacea to tackle these issues. For students simply to access the Internet or the World Wide Web may result in valuable learning, but more often than not it is a very hit-and-miss affair. There is too much misinformation out there and students may not be adept at sorting the wheat from the chaff. On the other hand, a well-designed electronic learning environment has the potential to work effectively to promote student learning even without the usual class contact and where the students are learning at a distance.

There are other reasons why learning in an electronic environment can add value to the student experience. Already in some disciplines, law and geography for example, key ICT skills in the form of benchmarks have become essential features of academic programmes. Course designers will need to provide students with opportunities to learn or hone these technology competence based skills

To manage both ICT skills and subject learning in one design will appeal to many practitioners. As they become more confident with Web based learning, students might learn the ICT skills almost unconsciously. Later, they may find these skills invaluable as they move from being autonomous learners to become autonomous earners in an increasingly cyber-dependent world of careers. Being able to e-mail, conference and maintain Webs, and all in a multi-task environment, would be career-relevant preparation for fast-moving change. Promoting such abilities places additional demands on higher education institutions. In the words of Barnett (2000), 'How do we prepare human beings for a crazy world and to add something to that crazy world?'

A number of experiments in learning in cyberspace provide good evidence that there are certain advantages over traditional methods. These include the facts that:

- Students can learn at their own pace and in their own time (Lapham, 1999).

- The use of e-mail and discussion fora can improve the quality of student contributions to the learning endeavour (Ehrmann, 1999).

- Students appreciate the availability of instant Web feedback on their efforts to learn (Grantham and Hunt, 1999).

- Learners who show a marked reluctance to contribute in face to face discussion are quite happy to communicate electronically (Grantham, 2000).

However, none of these experiments make positive claims about tackling the resource issues currently facing higher education. On the contrary, there are strong arguments that designing electronic learning costs more, rather than less, and may do little to reduce unit costs or staff workload.

Whatever the resource arguments, however, poorly designed electronic learning is always likely to be perceived by technology sceptics as inferior to tried and trusted methods. Arguments for developing electronic environments will fail to persuade anyone of their worth unless the designer can mobilize sound pedagogy. Electronic learning should not just be a substitute for, or adjunct to, traditional learning; it should be able to offer some positive advantages to the learner.

The issue addressed in this chapter is that of designing the kind of Web that has potential for meaningful student learning: a Web that allows tutors to incorporate the best that modern pedagogy has to offer, but in the context of an information revolution. There is nothing particularly innovative about most of the pedagogy. It is, arguably, the kind of pedagogy that underpins many of the best practices in a non-electronic learning milieu. Unashamedly, the ideas that follow are driven by a philosophy that values student autonomy in learning and reflects some of the practical pedagogical ideas of Ausubel *et al* (1978), Knowles (1984), Boud (1988), Laurillard (1993) and Entwistle and Walker (2000). In essence, these philosophies value the processes of learning and the development of generic student abilities at least as much as subject knowledge.

From the practitioner perspective, the practical suggestions are examples of 'reflective practice' drawing upon such technical and pedagogical skills that the author has at the time of writing. It is based upon action research over the past three years conducted as a member of the Coventry University Learning, Teaching and Assessment Task Force. Each development came under the constructively critical scrutiny of colleagues both within and outside the university. This process, described by Carr and Kemmis (1986) as 'critical reflection', is also described in the work of Schon (1987) and Beaty (1997).

Practitioners can drop into the suggested scheme at any point. The step-by-step approach is also linear in that it begins with relatively easily applied technology and works up to quite sophisticated applications.

TRENDS IN PRACTICE

Professionals can put ICT to work in a way that merely adds even more content to an already crowded curriculum. This is exemplified in the several requests I have had from colleagues from a variety of disciplines to the effect that they would like help in putting their lecture notes on the Web. Many will be familiar with the old chestnut, now augmented to suit the post-modern age: 'Lecturing is the process by which the lecture notes [now on the course or module Web site] become the notes of the student without passing through the minds of either.'

There are a number of Web sites world-wide where such notes can be found, sometimes with suggested answers to problems. Such sites described by Ritalis, Papaspyrou and Skordalakis (1998) as 'information-based models of Web design', have the propensity to encourage the student towards a passive, rather than an interactive mode of learning. Students will tend to be instrumental in their learning, constantly seeking clues for what is minimally required of them for assessment purposes (Miller and Parlett, 1974). The growth of sites offering to write student assignments through what may be termed 'cyber-plagiarism' or 'cyber-ghosting' is clearly a worrying trend and will no doubt survive the best software designed to defeat it.

It is the purpose of this chapter to argue that the key to meaningful electronic learning environments lies in the hands of the learning and teaching professionals. Sound pedagogical theory ought to lead to sound pedagogical practice. This argument should hold true in both the electronic and the non-electronic learning contexts. In designing a Web based curriculum it is essential that the same design skills should be brought to bear on the project as would be utilized in constructing a curriculum in any other medium. Poor design in a traditional learning and teaching environment will work no better in an electronic one. Of course, even the most professional curriculum design may fail simply because the students who use it may not respond positively to it. They may not be properly inducted into electronic learning, or the technology may fail or for a number of other reasons the project flounders. However, if the design is not properly thought out and tested beforehand then the likelihood of shipwreck is markedly increased.

There are a number of commercially available Web based learning environments that provide shells into which material and student data can be added. WebCT is the current market leader in the United Kingdom, and Coventry University was one of the first adopters in September 1999. All modules offered at the university now have their own Web site, albeit in different stages of development. As far as my own particular work on Web based learning is concerned, a research background in curriculum development and design has been of considerable help in wrestling with the issues. My main learning and teaching interests, perhaps unusually, lie in two fields, law and education, and it is in both of these areas that the Web design has been focused. Curiously, the module involved in the education field is Curriculum Evaluation, Design and Research. Therefore, I have to construct a Web that is supposed to be an exemplar of good practice. I have to 'walk the talk'.

This guide does not pretend to be the last word on Web design. Indeed, I have now begun to explore the use of video and audio in Web design and the scheme outlined may simply be the overture to a much more developed multimedia approach. The suggestions presume a rudimentary understanding of how Webs can be put together and a simple working knowledge of a Web editor, such as Netscape Composer or Microsoft Front Page.

Throughout the scheme a horticultural or botanical analogy has been used. The choice of analogy was mostly determined by a cherished one employed by Northedge (1976) in describing some teachers' metaphors for the process of learning and teaching. One metaphor describes the tutor as a kind of gardener who provides all the necessary know-how, nutrients and conditions in which growth is likely to occur. However, Northedge recognizes that the students come from a wide range of educational backgrounds, have already been tended by previous gardeners and will thus require different kinds and levels of growth agent at strategic times:

> The gardener does not work to a precisely defined end... He has broad plans as to how he wants the garden to develop (probably rather flexible ones, which change as possibilities within the garden reveal themselves), but he does not attempt to specify the exact dimensions that each plant (or concept structure) is to achieve... there is never a stage when further constructive activity is not anticipated.

A Web can also be viewed as a garden where students can grow their understanding of the subject and develop a range of skills. They can gather such growth agent as each requires at the time it is needed. Some will need more resources than others and at different times to others. Whether as a supplement to, or as an alternative to, more traditional methods, a thoughtfully designed Web can be a very valuable environment for student development.

Examples of the contents of Web pages are taken from a Web site for law students but most, if not all, of the pedagogy and page design may be relevant to many disciplines. This may be particularly true where the intention of the tutor is to get the students to take a critical view of the subject and promote the necessary 'deep learning' (Marton and Saljo, 1976).

THE 'SEEDBED' (FIRST STAGE IN WEB DEVELOPMENT)

A primary pedagogical objective of the whole scheme is to encourage the student out of 'passive' mode into interacting with the material to improve understanding. The degree of interaction available is increased as the scheme develops. Perhaps this is really not very different from the traditional lecture situation. A new lecturer will tend to lecture from carefully prepared notes, and encourage more interaction as confidence grows.

For this first stage, the skills required are explained in the online help that can be found in most Web editors or electronic learning shells like WebCT. In practical terms, the tutor loads lecture notes onto a Web (or into a Web editor) but only as a first step in the process of the design. This will provide the seedbed for what is to follow. A Web site can then grow according to the philosophy and practices of the tutor concerned. As a first step, the lecture notes can then be made minimally interactive so that the students can do something with the notes, even if it is only to find their way more quickly around them. Two features can be added at this stage:

1.   hypertext links;

2.   a glossary.

Hypertext links are usually easily accomplished through a Web editor and allow the user to click quickly through to different parts of the Web pages. By this means, tutors can direct students to particular material, easily located via one mouse click on the hypertext link.

Tutors must decide how to segment their notes, though often this is a natural process requiring very little additional effort. Most Web based electronic learning environments have a facility for students to make their own notes on each Web page. This important feature empowers the student to make customized comments on the page, encouraging a sense of ownership in the process.

Glossary entries provide a golden opportunity to define words or concepts that are known from the tutor's experience to cause difficulties for students. The glossary in WebCT allows the tutor/designer to hypertext a particular word or words so that one click by the student will reveal the glossary entry. Just looking through uploaded lecture notes for potential glossary needs can be a revealing exercise for a reflective practitioner. So often in the rush and tumble of getting through a lecture it is only too easy to overlook the needs of the students, especially where technical terms are liberally employed. Evaluations with my students (Grantham, 1999) confirm that students, especially those for whom English is an additional language, find the glossary an indispensable learning aid.

'SHOOTS' (SECOND STAGE IN WEB DEVELOPMENT)

Here the pedagogical objective of interactivity is supported by various ways of involving students with the material by the setting of tasks within the text. Tasks are of different kinds to promote different kinds of learning.

Awareness

Here, the purpose is to raise student awareness of some factor or context. In the example, it is to help students to understand the significance of changes in law in response to the socio-economic context. The pedagogical aim here is to introduce into the learning a deeper level of appreciation of relationships between real world learning, in the form of real world change, and scholarship. Research evidence shows that students learn best when questions, or tasks, are authentic in the sense that they are 'situated' in a world to which the student can relate (Seeley Brown, Collins and Duguid, 1989; Bradshaw, 1995).

Puzzle

This is the tutor's opportunity to ask questions about things that often puzzle students and can sometimes even tax the tutor herself. Puzzle questions are arguably at their very best when they question something that has been learned previously,yet the new understanding to be revealed does not sit easily with that prior learning. Law abounds with such puzzles, but other disciplines will have their own areas of real or apparent conflict.

The underpinning pedagogy for this kind of question is to give the student an opportunity to examine dissonance. The lack of 'fit' (Snyder, 1971) with the student's prior learning often reveals that things do not always rhyme as they perhaps should. Recognizing that there is such a dissonance puzzle is also an important transferable skill.

Revision

Tutors will recognise this type of task. Gilbert (1962) refers to this process as 'backward chaining', enabling students to test how well they have grasped important prior learning. In the example, the previous learning was encountered some months before, so additional help is given in the form of a clue. The pedagogy also reflects work of Ausubel *et al* (1978), who argue that the most important thing about learning is what the student already knows.

Linking with prior learning can also enable students to 'integrate' their understanding and to think more holistically. A pedagogical assumption here is that holistic learning is more valuable to the student than 'atomized' learning, where bits of understanding are often not related to each other. The assumption is supported by Biggs (1989):

> The structure of knowledge is more visible to, and more useful to, students where it is clearly displayed, where content is taught in integrated wholes rather than in small separate pieces, and where knowledge is required to be related to other knowledge rather than learned in isolation.

Atomistic learning is one of the dangers of the modular system now adopted in many modern universities that integrative questions seek to remedy. In the example there is also a 'puzzle' type question, demonstrating how different types of task can sometimes be usefully combined.

Links

Such questions attempt to draw upon understanding from other parts of the subject (or module), or in this case, from another subject or module. The student is asked to consider a more ambitious aim of constructing cognitive bridges between what may have been viewed previously as discrete territories.

Pedagogical theory here is to foster even greater 'holism' and encourage more of an overview of the discipline. The breaking down of subject barriers should help the learner in applying a synthesis of ideas and concepts to new problems; to construct their own learning. Encouraging this kind of student behaviour should better enable the students to explore new territory and draw their own maps.

Problem solving

In this task the students are faced with applying first principles to a fact situation. Skills in problem solving are not peculiar to law. However, such skills are essential if the student is to embark on a legal career. This will certainly hold true for many other careers, both now and in the future.

Ability to apply learning to unfamiliar situations is the pedagogy behind this task and, if based on real-world events, can provide an excellent example of 'situated' learning (Seeley Brown *et al*, 1989; Bradshaw, 1995; Gibbs, 1992).

Reconciliation

The focus here is to draw together the characteristics of 'puzzles', 'links' and 'problem solving' type questions. Here, the student has to apply careful reasoning in an attempt to explain apparently irreconcilable decisions. This is a difficult task and will involve the student in extensive research, not to mention a tolerance of uncertainty. It is yet another exercise that is inviting the student to explain dissonance within the body of the discipline, but with more reliance on prior learning and a real world context. Pedagogically speaking, this kind of learning compendium of 'learning goodies' will test even the most able of students. A series of judiciously selected clues, revealed via a discussion forum, could assist those students who have need of such legal aid. Of particular importance is the critical role such questions play in introducing the student to the possibly discomforting idea that experts (in this case, judges) can sometimes get it wrong! Are there any disciplines that are not littered with the opinions of experts who got it wrong?

Support for the student is important at every stage of the learning process, but here it takes on special significance. Not only is the task a demanding one for students but, as explored in the work of Gardner (1983, 1991), it is both a cognitive and often emotional process. Some students, and especially those from a 'rote' learning culture, will have difficulty with the revelation that experts can be questioned.

Student responses could be prepared for seminars or postings could be made to a discussion forum or chat room. Both of these communications media are available in most electronic learning environments. Chat rooms might be difficult for the tutor to manage if all students were to make individual contributions. Even the discussion forum can present this kind of management problem. One way to reduce these is to have student sub-groups, of say five or six students, who make 'group entries' to the fora.

'FLOWER BUDS' (THIRD STAGE OF WEB DEVELOPMENT)

Pedagogical objectives

The feature of this development is the provision of feedback to students via the pop-up window provided by the glossary function. Feedback in this learning environment aims to reassure the tutee that he or she is on the right track, and is a timely tool for course corrections en route. Toohey (1999) argues that students who compare their work with that of an expert, or panel of experts, is likely to find this form of feedback less confronting than direct comment on individual performance. Not all tasks have instant feedback since some of them require more dialogue between students and tutor in the discussion forum. Here, course corrections can be made gradually, almost half a degree at a time if necessary, so that tutees can be brought back on track with appropriate and timely tutor interventions.

Advantages of instant feedback are:

- Students can quickly check their understanding.
- It can boost student confidence ready for the next learning task.
- It can instantly reveal any misunderstanding requiring remedial action.

Disadvantages of instant feedback are:

- Students can beat the system and look at the feedback without putting in much, or any, learning effort.

- Students could be led into thinking that the response reveals all that needs to be known, or that there is to know, about the subject-matter.

Both of these 'down-sides' can be countered by including in the feedback some questions prompting further enquiry. There is, of course, no guarantee that the student will follow through with the enquiry! Another counter to the 'let's have a peep at the feedback' syndrome is that much of the feedback can only be fully understood if the essential prior groundwork is done. This latter factor is likely to be the more influential if the original question is carefully constructed.

'FLOWERS' (THE FOURTH STAGE OF WEB DEVELOPMENT)

For this final stage of development there are six additions to the design of the Web page. Each of the enhancements has its own pedagogical basis.

1) Prior learning

Although a number of the student activities are designed to probe previous understanding, this by contrast sets out underpinning learning as preconditions to the present study. A hypertext link could return the self-doubting student to any Web page where relevant previous study can be found.

2) Learning objectives

There are arguments for and against these and space dictates that these cannot be rehearsed here. Readers interested in the objectives debate can get much food for thought from the work of Stenhouse (1975), Popham (1974) and MacDonald-Ross (1973). However, for good or ill, for Coventry University students and tutors, learning objectives became a stark reality when the university management decided that all modules should have them.

Whatever the arguments against them, learning objectives do have the advantage of providing students with a checklist of what they should know and be able to do at the end of the study. They also provide a blueprint for tutors to design learning activities to meet the objectives. Some of the objectives in the development Web have been drafted in very broad terms. This is deliberate. Practitioners should be mindful of a real drawback of objectives: the limiting of the learning experience. More recently, the university has moved towards specifying outcomes rather than objectives.

3) Frequently occurring misunderstandings ('FOMs')

These alert the student to a range of misunderstandings that commonly arise in learning in this area of the law. They have been gathered together from the tutor's experience of holding seminars and assessing student work over a number of years. Any practitioner will testify that there are no limits to the number of ways a discipline can be misunderstood. Based upon 'frequently asked questions' on many Web sites, they act as a kind of map of the minefield, indicating to the unwary the whereabouts of the dangers. Students can, of course, enter the mine-field without reference to the map – and some no doubt will!

4) Learning groups

If there is concern that the tutor may be unable to respond to each student in the discussion forum, then students could be divided into learning groups. Students must learn how to e-mail each other with ideas and then how to make group postings to the discussion forum. Alternatively, a discussion forum could be set up for each group, or sub-group, postings being visible only to the members of the group and the tutor.

Tutors should allow free dialogue between the students and only intervene strategically. Examples of such interventions include when the dialogue is 'off-task', or flagging and in need of new input, or is simply going in the wrong direction. Whatever the reason, professional judgement needs to be sound, otherwise tutor postings may risk hampering or completely stopping ongoing dialogue.

Learning groups can also be mobilized for assessment purposes. Groups could be asked to gather together materials and write a commentary for their own Web site, or to create a news group where all would contribute to the matter under discussion. A measure of peer assessment could be introduced here, where the students both contribute to and apply the criteria for assessment. Such a student centred approach to assessment would seem to address the important issue raised by Boud (1988) that students ought to acquire the capacity both to get to know and to recognize when they have got to know. The creation and empowering of learning groups enhances cooperative or collaborative learning between students and tutors of the kind explored in the work of Knight and Bohlmeyer (1990) and McConnell (2000).

5) Links to the Internet

These can be added to a Web page relatively easily. Here the link is to an article on relevant issues on an electronic journal site. Students' attention can be drawn to the link and additional tasks, relating directly to the link, can be set. (See Figure 17.1.)

6) Graphics

These add interest to the pages and introduce something of an element of fun. Gathered from various free graphics Web sites, they can light up what might otherwise be a dull page. More than this, they can act as a prompt to learning, especially for students who are motivated by visual stimuli. (See Figure 17.2.)

CONCLUSION

Web-based learning environments provide a context in which higher education practitioners can conduct action research and design a curriculum within which meaningful learning can take place. Reflection, alone or in a

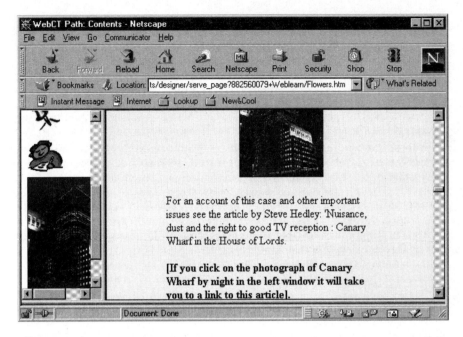

Figure 17.1   *Links to Web pages*

Figure 17.2   *Graphics on Web pages*

collaboration with colleagues, is a necessary but, on its own, an insufficient condition for sound design. Some training in the technology is necessary if tutors are to take advantage of the vast and still expanding cyber-resources. Being able to teach face to face, as Rowntree (1995) exhorts, is no real indicator of online teaching ability. Institutional investment in computer hardware and software will not yield excellence in facilitators of online learning without similar input into the funding of staff development in the necessary skills. Stenhouse (1975) reminds us that there can be no curriculum development without the development of tutors.

Even so, well-honed technical skills may not guarantee well-constructed online learning. Webs can look good and students can be falsely persuaded of their value by all kinds of technical 'whizzythings'. The main purpose of this chapter has been to argue that sound online learning must first be supported by sound pedagogy. In giving practical, working examples of the pedagogy/technology in action it has attempted to demonstrate one instance of how this argument can be operationalized. One of the major attributes of the step-by-step approach is that it gives interested colleagues the opportunity to try the scheme at whatever point of entry is appropriate for them.

REFERENCES

Ausubel, D P, Novak, J S and Hanesian, H (1978) *Educational Psychology: A cognitive view*, Holt, Rinehart and Winston, New York

Barnett, R (2000), ESRC seminar on Networked Learning, Sheffield University, 10/11 July

Beaty, E (1997), *Developing Your Teaching Through Reflective Practice*, Staff and Educational Development Association, Birmingham

Biggs, J B (1989), Does learning about learning help teachers with teaching? Psychology and the tertiary teacher, *The Gazette (Supplement)*, 26 (1), University of Hong Kong

Boud, D (ed) (1988), *Developing Student Autonomy in Learning*, Kogan Page, London

Bradshaw, D C A (1995) Learning theory: harnessing the strength of a neglected resource, in *Bringing Learning to Life: The learning revolution, the economy, and the individual*, ed D C A Bradshaw, pp 79–82, Falmer Press, London

Carr, W and Kemmis, S (1986) *Becoming Critical: Education, knowledge and action research*, Falmer Press, London

Ehrmann, S C (1999) Access and/or quality?, *Educom Review*, September/October, p 27

Entwistle, N and Walker, P (2000) Strategic alertness and expanded awareness within sophisticated conceptions of teaching, in *Teaching for Effective Learning in Higher Education*, ed N Haviva, D M Osheroff and W M McKeachie, Kluwer, London

Gardner H (1983) *Frames of Mind: The theory of multiple intelligences*, Basic books, New York

Gardner H (1991) *The Unschooled Mind: How children think and how schools should teach*, Basic Books, New York

Gibbs, G (1992) Improving the quality of student learning through course design, in *Learning to Effect*, ed R Barnett, Society for Research into Higher Education/Open University Press, Buckingham

Gilbert, T F (1962) Mathetics: the technology of education, *Journal of Mathetics*, 1, reprinted as a supplement to *Recall* (1970), Longman, London

Grantham, D J (1999) 'IOLISplus – extending the electronic learning environment', *Journal of Information Law and Technology*, **1**

Grantham, D J (2000) IOLISplus – the second chapter, *Journal of Information Law and Technology*, **11** [online] http://www.law.warwick.ac.uk/jilt/99-1/grantham.html [accessed 28 January 2002]

Grantham, D J and Hunt, N (1999) Web interfaces to enhance CAL materials; case studies from law and statistics, *ALT-J*, 7 (3)

Knight, G P and Bohlmeyer, E M (1990) Cooperative learning and achievement: methods for assessing causal mechanisms, in *Cooperative Learning: Theory and research*, ed S Sharan, Praegar, New York

Knowles, M S (1984), *Andragogy in Action*, Jossey-Bass, San Francisco

Lapham, A (1999) Reflections on the groupware experience: a content analysis of student module evaluations, *Active Learning*, 10 (July), pp 14–20

Laurillard, D (1993), *Rethinking University Teaching: A framework for the effective use of educational technology*, Routledge, London

MacDonald-Ross, M (1973) Behavioural objectives: a critical review, *Instructional Science 2*, Elsevier, Amsterdam

Marton, F and Saljo, R (1976) On qualitative differences in learning: I. Outcome and process, *British Journal of Educational Psychology*, 46, pp 4–11

McConnell, D (2000) *Implementing Computer Supported Cooperative Learning* (2nd edn), Kogan Page, London

Miller, C M L and Parlett, M (1974) *Up to The Mark: A study of the examination game*, Society for Research in Higher Education, London

Northedge, A (1976) Examining our implicit analogies for learning processes, *Programmed Learning and Educational Technology*, 13 (4), pp 67–78

Popham, W J (1974) Curriculum design: the problem of specifying intended learning outcomes, in *Program Development in Education*, ed J Blaney *et al*, Education-Extension, Centre for Continuing Education, University of British Columbia, Canada

Ritalis, S, Papaspyrou, N and Skordalakis, M (1998) A case study of an enriched classroom model on the World Wide Web, *Active Learning*, 8, pp 15–19

Rowntree, D (1995) Teaching and learning online: a correspondence education for the 21st century?, *British Journal of Educational Technology*, 26 (3), pp 205–15

Schon, D A (1987) *Educating the Reflective Practitioner*, Jossey-Bass, San Francisco

Seeley Brown, J, Collins, A and Duguid, P (1989) Stolen knowledge, *Educational Technology* (March), pp 10–15

Snyder, B R (1971) *The Hidden Curriculum*, Knopf, New York

Stenhouse, L (1975) A critique of the objectives model, ch 6 in *An Introduction to Curriculum Research and Development*, pp 71–83, Heinemann Educational, London

Toohey, S (1999) *Designing Courses for Higher Education*, Society for Research into Higher Education/Open University Press, Buckingham

ICT: a threat to the traditional university?

Rakesh Bhanot and Stephen Fallows

> When the winds of change blow, some build walls while others build
> windmills
>
> (Chinese proverb)

INTRODUCTION

This chapter highlights a selection of the issues surrounding educational development which need to be tackled if ICT is to maximize its potential for
improving the educational process while avoiding some of the obvious pitfalls.
We are not necessarily seeking to draw summarizing conclusions, but will map
some of the problems and possibilities of the adoption of ICT into higher
education. However, the tentative generalizations canvassed here are intended
to be no more than suggestive, and it is left to the readers to adjudicate the
extent to which they can be considered relevant to their particular contexts.
This caution is quite normal in considering the appropriateness of drawing
inferences from a series of case studies, and has been referred to by Stake
(1988) as involving 'naturalistic' rather then 'formalistic' generalizations.

One overriding question is the extent to which the changes permitted by an
extensive involvement of ICT may lead to the advent of novel institutions that
may still be called 'universities', but which may not be 'universities as we know
them'. This was a major consideration in the question posed by Lord Dearing
in his keynote address to the 2000 SEDA conference: 'Can the university
survive the future?' Indeed, the ICT revolution has already had a major impact
on the common practices of a university, leading several commentators (eg
Laurillard, 1994; Barnett, 2000) to require of its practitioners a 'rethinking' or
're-invention' of the notion of a university. At the same time, there is no
shortage of technological enthusiasts who are telling us that the adoption of
ICT solutions is perhaps the only way for universities to survive. Thus Carole
Barone, Vice President of EDUCAUSE, argues that:

> The new sociotechnological context for working and learning (even for
> 'playing') calls for new ways of conceptualizing the learning and

decision-making environments of colleges and universities today. Change at such a fundamental level is transformative and disruptive but also ultimately essential if the powerful and socially positive – though not necessarily profitable – values of higher education are to persist in the information age.

(Barone 2001: 41)

In practice, however, the likely scenario in higher education for years to come will be a mix of approaches to teaching and learning in which ICT will play an increasing role. One of its many consequences may be to increase the 'digital divide' between the (technological) rich and poor universities.

Other perceived threats to the modus operandi of universities are rooted in several large-scale social changes, including considerations of academic globalization and the increasing 'massification' of higher education (Scott, 1995). However, the new ICT is seen as a solution to some of the problems of this massification, acting as a kind of relieving cavalry as student numbers escalate. Already there are universities with substantially more students than seats, now that the advantages of online learning are more clearly understood as allowing savings on plant. The suspicion that the new circumstances may disadvantage students by undermining the person-to-person pedagogy is already being challenged by those who argue that online learning can actually enhance student–student and student–teacher interactions (personal communication from colleagues in Coventry University using WebCT with large groups of students on a variety of courses). We are aware that there are pockets of resistance but these are more to do with pressures of work and the speed of change rather than any ideological positions.

The thrust of this volume, however, is a decidedly optimistic one: that technological developments offer more advantageous possibilities than they create problems, and the contributors seem to agree in arguing that the latter can be overcome. Nevertheless, there is also a wide acceptance of the fact that a number of difficult issues remain. For example, the promise of ICT to accommodate increasing student numbers (many so-called 'first generation students') may have unpredictable effects on staff/student relationships. Equally, technological developments in Web based learning will involve major changes in the way in which knowledge is generated and disseminated. Thus, the new technologies not only offer additional tools for teachers and students to interact at great distances and at different times but, as Resnick (1995) points out, we are witnessing a paradigmatic shift in the way we view knowledge and its production.

> The best computational tools do not simply offer the same content in new clothing; rather, they aim to recast areas of knowledge, suggesting fundamentally new ways of thinking about the concepts in that domain, allowing learners to explore concepts that were previously inaccessible.

Similarly, Sharples (1999) argues that the new technologies are not only changing the way we write but also the 'very nature of writing'.

These shifts will carry consequences for the way in which structured or semi-structured academic and practical domains are conceptualized and mapped by the technology. However, as the preceding chapters show, in addition to highlighting an array of issues and problems, the new developments in ICT hold out a number of promises for higher education in an age of rapid contextual changes. It would be rash to suggest that technology has already captured this educational sector because, as Wood McCarty (Chapter 4) points out, relatively few institutions have so far made ICT 'a ubiquitous part of campus life'. Although adoption of ICT varies both across national sectors and globally, all the signs suggest that even the most ardent academic technophobe is going to have to engage with the information and knowledge revolution.

In this tempestuous climate of change, some educational developers see ICT as an extra burden. Others welcome it as a kind of midwife that will aid the eventual rebirth of the university as a more accessible and flexible institution in which teacher–student and other relations (technical–academic staff, administrative–academic staff) will be reconfigured. Such a vision could be said to unite the contributors to this volume. ICT does indeed offer educational developers both an opportunity and a challenge to reconsider issues concerning both epistemology and pedagogy/andragogy within the context of rethinking university education. With its new configurations of time and space, ICT can link us directly to colleagues and students on the other side of the world, allowing us to share experiences and differences in unprecedented ways. It is this radical potential of ICT in education that will move us away from the idea of higher education as a multiplicity of localized 'cottage industries', each with individual character, towards global reach, if not uniformity.

How and to what extent we adapt to this new landscape will depend not merely on the advances in technology but on developing and transforming pedagogic practices that can harness its potential. In the new universities of the 21st century, the roles of those who support learning in universities (teachers/lecturers/technicians/administrators and so on) are likely to undergo profound changes, and many of us are in for a fairly bumpy ride. Can educational developers make the ride smoother, more comfortable, more worthwhile?

The contributors to this book provide a selection of stories or case studies that illustrate a diversity of contexts in which ICT has been adopted in their individual institutions. While there is a variety of experiences, they do have common features. For example, there is an underlying assumption of an increasing acceptance of the role of ICT in education. Many argue that, if properly managed, the new technologies will empower both teachers and students, as well as managers and administrators, enabling them all to benefit from the changed scenarios. Several contributors provide both guidelines for good practice and also point out some of the pitfalls in adopting ICT in higher education.

The sections below consider some of the ramifications and challenges involved in the adoption of ICT into higher education.

REDEFINING ROLES

The studies in this volume demonstrate that a strong interdependence is emerging between technology and pedagogy; between teachers and technologists. What is likely to develop, and indeed is already taking place, is a redefinition of professional categories and the contractual arrangements that support them. As the examples show, collaboration between different kinds of expertise is becoming key to the effective implementation and integration of ICT. In general terms, the teacher is required to become proficient with the technology, while the ICT professional is drawn more closely into the educational process. New professions are evolving, for example learning technologists, course designers and educational Web specialists, and they are drawing recruits from the two broad categories mentioned above.

There are also likely to be changes in the ways in which academics are expected to manage their time. Decisions here will involve deciding on whether academics are resource makers or resource presenters; whether they are in partnership with their students in constructing knowledge or whether they are simply vehicles for its transmission. (Doubtless there will be a role for both.)

These changes have profound implications for the role of educational developers who are likely to have to play a pivotal role in the integration of ICT into the fabric of university life. For instance, they need to be fully aware of the possibilities, potential and pitfalls inherent in adopting the new tools. It is important for educational developers to be 'ahead of the game' and to 'walk the talk' by delivering development programmes that make use of the new technologies. They will also have a key role in monitoring and evaluating the effectiveness of new educational initiatives and practices. It is important to assess whether the promises made in the name of ICT are actually being fulfilled.

Clearly, the expected benefits cannot come about without 'intensive and rigorous training' for both staff and students in order to make the best use of ICT (Steven and Zakrzewski, Chapter 11). The current technological revolution has to be accompanied by a pedagogic reformation (Grantham, Chapter 17) which in turn has ramifications for all those working and learning in HE. In view of this, the implications of the above for educational developers are best considered in an overall institutional context, since to advocate change without concomitant adjustments on the other two sides of the model given in Figure 18.1 is likely to prove ineffective and inefficient.

INSTITUTIONAL DEVELOPMENT

The introduction of, for example, an online learning environment will require major (infra)structural changes in order for the new types of learning to take place. This may mean a refocusing of the university mission or vision, not to mention a review of resource allocations and indeed a shift in who makes the key decisions. In addition to providing enhanced pedagogic practice, it has been argued that ICT offers HE institutions more efficient and economical means of dealing with the increased bureaucracy brought about by larger

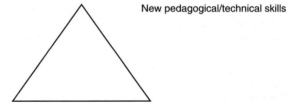

Institutional development

New mission/vision
(including ICT strategy)
New administrative structures

**Staff/student
development**

New pedagogical/technical skills

Curriculum development

New forms of content/delivery/assessment/research

Figure 18.1   *Model for educational development*

numbers of students and the more flexible, individual, learner-centred forms
of education.

> The accumulating evidence suggests that although it is certainly
> possible to teach people things online – sometimes with better results
> than in conventional classes – the main benefit to universities of the
> communications revolution is unlikely to lie in that area. Instead, for
> the foreseeable future, the main effect of new technology will be on the
> administration of universities.
>
> *(THES*, 6 April 2001)

Perhaps the driving force behind the introduction of ICT in a university will
be the economic advantage it offers through teaching more students. It will
thus be business-led rather than pedagogically driven. Will there be a
conflict of interests between the business and scholarship aspects of a
university? It would be a shame if the main benefit of the new ICT will
merely be the potential to run a university more efficiently, since the possibilities and challenges offered by ICT in developing new educational paradigms should be the focus of attention. But whatever the motivation
(perceived administrative benefits and/or educational enhancement), HE
institutions will need to adopt a strategic approach in moving from a traditional to a more electronically based delivery of their services. While many
universities have documented an institutional teaching and learning
strategy, not all include an explicit statement on the role of ICT in creating a
modern learning environment. A key function of educational developers is
to take a lead in ensuring that the use of ICT in higher education is based on

sound educational principles and not driven by technological or administrative considerations only.

> The use of C&IT does not itself produce quality outcomes. The focus must be on pedagogy rather than technology.
>
> (Beaty and Thomas, 1998: 6)

The need for a strategic approach with a full commitment from senior management is key, since without a whole-institutional implementation programme, the developments are likely to remain with the enthusiasts without impacting on the mainstream (Stiles and Orsmond, Chapter 5).

Here, the role of educational development units (EDUs) becomes crucial, but it is worth remembering that the creation of EDUs in universities is a fairly recent phenomenon (Gosling, 2000; Jenkins, Cousin and Bhanot, 2000) that was initially premised on prioritizing student learning by paying more attention to student centred learning. Its typical mantra was in support of 'active learning' and the encouragement of exploratory pedagogies involving the interrogation of direct experience or symbolic representations of the world; the task of the student was typically to generate cognitive and evaluative maps rather than assimilate information. In this equation, dialogue and discussion moved closer to the centre of the pedagogic enterprise with negotiated learning, based on constructivist principles. Yet can the online bulletin board replicate the power of the university seminar? The answer may to some extent depend on whether online learning is an add-on or a substitute, a choice that will deeply affect the outcome of any cost/benefit analysis and the direction of strategic management decisions.

Moreover, many newly appointed EDU staff, often with a humanities bias, now find themselves facing a new challenge. How can they assist in the integration of online learning into the new higher education landscape? A number of EDUs have responded by opening up a technological wing and collaborating with their new ICT 'bedfellows'. In order to achieve an appropriate balance between technology and learning, they are being called upon to assist both 'front line' teachers and those with responsibility for integrating new forms of technology into the fabric of higher education. Their role is to ensure that the focus on technological advances does not detract from the need to maintain sound educational practices. The 'geeks' should not be left to inherit the entire earth.

The changes brought about by introducing ICT are inevitably shifting the centres of power in HE institutions, with the development of new forms of expertise and new hierarchies (Barone, 2001), and this may have a temporary unsettling effect on all staff. Hence the need for careful and sensitive programmes of staff and student development.

STAFF/STUDENT DEVELOPMENT

Given the developments in ICT and the changing nature of the students entering higher education, many of whom are comfortable using the Internet, the majority of academic staff (who themselves may not have this familiarity with ICT) are having to review their practices. This is even the case in residential campus universities where not all the teaching and learning is carried out in traditional classrooms. The adoption of ICT in the learning and teaching process in this new scenario brings new challenges for both teachers and educational developers. Traditionally, many of the latter have come from a teaching background; perhaps the new educational developers may hail from a background in technology. Of course, the ideal solution would be to have a multi-skilled team comprising colleagues from a variety of backgrounds. However, in the near future the task for the educational developer may be to perform a kind of circus trick and to ride both horses (the pedagogic and the technological) successfully at the same time.

Thus, in order to realize the benefits arising from the new ICT outlined in this volume, educational developers will have to help teachers to develop and enhance their pedagogic and IT skills so that they are able to teach both face to face and online (Grantham, Chapter 17). Students will need to develop strategies for independent learning as well as other skills, for example, of sifting what is and what is not useful information and knowledge on the Internet (Bostock, 2001).

Both learners and teachers will have to find ways of working even more closely with librarians and technical staff in order to make the most of what ICT offers. Indeed, this is likely to lead to new forms of collaboration which many of the authors in this volume see as positive spin-offs arising from the new developments.

Clearly, not all colleagues will want to go along with new developments (Brosnan, 1998) and we have to find ways of dealing with the resistance to change by motivating colleagues to make use of the new resources available, and by fostering skills for teaching in an online environment (Sharpe, 2000). Wood McCarty (Chapter 4) argues that development activities for staff and students have to be gradual and ongoing. Individuals must be allowed to develop at their own pace to reach what she refers to as the 'comfort zone' before moving on to more complex uses of ICT. The following suggestions may be considered, but as with all management of change strategies, the local context will determine the best course of action.

- Gradually involve all colleagues (including administrative, technical, librarians) in the implementation process.

- Reward colleagues who acquire new skills. This may mean developing new sorts of qualifications and accreditation.

- Use mentors with knowledge of ICT and pair them with 'novices' (Paget and Chandler, Chapter 15).

- Develop ICT skills in the students.

Students (in case they do not already come with them) will clearly need to acquire 'modern' skills that will prepare them not just for their studies but also for an uncertain future in what will probably be a life of serial careers. These skills will almost certainly include being able to handle e-mail, Internet searches, mail groups, Internet conferencing and, no doubt, other means of communication and decision making yet to be unveiled.

According to the Dearing Report (NCIHE,1997) 'by the year 2005/2006 every student will be required to have access to their own laptop'. Most students are already beginning to buy PCs without exhortation from universities. It was reported that three-quarters of the 1999 intake at Oxford Brookes University had access to their own PCs and the owners believe that PCs are 'essential learning tools'. (Breen *et al*, 2001). The article also reports that university staff recognize the value of computer use that 'involves high-level creative activity and goes well beyond repetitive practice of manual skills' (Breen *et al*, 2001). Some of the contributors to this volume emphasize that using ICT can and does encourage 'deep learning' and the development of higher order cognitive skills, as well as enhancing communication skills (Blackmore, Roach and Dempster, Chapter 12). ICT allows students to become more independent learners, or co-learners, where the emphasis is not so much on knowledge transfer as on knowledge construction.

Educational developers need to be proactive by adopting an integrated development policy so that both staff and students acquire the necessary skills for the new learning context. They will have to ensure that their own personal and professional development programme includes a direct understanding of the role of ICT in higher education. In order to do this effectively, it may be necessary for them to experience online learning for themselves.

While it may seem unreasonable to some, it may soon be expected that all academic staff should have some expertise in all three areas: ICT, instructional design and their subject disciplines. Perhaps in the near future some will need to work with technical staff, and this will encourage more collaboration between academic and other staff than has traditionally been the case. As indicated earlier, such developments are likely to lead to a redefinition of the roles of all those who support learning in universities (Drew, Chapter 10).

CURRICULUM DEVELOPMENT

As stated above, changes at any one side of the model in Figure 18.1 will necessitate reconsideration at the other two sides. Curriculum developers, packaging a curriculum for online learning and teaching, will no longer be able to defend against the erosion of the boundary between the Web space they create and the Internet in general.

When trawling the huge resources of the Web, students will no longer have the security of a designed curriculum as 'pre-digested pabulum' but may perhaps be more like hunters after raw meat. At the same time, postmodernism's collapse of the canons by which the truths of academic propositions may be determined has become exacerbated by the profligacy of competing voices on the WWW where arguments for the democracy of knowledge and its customization according to the whims of individual learners are virtually cultural norms. A curriculum developer trapped within Ralph Tyler's (1949) coherence of objectives and outcomes model is likely to experience some degree of discomfort in this scenario.

Coulby (1993) is undoubtedly correct in asserting that 'any curriculum... can only be a small selection from what humanity knows or claims to know'. The point here is that the curriculum developer is no longer in a position unequivocally to control the selection; furthermore, Web based learning involves a wider potential selection, the responsibility for which has partly moved to the learner. In Coulby's account (1993), 'cultural and epistemological relativism seem both theoretical and abstruse [but]... despite their complexity and lack of resolution these debates are centrally relevant' (particularly to online learning, even though Coulby's paper was published before the advent of the Internet). In the light of the issues raised by Resnick and Sharples (see above), Coulby's point becomes even more pertinent.

In addition there are two other issues located within current educational debate, concerning diversity and inclusion, that need to be addressed. The first is, to what extent does the adoption of an ICT-based, predominantly Western curriculum play a part in perpetuating notions of cultural hegemony and the dominance of male discourse? Second, how will the adoption of the new technologies affect 'disadvantaged' students (such as the poor, the disabled and international students studying in a second language)?

The potential richness of ICT resources can itself be of help in forming solutions to the problems posed above, and this volume gives space to those who believe that they have found halfway decent practical solutions to some of these difficulties and challenges. For example, recently available adaptive technologies have been integrated into instructional design, thereby mirroring the interactivity of face to face teaching. One advantage of this technological customization is that disabled students have been enabled to participate more successfully in higher education programmes. (See for instance the following websites: http://wwwz.rit.edu/ easi/ and http://www.disinhe.ac.uk/)

The recent move towards modular degree structures, together with the growth of inter-disciplinary/multi-disciplinary courses and problem-based learning, have led to a repackaging of knowledge and experience using flexible forms of delivery and assessment in order to prepare students for both the 'real' and the 'virtual' worlds. This new order is proving to be a ready midwife for new forms of pedagogy (work based learning and resource based learning) which have just been waiting for their time to come. It may prove to be the case that ICT will be the ideal catalyst for realizing the full potential of these 'modern' approaches to learning.

Another area in which ICT has a growing impact is assessment, especially in those disciplines that face large cohorts of students. Steven and Zakrzewski (Chapter 11) point to the increasing use of ICT in assessment (both summative and formative) and how it can provide long-term benefits. However, while there are benefits from the 'automatic' marking of some student work, there is growing concern about the potential for plagiarism and other forms of cheating.

LESSONS FOR EDUCATIONAL DEVELOPMENT ORGANIZATIONS

The points raised in this final chapter, and elsewhere in the book, highlight the changing state of higher education in general, and of educational development in particular, which has come about as a result of the increased use of ICT in curriculum delivery, information management and assessment. These changes have onward implications not only for individuals but also for those national and international organizations that support the work of educational developers. Organizations such as the Staff and Educational Development Association (SEDA) in the UK (HERDSA in Australia, POD in the USA and ICED at an international level) will be called upon to take account of changed educational methodologies and will have to respond accordingly. ICT skills seem to be moving to the heart of the educational developer's repertoire, and this role is partly to help manage the transition to a more technological-based curriculum. Thus bodies such as SEDA , and its sister organizations throughout the world, may need to review and to revise their objectives and values.

The new hybrid professions mentioned above will inevitably lead to new constituencies of membership. However, are such bodies changing (fast enough) to accommodate/embrace the changes brought about by ICT? Should they lead the way? If so, how far do they need to adjust their mission or vision statements and/or to recast their thinking? If ICT is to become a fundamental/integral part of the landscape of HE, then other organizations, such as the recently established Institute for Learning and Teaching in the UK, may also need to review their criteria for membership.

CONCLUDING COMMENTS

The pace of change may be such that some feel uncomfortable and others may choose to drag their feet for a while. However, the evidence from the chapters in this book seems to point to teams of higher education staff busy designing, building and indeed using their 'new windmills' in order to harness the possibilities offered by the new ICT for a variety of educational and administrative purposes. In this new context, the roles of staff and students are being re-invented, and we shall need to develop standards, conventions, rules and etiquette for electronic communication, for example, how to contribute to and to manage an electronic discussion forum (Duggleby, 2000).

Even with the exciting possibilities offered by ICT, we still need to understand that students learn in a variety of ways. Electronic machines may be able to perform certain operations faster than humans, but they do not offer automatic solutions to the perennial problems of pedagogy. This is an area that is still poorly understood, and there is a need for rigorous research into how students learn, particularly using online learning environments, and to compare the results with traditional forms of learning and teaching. Some studies indicate that online learning appears to be particularly effective when it is combined with face to face delivery. For example, students at Glasgow University who had a structured discussion led by a tutor after listening to an online lecture received better grades than their counterparts who did not have this extra facility (*THES*, April 2001). There may be financial implications in providing such services that may militate against their universal adoption.

It is not our aim to predict what will happen in the coming years, but let us remember how far we have travelled during the first decade following the introduction of ICT initiatives in university life. How many of us can now manage without a (networked) PC/laptop? Or without access to e-mail and the Internet? Some of the new technologies are already indispensable, and as more and more of these become 'invisible', much of the fear and anxiety they induce in some may disappear, so that we can begin to exploit their full potential.

Indeed, it is difficult to see how one can follow courses in engineering design without the use of computer aided graphics. Increasingly fewer students and staff coming into universities are likely to be suffering from technophobia, although it has to be recognized that for some of the present generation of both groups, this may prove to be a genuine problem (Brosnan, 1998). Thus, while some disciplines have found it easy to accept and adopt the possibilities offered through ICT, in other areas, such as performing arts, colleagues may still need to be convinced about the potential uses of computers: for example to simulate a dance routine, or, in the case of fine arts teachers, to exploit the wealth of digital images available on the Internet.

Before we become too excited (or frightened) by the new developments, let us consider a parallel from another sector of society. It was not very long ago that the international stock market experienced a huge boom in its shares based on some dot.com companies. The promises that were made in the name of the new ICTs led to massive euphoria and a kind of stampede in the international marketplace. However, when the dust had settled, one could witness the results of the inevitable crash, with a small number of players having made significant gains and the vast majority as the losers. Are we likely to witness a similar phenomenon in higher education? In the rush to introduce ICT into university education, there may be a small number of winners at the expense of lots of losers. Until we have some hard-nosed evidence of the cost and benefit analysis of ICT, there will always be a slight suspicion that the whole enterprise could suffer the same fate as the dot.com collapse. Can we afford to run on faith that this is the only way ahead? Will the huge investments bear fruit?

Higher education institutions throughout the world have always been seen as forming a caste system or a kind of (Ivy) league table. Given the increasing cost of higher education, is there a danger that elite residential universities will emerge for the rich, combining the best of face to face and electronic learning, leaving the possibility of open/distant learning for the poor? Will the rapid introduction of the new ICT into university teaching and administration systems lead to a furthering of the divisions of the technologically rich and poor institutions? Will the old and the new Ivy League institutions be able to recruit the most able students (or the ones who can pay the most?), by offering the best combination of face to face and online learning?

How exactly the role of teachers and education developers will change is not easy to predict, since many issues remain unresolved. One thing is certain, however, and that is that there will be a role for both. It is worth remembering that new technologies for educational purposes have always tended to create a kind of euphoria, but not all of them have lived up to their promises (for example, language laboratories). However, in the long term technology is likely to enhance teaching rather than to replace it.

> There is an often-expressed fact that technology will replace teachers. I can say emphatically and unequivocally, IT WON'T... However, technology will be pivotal in the future role of teachers.
>
> (Gates, 1995)

REFERENCES

Barnett, R (2000) *Realizing the University in an Age of Supercomplexity*, Open University Press, Buckingham

Barone C A (2001) Conditions for transformation: infrastructure is not the issue, *EDUCAUSE Review*, **36** (3)

Beaty, L and Thomas, G (1998) *Coventry University Teaching and Learning Strategy*, Coventry University

Breen, R, Lindsay, R, Jenkins, A and Smith, P (2001) The role of ICT in a university learning environment, *Studies in Higher Education*, **26** (1), 95–114

Bostock, S (2001) Online resources to help students to evaluate online resources, *Educational Developments*, vol **2** (2), 15

Brosnan, M (1998) *Technophobia: The psychological impact of information technology*, Routledge, London and New York

Coulby, D (1993) Cultural and epistemological relativism and European curricula, *European Journal of Intercultural Studies*, **3** (2/3), 17–18

Duggleby, J (2000) *How to be an Online Tutor*, Gower, Aldershot

Gates, B (1995) *The Road Ahead*, Viking, London

Gosling, D (2000) Educational development units in the UK – what are they doing five years on? *International Journal for Academic Development*, **6** (1)

Jenkins, D, Cousin, G and Bhanot, R (2000) The literal and the metaphysical: accounts of educational development units, in *Educational Developments*, **1** (4)

Laurillard, D. (1994) *Rethinking University Teaching: A framework for effective use of educational technology*, Routledge, London

National Committee of Enquiry into Higher Education (1997) *Higher Education in the Learning Society: Report of the National Committee* (the Dearing Report), The Stationery Office, London

Resnick, M (1995) New paradigms for computing, new paradigms for thinking, in *Computers and Exploratory Learning*, ed A diSessa, C Hoyles and R Noss, Springer-Verlag [online] http://www.media.mit.edu/mres/papers/new_paradigms/new_paradigms.html [accessed 28 January 2002]

Scott, P (1995) *The Meanings of Mass Higher Education*, Society for Research in Higher Education/Open University Press, Buckingham

Sharpe, R (2000) A review of Web resources for online tutors, in *Educational Development*, **1** (4), 12–13

Sharples, M (1999) *How We Write: Writing as creative design*, Routledge, London

Stake, B (1988) Case study research, in Jaeger, R (ed) *Complementary Methods for Research*, American Research Association

Times Higher Education Supplement (*THES*) 6 April 2001

Tyler, R W (1949) Basic Principles of Curriculum and Instruction, *University of Chicago Press*, London

APPENDIX: A CHECKLIST OF QUESTIONS FOR EDUCATIONAL DEVELOPERS

This list is not intended to be exhaustive. Rather, it is a start from which educational developers can build their own resource as appropriate to the needs of their home institution, its circumstances, its students and staff, and perhaps most important, its local vision for the future.

- What counts as good practice in the new technologically based curriculum?

- Is good teaching just good teaching whether it is delivered face to face or via the Internet?

- How much can be extrapolated from traditional (and new) distance learning packages?

- Do the advantages offered by ICT outweigh the disadvantages?

- Is the technology robust enough to deal with increasing numbers of students?

- Should the staff development needed to implement the technologically based curriculum be delivered (partly) online?

- Can one (still) deliver courses without the new ICT?

- Does everyone in an institution have to follow suit or are we looking at a mixed mode of delivery where some of the staff deliver part or all of their courses online?

- Does it actually matter that others do not use ICT?

- Is the UK Open University model the future for all universities? If so, what follows?

- Given that both staff and students can communicate with one another, irrespective of time and place, how will teachers calculate their working hours?

- Will the contractual agreements between universities have to be reviewed?

- If support staff such as technical and library colleagues become part of the delivery team, will their pay structures be reviewed to bring them into line with academic colleagues?

- Some issues, for example intellectual property rights, remain unsolved. Who will own the materials on the Web? Do individuals take their material with them when they move to another institution? Will publishers make all new books available online? If so, what will be the role of the library and the university bookshop?

Contributor contact details

The contributions included in this book have all been presented by practitioners whose work falls within the broad definition of higher education: these details are provided for the benefit of their colleagues worldwide.

It is increasingly the case that the primary mode of communication within the international higher education community is by means of e-mail. This mode has been utilized extensively throughout the development of this book. For many authors, the sole mode of communication with the editors has been via e-mail. Since e-mail is a preferred and rapid mode of communication for our contributing authors we list the e-mail addresses of all contributors.

For readers who prefer to use more traditional communications routes, postal addresses are also given.

Kyriaki Anagnostopoulou
Centre for Learning Development
Middlesex University
Bounds Green Road
London N11 2NQ
England
kyriaki2@mdx.ac.uk

Rakesh Bhanot
Centre for Higher Education Development
Coventry University
Coventry CV1 5FB
England
r.bhanot@coventry.ac.uk

Paul Blackmore
Centre for Academic Practice
University of Warwick
Coventry CV4 7AL
England
p.blackmore@warwick.ac.uk

Susan Chandler
Learning Facilitation Programs
Royal Roads University
2005 Sooke Road
Victoria, BC
V9B 5Y2
Canada
susan.chandler@royalroads.ca

Anne Davidson
School of Health and Social Sciences
Coventry University
Coventry CV1 5FB
England
a.davidson@cov.ac.uk

Jacqueline Dempster
Centre for Academic Practice
University of Warwick
Coventry CV4 7AL
England
jay.dempster@warwick.ac.uk

Sue Drew
Learning and Teaching Institute
Sheffield Hallam University
City Campus
Sheffield S1 1WB
England
s.k.drew@shu.ac.uk

Stephen Fallows
Chester College of Higher Education
Parkgate Road
Chester CH1 4BJ
England
s.fallows@chester.ac.uk
steve@sjfallows.co.uk

Susan Foster
Vice President for Information Technologies
University of Delaware
Suite 200, 192 South Chapel Street
Newark, DE 19711–4321
USA
sfoster@udel.edu

Mike Fuller
Canterbury Business School
University of Kent at Canterbury
Canterbury, Kent CT2 7PE
England
m.f.fuller@ukc.ac.uk

David Grantham
School of International Studies and Law
Coventry University
Coventry CV1 5FB
England
d.grantham@cov.ac.uk

Michelle Haynes
Centre for Learning Development
Middlesex University
Bounds Green Road
London N11 2NQ
England
m.haynes@mdx.ac.uk

Raja Maznah Raja Hussain
Faculty of Education
University of Malaya
50603 Kuala Lumpur
Malaysia
maznah@tm.net.my, rajamaznah@maxis.net.my

Maggie Hutchings
Learning Design Studio
Bournemouth University
Talbot Campus
Poole, Dorset BH12 5BB
England
mhutchin@bournemouth.ac.uk

Gillian Jordan
School of Health
Mansion Site
University of Greenwich
London SE9 2PQ
England
g.g.jordan@greenwich.ac.uk

Donna Wood McCarty
School of Arts and Sciences
Clayton College and State University
5900 N Lee Street
Morrow, GA 30260
USA
donna.mccarty@mail.clayton.edu

Marina Möller
Department of Professional Education
Vista University
Sebokeng Campus, Private Bag X050
Vanderbiljpark 1900
South Africa
mollr-hm@serval.vista.ac.za

Ivan Moore
University of Portsmouth
University House
Winston Churchill Avenue
Portsmouth PO1 2UP
England
ivan.moore@port.ac.uk

Marina Orsini-Jones
School of International Studies and Law
Coventry University
Coventry CV1 5FB
England
m.orsini@cov.ac.uk

Paul Orsmond
The Learning Development Centre
Staffordshire University
The Octagon, Beaconside
Stafford ST18 0AD
England
p.orsmond@staffs.ac.uk

Estelle Paget
Learning Facilitation Programs
Royal Roads University
2005 Sooke Road
Victoria, BC
V9B 5Y2
Canada
estelle.paget@royalroads.ca

Mick Roach
Centre for Academic Practice
University of Warwick
Coventry CV4 7AL
England
m.p.roach@warwick.ac.uk

Christine Steven
Folkestone School for Girls
Folkestone
Kent CT20 3RB
England
CSteven@folkestonegirls.kent.sch.uk

Mark Stiles
The Learning Development Centre
Staffordshire University
The Octagon, Beaconside
Stafford ST18 0AD
England
m.j.stiles@staffs.ac.uk

Stan Zakrzewski
Dept of Computing, Information Systems & Mathematics
London Guildhall University
London EC3N 1JY
England
stanz@lgu.ac.uk

Index